"FOLLOW THE PERSON"

Before you start to read this book, take this moment to think about making a donation to punctum books, an independent non-profit press,

@ https://punctumbooks.com/support/

If you're reading the e-book, you can click on the image below to go directly to our donations site. Any amount, no matter the size, is appreciated and will help us to keep our ship of fools afloat. Contributions from dedicated readers will also help us to keep our commons open and to cultivate new work that can't find a welcoming port elsewhere. Our adventure is not possible without your support.

Vive la Open Access.

Fig. 1. Detail from Hieronymus Bosch, *Ship of Fools* (1490–1500)

"FOLLOW THE PERSON": ARCHIVAL ENCOUNTERS. Copyright © 2025 by Ammiel Alcalay. This work carries a Creative Commons BY-NC-SA 4.0 International license, which means that you are free to copy and redistribute the material in any medium or format, and you may also remix, transform, and build upon the material, as long as you clearly attribute the work to the author (but not in a way that suggests the author or punctum books endorses you and your work), you do not use this work for commercial gain in any form whatsoever, and that for any remixing and transformation, you distribute your rebuild under the same license. http://creativecommons.org/licenses/by-nc-sa/4.0/

Published in 2025 by punctum books, Earth, Milky Way
https://punctumbooks.com
In collaboration with *Lost & Found: The CUNY Poetics Document Initiative*, https://centerforthehumanities.org/person/lost-found-the-cuny-poetics-document-initiative/

ISBN-13: 978-1-68571-286-0 (paperbound)
ISBN-13: 978-1-68571-287-7 (PDF)
ISBN-13: 978-1-68571-296-9 (EPUB)

DOI: 10.53288/0395.1.00

LCCN: 2025942821
Library of Congress Cataloging Data is available from the Library of Congress

Editing: SAJ and Eileen A. Fradenburg Joy
Book design: Hatim Eujayl
Cover image: Chris Russell
Cover design: Vincent W.J. van Gerven Oei

HIC SVNT MONSTRA

Ammiel
Alcalay

"FOLLOW THE PERSON"
Archival Encounters

Contents

Introduction by Miriam Nichols — 13

Manifesto — 31

I. THE GROUND

"Let me show you something" — 35
"What I Found Out" — 51
Relieving the National Debt: W.D. Ehrhart &
   the Wages of Memory — 57
"The Body is a House" — 71

II. OUT OF THE SCHOLOLS AND INTO THE ARCHIVES

Interview with David Hadbawnik — 83
Peter Anastas: A Walker in the City — 99
"Out of the Schools and into the Archives" — 105
On Robert Creeley's "Contexts of Poetry" — 111
On Diane di Prima's *R.D.'s H.D.* — 117
Confluences — 127
"the whole thing has no meaning if it is not signed" — 139
Letters to & from Joanne Kyger — 145
"Querido Pablito"/"Julissimo querido": Paul Blackburn &
   Julio Cortázar's Selected Correspondence, 1958–1971 — 151
Of Suckers and Gulls — 169
Vincent Ferrini: *Before Gloucester* — 175

Rimbaud via Rukeyser: An Editorial Note	197
You Don't Know Jack: On Jack Kerouac	205
Introduction for Amiri Baraka's Olson Lecture	209
On Amiri Baraka: An Interview with Özge Özbek Akıman	215
For Jimmie Durham, Poet	225
Getting Out of the Western Box: Dennis Tedlock's *The Olson Codex*	229
Digging Our Way through the Data Midden	233
An Interview with Marwa Helal	241

III. IN FRIENDSHIP

"a dance of freedom" / In the Worlds of Etel Adnan	253
In Friendship, for John Wieners	271
Still Standing, for Gil Sorrentino	277
In & Out of Place: Memories of Nissim Rejwan, Shimon Ballas, and Samir Naqqash	289
From the Citadel: "I must have been an Arab once…"	295
CODA: Following the Person	311
Bibliography	319

Acknowledgments

I begin with thanks to the team at punctum; on my first book with punctum I worked with Eileen A. Fradenburg Joy and Vincent W.J. van Gerven Oei, and on this, also with SAJ and Livy Snyder; they have all made punctum a haven for unusual work. With heartfelt thanks to the many collaborators and editors with whom I worked, as well as the publishers, editors, and venues where some of the texts included in *"FOLLOW THE PERSON": Archival Encounters* previously appeared; and with apologies to anyone I may not have mentioned: The Academy of American Poets; Etel Adnan, for asking me to write an introduction to her work, and Nightboat Books, where it appeared; Özge Özbek Akıman and the *Turkish Journal of American Studies*; Peter and Benjamin Anastas and Back Shore Books; the Cape Ann Museum, particularly archivists Fred and Stephanie Buck; the Carmen Ballcells Literary Agency; *Banipal* magazine, especially its founders Margaret Obank and Samuel Shimon; to everyone at *BOMB* magazine; to everyone at City Lights, especially Elaine Katzenberger and Garrett Caples; Michael Boughn, Kent Johnson, and Andrè Spears at *Dispatches from the Poetry Wars;* Karim Dounane, for soliciting a piece for the *French Journal of American Studies;* Jimmie Durham for asking me to write liner notes for an LP of his readings, and Sergio Edelsztein for producing the record; Geoffrey Gatza at BlazeVOX books, and Kenneth Warren for asking me to write about his work; the Gloucester Writers Center, and Henry Ferrini; David Hadbawnik and his journal *Kadar Koli;* Marwa Helal and everyone at the *Poetry Project Newsletter;* to everyone over the years at *Lost & Found,* and particularly Ana Božičević, Shea'la Finch, Tonya Foster, Stephon Lawrence, Kate Tarlow Morgan, Sampson Starkweather, Kendra Sullivan, and Aoibheann Sweeney, as well as editors Chris Clarke, Jacqui Cornetta, Meira Levinson, Bradley Lubin, Allison Macomber, Alexander Soria, Kyle Waugh, and Rachael Wilson; to Diane di Prima, Joanne Kyger, Megan Paslawski, Michael Rumaker, Ed Sanders, and Michael Seth Stewart, for their work on *Lost & Found* projects, as well as Amiri Baraka, Joan Blackburn, Penelope Creeley, Jennifer Dunbar Dorn, and William Rukeyser for their help and attention; J.J. Malo, for asking me to contribute to a book of essays on poet W.D. Ehrhart; Irakli Qolbaia and Dato Barbakadze, for being inspired by a short essay of mine and translating my work into Georgian; Jayce Salloum, for asking me to write on his work for a catalogue, and Jen Budney for her editing and production; Stefanie Sobelle and Christopher Sorrentino, for asking me to participate in a Festschrift for Gilbert Sorrentino at the *Review of Contemporary Fiction;* Shareah Taleghani for inviting me to a conference she organized on political prisoners in the Middle East; and Lydia Wilson at the *Cambridge Review.*

Introduction

Miriam Nichols

> Untangling the strands of the past is not simply an act of
> recognition, of fitting events into fixed patterns, of just seeing
> the light; it begins, rather, by apprehending the source of light
> and follows with an active, incessant engagement in the process
> of naming and renaming.
> — Ammiel Alcalay, "The Quill's Embroidery:
> Untangling a Tradition"[1]

> Everywhere we look our history / histories, distorted to the
> point of caricature.
> — Ammiel Alcalay, "'Follow the person':
> A Manifesto for *Lost & Found*"[2]

Ammiel Alcalay has been "untangling the strands of the past" for more than thirty years in essays, poems, anthologies, interviews, translations, journal articles, publishing projects, and pedagogy. The present collection, *"FOLLOW THE PERSON": Archival Encounters,* adds another chapter to this lifework in progress. As a sorter of histories, Alcalay is also necessarily a

---

1 Ammiel Alcalay, *Memories of Our Future* (City Lights Books, 1999), 33.
2 Ammiel Alcalay, "'Follow the person': A Manifesto for *Lost & Found*," *Cambridge Literary Review* 11 (2018): 14.

mapper of cultural and geopolitical spaces, particularly those that have been buried, forgotten, or repressed. In an introduction to his essay collection of 1999, *Memories of Our Future,* he says it this way:

> Both the idea of place and particular places play an enormous role in this itinerant work and in my choices as a writer and translator. I have very consciously striven to stretch what might be thought possible in an American context; that is, I look for work that I would like to have seen somebody write here, but they can't, or haven't, or wouldn't be able to because the circumstances for that writing don't exist in quite such a configuration.[3]

Alcalay's "configurations" cross social identities, schools, generations, places, and times. This is a key feature of the present volume; it includes commentary on and a collaging of works ranging from artists Jayce Salloum and Etel Adnan, Baghdadi-born writers Nissim Rejwan, Shimon Ballas, and Samir Naqqash, to Americans Robert Creeley, Charles Olson, Diane di Prima, Robert Duncan, Joanne Kyger, Amiri Baraka, Jack Kerouac, Gil Sorrentino, Dennis Tedlock, Ed Dorn, and John Wieners. Vietnam vet W.D. Ehrhart, Gloucester poet Vincent Ferrini, and artist, poet, and AIM activist Jimmie Durham come in for attention as important figures belonging to the same historical terrain as their better known peers. The late Ken Warren is reviewed for his exemplary critical intelligence in *Captain Poetry's Sucker Punch* and his respect for authorial intent, contra theoretical fashions.[4] Alcalay does not partition his cultural landscapes into traditional versus avant-garde, political versus formalist, nor does he offer exegesis. Instead, he locates the writers and artists that draw his attention in their historical habitats. "Follow the

---

3 Alcalay, *Memories of Our Future,* xiii.
4 What Alcalay sees in Warren's work, in Chapter 14, is pretty clear: "a huge sigh of relief in the monotonous, jargon-filled, mystifying, pretentious, back-scratching, ass-kissing terrain that purports to consider itself criticism these days."

person" and you will find a world; discover a world and you will find particular persons and places. Alcalay's writings repeatedly perform the mutual constitution and illumination of figure and ground.

The Wheat Is Poisoned: Places of Return

As a scholar of both Middle Eastern and American studies as well as a correspondent and translator during the Bosnian war, Alcalay ranges widely,[5] but he does have his places of return. With family ties to the former Yugoslavia, Alcalay translated Bosnian voices into English for American audiences during the 1992–1995 war, and wrote columns and gave interviews on American politics for Bosnian papers. Bosnia is a permanent locus. Another is Palestine. Alcalay spent eight years in Jerusalem, immersing himself in worlds little known and under great duress.[6] His *After Jews and Arabs* (1993), *Keys to the Garden* (1996), and *Memories of Our Future* (1999) challenge the cultural maps that separate Israelis, Palestinians, and Arab Jews, finding in his colloquy with political prisoners, forgotten musicians, or neighborhood activists the energies and models that have become all too rare in academic and intellectual realms. There are also the American places. Vietnam, of course, and Iraq. Although he was too young for the Vietnam draft, Alcalay has an abiding interest in American wars and in public policy, which he traces back to devastating colonial encounters with Indigenous nations. In his numerous traversals and remappings

---

5 In "Local Politics," from page xii of *Memories of Our Future:* "[M]y experience in presenting unknown or marginalized literatures has taught me that an extremely wide net needs to be cast in order to create the conditions through which such work can find a productive space in American culture, a place where poets and writers can get to it and begin relating to distinctly new forms, idioms, sensibilities, and experiences as part of their own vocabulary."

6 In an interview with Benjamin Hollander, included as back matter in Ammiel Alcalay, *from the warring factions*, ed. Fred Dewey (Re:public/UpSet Press, 2012), Alcalay discusses his time in Jerusalem (173–212). See especially 176–80.

of these geo-historical trouble spots, Alcalay counts the New American poets as allies. Olson was a family friend from childhood; the next-generation crowd, including Wieners, di Prima, Baraka, Anne Waldman, and Ed Sanders, are fellow travelers.

The point that needs making here is that however rangy Alcalay's references may be, the intent and method are steady. As is obvious, Alcalay is a poet who stays with the trouble. With a journalist's commitment to investigative reporting and a poet's engagement with fable making, Alcalay seeks out places of conflict and animates voices that have been silenced. In "Why Israel," an essay from *Memories of Our Future,* he writes about it this way:

> The crisis we have been brought to demands that we use our past to re-create new memories of our future, to reject versions of history that banish Arabs and Jews, Israelis and Palestinians, to separate realms where there will be no intimacy or ambivalence, no love or jealousy, no respect or common destiny, where the full range of complex emotions, intentions, conscious and subconscious traces inherited through a long life lived in common will either simply be shelved in the name of some impersonal and polite forms of "cooperation" or, perhaps even worse, just deemed unimaginable. Any relationship to Israel must include a relationship to the Middle East, to Arabs, to Islam, to unemployment in Algeria, censorship and torture in Egypt, the abandonment of Muslims in Bosnia, to efforts at rebuilding Beirut, to the effect of sanctions against Iraqi children.[7]

Notice the connecting threads in this passage, from the Israeli–Palestinian conflict to Algeria, Egypt, Bosnia, and US sanctions against Iraq. Whether we follow Alcalay to Jerusalem, Sarajevo, Srebrenica, Baghdad, Gloucester, or New York, we will find him unhiding the hidden, making visible the orders that are and those that are not, but were, perhaps, and might be if we were

---

7   Alcalay, *Memories of Our Future,* 208.

to search out buried or broken lines of connection. The past we choose is the future we will get: The stakes are that high.[8]

Follow the leads in Alcalay's writings and you will find a curriculum. To demonstrate, here is just one trail of breadcrumbs from the "Manifesto" that opens this collection of writings: "THE WHEAT IS POISONED." This line references a long poem by Michael McClure, "Poisoned Wheat," an anti-Vietnam War poem published in 1965. In Operation Ranch Hand, between 1961 and 1971, the US sprayed 73 million liters of herbicides over forests and farmlands in Vietnam.[9] The purpose was to reduce forest cover and render crops unfit for consumption; the effect was to curse generations of Vietnamese and American soldiers with cancer and birth defects. The soil is still contaminated and some forests are irretrievable. McClure's poem begins with Vietnam, but it quickly expands to a critique of the major political systems of the twentieth century: capitalism, communism, and fascism. As an alternative to these systems, McClure proposes bio-culture, meaning, in his context, the reintegration of humanity with the rest of nature. If the species cannot change course, McClure says, the result will be starvation from overcrowding and war.[10] Here he points to the long and appalling

---

8 When the traditions of culture cannot be taken for granted — when tribal memory is lost or severed or when the tribe itself has dispersed as in the twentieth century — the past has to be actively remembered and chosen. As I understand it, this is what modernism was about. Pound begins *The Cantos* with a rewrite of Odysseus's descent to Hades. That descent kicks off a long poem with history in it, as Pound described his epic: In the absence of collective memory, the bard takes on the task of searching out historical modes of life that might illuminate and give identity to the present.

9 These numbers come from an article by Jason von Meding, "Fifty Years Later, Agent Orange Still Kills in Vietnam," *The National Interest*, November 28, 2020, https://nationalinterest.org/blog/buzz/americas-chemical-warfare-tour-how-agent-orange-destroyed-vietnam-100317.

10 "I AM SICKENED / by the oncoming MASS STARVATION / and concomitant revolting degree / of overpopulation, and the accompanying / production of incredible numbers / of useless physical objects / whose raw materials demand / a destruction of those parts of nature / I have come to think of as beautiful!" Michael McClure, *Star* (Grove Press, 1970), 91.

history of human aggression, to a species-level disregard for the living planet, and to the reckless use of technology. But the story of "poisoned wheat" does more. It brings to attention a thinking of life's physicality. This was an important focus in the 1960s, fundamental to McClure as it was to Olson and as it is to Alcalay as their inheritor. The writings that follow this "Manifesto" — "Let me show you something," "What I Found Out," and "The body is a house" — lay out a poetic method that requires the poet to inhabit the body.

"Let me show you something" is, as the title says, about showing. The piece draws into present contexts materials that may be obscure or forgotten but which nonetheless bear on a current state of affairs. Hence the importance of collage as a strategy for "[recalibrating] the relationship of existing materials to new conditions and interpretations dictated by events current or otherwise." Alcalay credits Lebanese-Canadian artist Jayce Salloum with inspiration, and Salloum's practice includes an ongoing investigation of modes of representation and reproduction. In a video that Alcalay cites, "This is Not Beirut/There was and there was not," Salloum ponders how to represent Beirut: postcards? street videos? handing the camera to other people? "The artists fumble," Alcalay says, "working their way through rooms and hallways, taking notes, trying to get to 'the people' as they discuss 'representation,' only to hear: 'There isn't a word for this in Arabic.'"

I don't know by which route Salloum arrived at his inquiry into representation — he has said in an interview Alcalay cites that it is a component of what he understands to be an art of resistance.[11] I do know, however, that Alcalay would have rec-

---

[11] Alcalay cites this passage from an interview with Salloum in "Occupied Territories: Mapping the Transgressions of Cultural Terrain," *Framework* 43, no. 3 (2002): 87–88. The question is about the role of "resistance" in Salloum's work: "In the work I've produced there is not only 'resistance' being represented — for instance, the resistance to the occupation of South Lebanon by the Israeli Army, the resistance to the continuity of misrepresentation, and resistance to the use of Lebanon as a product/subject and 'laboratory' for the West (in the testing of new & banned warfare technology, the

ognized Salloum's art through his lifelong attention to Olson. In *The Maximus Poems:*

> There are no hierarchies, no infinite, no such many as mass, there are
>
>   only
>
> eyes in all heads,
> to be looked out of

These lines from "Letter 6" are fundamental to Alcalay's "follow the person" directive. "Polis is / eyes," Olson wrote. There is no other kind of perspective to be had apart from such an assembly of various views-from-here.[12] Judgment comes from weighing the perspectives brought to bear on the common thing. Salloum's videos perform this space of assembly. In his video, *untitled,* another one that Alcalay cites, Salloum interviews Soha Bechara, a Lebanese activist incarcerated for ten years in Khiam prison, an Israeli detention center in South Lebanon. The point of the interview is to give space to her experience as a political prisoner—to create a public venue for that experience and to invite the viewer's attention to it as an issue of common concern. Alcalay's collage work is of the same order and end.

Read as method, "Let me show you something" is a call out to witnesses and an active listening to the words of others.[13]

    'coverage' by writers, journalists, travelers and 'experts' and as a case study for social/cultural studies)—but 'resistance' is also being (re)produced structurally, formally, and ideologically in the pieces themselves."

12 Hannah Arendt arrives at a similar conclusion, coming at the question of representation and public space from the perspective of political philosophy. Polis, she says, is a space of assembly around something of "interest, which lies between people and therefore can relate and bind them together." Hannah Arendt, *The Human Condition* (Doubleday, 1959), 162.

13 Alcalay makes the receptive element of his work very clear. The following passage is reproduced in Chapter 1 from an interview with Benjamin Hollander: "Coursing through everything is the simple question of transmission—how does memory survive? To what materials do we entrust it? Have we, in the cinematic and digital age, renounced claims to stable memory as materials we use to record this age implode and crumble

The essay immediately following, "What I Found Out," is about personal investigation. It begins like this: "Sometime around 1979, I remember driving out to a prison from Jerusalem with some friends." The first paragraph-length anecdote of this piece recounts "protests over the lack of housing and cuts in the subsidies on bread, milk, oil, flour, sugar" around the prison. Alcalay is in the company of a man who had been involved with the Israeli Black Panthers,[14] someone whose name translates to "Upright Son" — paths here leading to the American civil rights struggle, played out between Mizrahim and Palestinians on one hand and the Israeli administration on the other. The next story begins with the sentence, "The next time I lived in Jerusalem, I found out a lot more about what the word torture meant." More connecting lines, running between public policies in and on the Middle East and to American complicity in the repression of Palestinians. Following these leads as a poet-investigator means going someplace, meeting people, seeing for oneself, making face to face contact, even putting the body in harm's way: This kind of investigation is a last ditch defense against what Alcalay calls "the grand psy-ops dreamt up and practiced in the Cold

---

more rapidly than any papyrus or tablet? This led to meditations on film, on forms of propaganda, and the use of materials from newspapers. The more I thought about this, the more I felt that it would somehow be disrespectful, certainly to the dead if not to the living, to pretend that I, as an individual, could add anything to all that has been said or written about war, genocide, exile, memory, and loss. I felt that, by adding new words, I would become a polluter and obfuscate the directions my other work had taken me in, particularly the translation. The issue was not to 'say something' or impose an order upon the world but to recalibrate the relationship of existing materials to new conditions and interpretations dictated by events, current or otherwise." Originally appears in Alcalay, *from the warring factions*, 192.

14 In response to discrimination against Jews of Arab heritage and Palestinians, the Israeli Black Panther party was formed in 1971, taking the name from its American predecessor. It achieved sufficient prominence to occasion a Commission and win seats in the Israeli parliament. The party officially ceased to exist in 1992. See Jacob Max Goldberg, "The Mizrahi Black Panthers of Israel," *Ha'Am: UCLA's Jewish Newsmagazine*, https://haam.org/the-mizrahi-black-panthers-of-israel/.

War — the purpose of which were to sever people from experience and the consciousness of their experience." It is Alcalay's contention that the "psy-ops" were not limited to the post-war era, but were and are the regular, ongoing business of the Military Industrial Media Entertainment complex (MIME), practiced through the many wars of the twentieth and twenty-first centuries. The "lack of personal relationships between North American intellectuals and their counterparts in the Middle East," he writes "has made it that much easier for propaganda to tell the story."[15]

The dismissal of experience — and consequent alienation of people from their own manner of being in the world — is nothing new. In philosophy and science, it has been going on since Plato. Now, however, the experience of everyday life, never mind the academic disciplines, is almost unthinkable apart from the thick digital mediations with their little-understood algorithms that function like an ubiquitous background hum. It is important to see that, as Alcalay uses the term, experience is not passive, as in just-what-happens-to-me; it requires active receptivity and creative assemblage. Considered as method in Alcalay's work, "experience" has a precedent in Ezra Pound's story of a post-graduate student asked by a great savant to describe a sunfish. When the student returned with a textbook description, he was sent back to the task. "At the end of three weeks," Pound says, "the fish was in an advanced state of decomposition, but the student knew something about it."[16] Pound's story is aimed at decontextualized ways of knowing things and to my ear, it remains even more relevant than when it was written. Pound says that the modern European idea of how to know something leads to abstraction. "If you ask a man to define anything," he says,

---

15 See references in Chapter 2, "What I Found Out," to Alcalay's personal friendships and correspondence with political prisoners Abraham Serfaty (Morocco), Abdellatif Laâbi (Morocco), and Faraj Bayrakdar (Syria).
16 Ezra Pound, *ABC of Reading* (New Directions, 1960), 18.

> his definition always moves away from the simple things that he knows perfectly well,
>   it recedes into an unknown region, that is a region of remoter and progressively remoter abstraction.
>   Thus if you ask him what red is, he says it is a "color."
>   If you ask him what a color is, he tells you it is a vibration or a refraction of light, or a division of the spectrum.[17]

The tale of the student and the sunfish proposes an alternative to this process of abstraction in the knowing of a thing in situ: Where is it? How does it work? What or whom does it affect? What is the company it keeps? This is not at all to disregard the scientific explanation, but to situate it in what Olson called the human universe.

Alcalay's essay on W.D. Ehrhart shows what can be achieved when one honors situated knowledge. As a Vietnam vet, Ehrhart is usually slotted as a war poet. Alcalay repositions his work in the civil rights decade and places him beside Olson, Muriel Rukeyser, Kerouac, and McClure because he comes from and addresses the same historical ground as they do. The Ehrhart essay makes a double claim: First, this work is essential to the cultural and political fabric of the US at mid-twentieth century. Ehrhart's brief essay, "The United States Screw & Bolt Company," consists of a list of names of persons involved in Vietnam and a brief description of what they did and where they went after the war. It is an investigative piece of writing and Alcalay says that it presents "as accurate a picture of power relations in the United States as we have." The second claim is that the parceling out of poetry into categories or schools or ethnicities bars access to American history and tradition. Alcalay writes that "our history has been atomized, made illegible, as if there were neither connection nor consequence between one era or another, between one phenomenon and another." From this perspective, Vietnam is not a discrete event but part of a historical continuum stretching back to the colonizing of North America. Ehrhart's writings

---

17 Ibid, 19.

contribute to a tradition that includes Frederick Douglas's *Autobiography,* Walt Whitman's civil war poems, *The Autobiography of Malcolm X,* and Allen Ginsberg's *Howl.* To detach the Vietnam era from its place in this continuum, Alcalay says, "would be like saying that Melville's *Moby Dick* is only about whaling."

The last piece I will look at from what I'm thinking of as the "method" trio of writings is "The Body is a House." This piece, written with Kate Tarlow Morgan, takes its title from Olson's "The Resistance," a short prose piece of the immediate post-war that moves from the reduction of the body to ash and soap at Auschwitz to the treatment of the flesh as dwelling place. Olson developed this thought of the body in his work on proprioception, the "space-time specifics" of human being-in-the-world.[18] At a time when the US was preparing to launch into space, Olson called humanity back to its physicality. If I read him rightly, the problem is not exactly technology as such, but technology detached from a broader perspective — technology as an expression of will without regard for planetary consequences. We are still on the trail of the "poisoned wheat." Think industrial fishing and farming and the oil and gas industry in Olson's time and then add Big Tech, Big Pharma, and rapid transport in its current state. Think of the coming "metaverse" in which we are invited to live online and the now ubiquitous practice of inventing and selling "experiences" on social media in order to attract clicks and "earn" advertising revenue. In "Song 3" from Book 1 of *The Maximus Poems,* Olson blessed the "difficulties" of daily life as he lived it in voluntary impoverishment — the leaky faucet, the faulty toilet, the car that didn't run. "In the land of plenty," he writes, "have / nothing to do with it."

Olson's apparent Luddism is about rescuing the creative imagination, because the body is where self and world meet. The interaction may be fresh if the senses and intellect are alert, or it can be stale and distant if channelled through ready-made constructs. The "difficulties" that attend inhabitation of the body

---

18 See Olson's "Proprioception," in *Collected Prose,* ed. Donald Allen and Benjamin Friedlander (University of California Press, 1997), 179–99.

and the work of finding something out for oneself are foundational to a poet's practice. In an "Afterword" to *A Walker in the City* by Gloucester writer Peter Anastas, Alcalay writes that, "The organic integration of newly acquired sights and sounds into the very fabric of one's being and behavior is a complex and intimate process that perhaps comes as close to defining what it means to be human, and inhabit a human universe, as anything that comes to mind. The journey can be as near as your hands pushing at the floor to stand up or as far as you can go once you've learned."

None of this thinking about the body and its relationship to the imagination is new, but living in one's own flesh remains a difficult and largely ignored practice. In the language arts, as in academia, it is ever so much easier to push the world around with words.

These four pieces ("Let me show you something," "What I Found Out," "The body is a house," and the Ehrhart essay) make up a short opening section of FOLLOW THE PERSON that Alcalay calls "The ground." So, to summarize — there are the territories, especially the Middle East and the US, in the present volume. There is the intent: whatever the territory, the intent is to unhide the hiddens that bear on the present moment. "The archival encounter," Alcalay writes, "can present [. . .] a much less mediated experience in which the pursuit of particular things (names, dates, titles, incidents), can explode a whole host of assumptions and received knowledge, creating a new set of relations." Archival activism is also a pedagogical practice and a curriculum. In an interview with David Hadbawnik included in FOLLOW THE PERSON, Alcalay discusses *Lost & Found*, a unique pedagogical, publishing, and public-oriented project founded by Alcalay that began in 2009. In addition to training students as archivists, editors, and writers for the general public, the project publishes an annual series of chapbooks as well as full-length works in collaboration with various publishers. Each chapbook features previously unpublished materials from well-known writers. Asked in the interview why people should care about poets' archives, Alcalay says that such research can change our view not only of the writer in question but also of his or her period: "So what has interested me more than anything, besides the dramatic discoveries, is the creation of dense networks that can truly reconfigure our historical conceptualization of things, making everything more dense and complicated." The "dense networks" — micro-histories — invade and complicate received cultural narratives.

Secondly, the essays in "The Ground" perform a compositional practice that combines collage (listening to others, gathering and contextualizing voices in their historical place-times) with reportage (finding out for oneself, bearing witness, drawing stories out of one's findings). Together, these creative gestures make up a "special view" of what it means to experience something and build an informed response to one's times. Alcalay's oeuvre is a study of this method in action. In addition to the present collection, Alcalay has been engaged, along with the late Shareah Taleghani, in bringing to completion a collaborative English translation of the prison poems of Faraj Bayrakdar (*A Dove in Free Flight,* 2021), originally smuggled out of a Syrian prison on cigarette papers. This publication came after a sixteen-year hiatus between translation and publication, during which time no publisher could be found.[19] Another example is Alcalay's editorial engagement and interview with Palestinian poet Mosab Abu Toha's award-winning 2022 collection *Things You May Find Hidden in My Ear: Poems from Gaza.* This practice of drawing other writers and artists into presence by collaging their voices into his writings, interviewing them, or editing their work, is both a generosity and a creative making of public space, and one can find Alcalay's mark in dozens of projects that he has guided and cajoled into the light of day. In my view, the

---

19 The English translation of Bayrakdar's book, *A Dove in Free Flight,* began in a 2002 seminar led by the late Lebanese novelist Elias Khoury. Bayrakdar's poems, smuggled out of prison on cigarette papers, had been published in Arabic and French (translated by Abdellatif Laâbi); members of the seminar translated them into English but the hiatus between completion of the project and publication actually stretched out to sixteen years.

significance of these gestures cannot really be overestimated. We live in a time when public space is not only absent but barely imaginable through the racket of social media and the emissions of mainstream news that junk up the public realm with chatter and vested interests. Alcalay offers a glimpse of what a polis might look like.

Eleutherarchy

The bulk of the essays, introductions, afterwords, and interviews that follow the section "The Ground" of *"FOLLOW THE PERSON"* are gathered under the title "Out of the schools and into the archives." There is Peter Anastas's "mapping of the ordinary"; points of convergence between Robert Creeley and George Jackson; the marvel of New College programs in San Francisco; exploration of a living tradition as fashioned by Diane di Prima and Robert Duncan; the small press world of the 1960s; Michael Rumaker's *Robert Duncan in San Francisco;* the letters of Joanne Kyger; a long collaborative introduction to the *Lost & Found* publication of letters between Paul Blackburn and Julio Cortázar; a review of Ken Warren's *Captain Poetry's Sucker Punch;* a note on Muriel Rukeyser's Arthur Rimbaud translation (another *Lost & Found* initiative); a review of Todd Tietchen's editions of *The Unknown Kerouac* and Jean-Christophe Cloutier's *La vie est d'hommage,* bringing out the Quebeçois Kerouac; an introduction to Baraka's Olson lecture of 2013; a piece for Durham, and on and on. The "lost and found" world that comes out of these writings remaps its times as it expands the imaginative possibilities of the present.

Two highlights for me are the essays on Ferrini and Sanders. Ferrini (1913–2007) was mentor to a youthful Alcalay who was just beginning to read important things and write himself. If he is known at all, Ferrini is usually associated with Olson, his better-known Gloucester townsman, because of Olson's admonitory address to him in "Letter 5" of *The Maximus Poems.* Yet Alcalay describes their friendship as "constant and life sustaining to both." In this essay, he follows Ferrini through some major historical events of the twentieth century: "immigration, industrialization, anarchism, Communism, the New Deal, the Cold War, deindustrialization, and the creation — through political and artistic involvement — of countercultures in face of the totalizing forces of repression." The "range of his associations," Alcalay says, "found in political and civic action, publications, letters, and personal relationships — is staggering and mapping it will greatly enrich our literary, political, and cultural history." Ferrini's poems appeared alongside those of William Carlos Williams, Marianne Moore, Lorine Niedecker, Louis Zukofsky, Kenneth Patchen, Rukeyser, and Russell Atkins. In his book *Hermit of the Clouds,* Ferrini remarks on reading Federico García Lorca, brought to his attention by Langston Hughes: "I am entranced, intoxicated," he writes. Or there is Ferrini's poem to Camille Paglia on the occasion of her book, *Break, Blow, Burn.* "[L]eaves me speechless," she wrote him. The "dense networks" that Alcalay uncovers not only give presence to a lesser-known poet-activist, but they also enrich our understanding of the "big" moderns.

The Ed Sanders piece, "Digging our way through the Data Midden," is a review of Sanders's *Investigative Poetry* and *Broken Glory: the Final Years of Robert F. Kennedy,* but it is really a think piece about Sanders's method. Sanders claims a role for poetry in history-making in these books and others like them: *America, A History in Verse; The Poetry and Life of Allen Ginsberg; Sharon Tate;* and *The Family* (on the Manson family). In *Investigative Poetry,* which Alcalay describes as "among some of the most important manifestos and documents in poetics of the 20th century," Sanders writes that "history is open to the citizenry, no case is fully closed, and it is the right and duty of any one of us to 'NEVER HESITATE TO OPEN / A CASE FILE / EVEN UPON THE BLOODIEST OF BEASTS OF PLOTS.'" Alcalay tells us that in researching the Kennedy book, Sanders accumulated some 4,000 pages of FBI files as well as news clippings and documents available in the Robert F. Kennedy Assassination Archive at the University of Massachusetts. From this data midden, Sanders "has hewn a new form of narrative glyph in his historical poems, an indelible data cluster delivered in the form of a story." He has accomplished that most difficult trick of the poet, in other words: the turning of fact to fable. This passage, cited from *Investigative Poetry*, makes the point and it could stand as an epigraph to Alcalay's own work:

> Lawyers have a term: "to make law." You "make law" when you're involved in a case or an appeal which, as in Supreme Court decisions which have expanded the scope of personal freedom, opens up new human avenues.
> You make law.
> Bards, in a similar way, "make reality," or, really, they "make freedom" or they create new modes of what we might term Eleutherarchy, or the dance of freedom.

Eleutherarchy — a space in which to think again.

In the interview with Marwa Helal which follows the Sanders essay, Alcalay makes a case for projects like his and Sanders's:

> We've lived in a kind of banking hell joined at the hip with the British Empire since the creation of the Federal Reserve in 1913. With manufacturing and production now almost fully outsourced, we have also, in so many ways, internally outsourced our own culture, begun thinking of it and relating to it in terms that actually have little or no relationship to the historical conditions in which it was produced.

Now, he says, "the work of poetry might not necessarily mean writing it." Instead, "being a poet" might mean picking up the task of historical transmission. So very much of Alcalay's work does just this. In the final section of this collection, "Friends," Alcalay remembers and transmits memories of Adnan, Wieners, Sorrentino, Rejwan, Ballas, Naqqash, Kamal Boullata, and many, many others. "I took the time to be with them," he says,

> to read their work, to come to an understanding of their worlds. I did this not just because we felt an affinity for each

other as people but because I understood how important they were, how much particular history they carried, and how much of that history has been decimated and relegated to oblivion. And yet, it is precisely these tenuous threads that hold our world together, and they unravel unless we each act to find ways to reconnect them, and it is in that spirit that I think of them now.

Follow the "tenuous threads" in this collection of writings and you may end up at the looted National Museum in Baghdad during the American invasion, or in the Hoover Institute at Stanford University where most Iraqi state archives wound up. You may find yourself at Bashcharshiya, the market in Sarajevo during the Bosnian war, or in Palestine on May 14, 1948. Maybe, if you are keen, you will pick up the thread that leads to seventeenth-century colonial Massachusetts, or perhaps you will stay in New York, rummaging through garbage cans with di Prima, looking for journals and letters tossed out by a lover.[20] "Do you even know what you'd want to save?" Alcalay asks.

> No time, then, to choose.
> Not much time now, either — [21]

---

[20] All of these places are referenced in the "Manifesto" that opens *FOLLOW THE PERSON:* "But the Tigris / the Oriental Institute / just off Bashcharshiya / the films and photos and books of Palestine / the voices of Massachusetts and in Massachusett / apartments 'cleaned out' and papers piled into dumpsters / looted archives at the Hoover Institute / the fine lawns of Leland Stanford / ArabicFarsiOttomanashes whirling."

[21] Alcalay attributes this last line to musician Albert Ayler.

1

Manifesto

"follow the person"

— a manifesto [2018]

Everywhere we look our history/histories, distorted to the point of caricature: morality tales told from the arrogant present, everyone hurtling like lemmings in a headlong race to victimhood, grander claims for and against, without judgment or discrimination — REMEMBER THE ROOT of each word/etymologies — REMEMBER:

<u>THE WHEAT IS POISONED!!!</u>

Why not? Why couldn't it? You mean it already happened?

The buildings, the vaults, the climate-
controlled rooms

no guarantee:

"los fonógrafos nos siegaron los garones"
("phonographs have cut our throats") 1922

"FOLLOW THE PERSON"

screens dissect our ears
the materials must be
handed over
mouth to ear
hand to hand
          in touch

          "the voice is all"
But the Tigris
the Oriental Institute
just off Bashcharshiya —
the films and photos and books of Palestine
the voices in Massachusetts and in Massachusett
apartments "cleaned out" and papers piled into dumpsters
looted archives at the Hoover Institute
the fine lawns of Leland Stanford —
ArabicFarsiOttoman ashes whirling
along the river
          narrow river / narrow city

easily besieged —

Have you thought about defense? Do you know where the exit doors are?
How much you'd be able to carry before the flames lick
at your synthetic clothes & you go up like a fireball?

How much can you remember, like Faraj's lines
carried out of prison / grand recitals
in the heads of his comrades?

Do you even know now what you'd want to save? No time, then, to choose.

Not much time now, either —

I

THE GROUND

2

"Let me show you something"

Inspired by Jayce Salloum, 2009

Certain people say we should always go back to nature. I notice they never say we should go forward to nature. It seems to me they are more concerned that we should go back, than about nature. If the models we use are the apparitions seen in a dream or the recollection of our prehistoric past, is this less a part of nature or realism than a cow in a field? I think not.

The role of the artist has always been that of image maker. Different times require different images.

Today, when our aspirations have been reduced to a desperate attempt to escape from evil, and times are out of joint, our obsessive, subterranean and pictographic images are the expression of the neurosis which is reality. To my mind certain so-called abstraction is not abstraction at all, on the contrary, it is the realism of our time.

— Adolph Gottlieb, 1947

Perhaps our epoch, unaccustomed to translating thought into emotional experience, can do no more than pose the question: Are the trajectories, as recorded by a production engineer, "to eliminate needless, ill-directed, and ineffective motions," in any way connected with the emotional impact of the signs that appear time and again in our contemporary art? Only in our

period, so unaccustomed to assimilating processes of thought
into the emotional domain, could serious doubt arise.
— Siegfried Giedion, 1948

1.

Assault and intimacy — two faces that meet in the faces we meet in this work. There is the assault of assembled imagery, a digitized cesspool of our collective lexicon of manufactured violence (guns, rockets, planes, bombs, explosions, strategic rooms, undisclosed locations, control panels, handles, levers, buttons, targets), the visual noise from which some testimony emerges, and the very limited catalogue of "human" response, "in the absence of heroes": embraces, farewells, remnants, souvenirs, gestures that point to some forgotten realm of pre-mechanical expression. And there is the stunning intimacy, in sweeping shots of mist and trees, in the morbid dignity of ruined cities and bodily remains, in the alertness of speaking eyes that both invite and resist the camera's aim.

2.

Origins: we should always try to keep in mind, in the industrial age, the relationship of technical innovation to speed, velocity, arms. As Ian Jeffrey writes in *ReVisions: An Alternative History of Photography* (1999):

> Gradually, however, it was realized that high-speed photography had relevance in industry, and especially in the manufacture of armaments, which depended on synchronization at high-speed. Using electrical sparks, scientists practiced on splashes (usually made by metal pellets entering milk) and bullets at the moment of discharge. There were famous names involved, such as that of Ernst Mach, who was Professor of Physics at the Physical Institute in Prague. From 1881 he studied the flight of projectiles. As the result of these purely

technical experiments, high-speed photography evolved a strange iconography of bullets and bubbles. (62)

In other words: "once you've shot the gun, you can't stop the bullet."

3.

In Part 2 of Sigfried Giedion's 1948 masterpiece *Mechanization Takes Command: A Contribution to Anonymous History,* in a section called "MOVEMENT," he traces the various developments leading to "the capturing of movement," most graphically represented through E.J. Marey's 1860 Sphygmograph, an invention "which inscribed on a smoke-blackened cylinder the form and frequency of the human pulse beat." After recounting some of Marey's work, along with that of Eadweard Muybridge, sometimes in collaboration, Giedion takes us to the beginnings of the assembly line through the work of Frank B. Gilbreth, an American production engineer who worked with relentless precision "to eliminate needless, ill-directed, and ineffective motions."

"Do you mean," Walid Raad asks the woman Jayce Salloum is filming, "that we will always fail?" The eye directs the finger to shoot ("terrorism is not only a matter of killing, I mean we are simplifying this notion when we reduce it to a matter of killing"), but the hand may no longer be ours:

The human hand is a prehensile tool, a grasping instrument. It can search and feel. Flexibility and articulation are its key words.

The triple-articulated fingers, the wrist, the elbow, the shoulders, and, on occasion, the trunk and legs lighten the flexibility and adaptability of the hand. Muscles and tendons determine how it will seize and hold the object. Its sensitive skin feels and recognizes materials. The eye steers its movement. But vital to all this integrated work is the mind that governs and the feelings that lend it life. The kneading of bread; the folding of a cloth; the moving of brush over

> canvas: each movement has its root in the mind. For all the complicated tasks to which this organic tool may rise, to one thing it is poorly suited: automatization. In its very way of performing movement, the hand is ill-fitted to work with mathematical precision and without pause. Each movement depends on an order that the brain must constantly repeat. It wholly contradicts the organic, based on growth and change, to suffer automatization. (Giedion 1948, 46)

The image is made before us, the image is captured as we are its captive audience: who holds whom hostage in such a situation?

> [M]echanization implanted itself more deeply. It impinged upon the very center of the human psyche, through all the senses. For the eye and the ear, doors to the emotions, media of mechanical reproduction were invented. The cinema, with its unlimited possibility of reproducing an optical-psychic process, displaces the theater. The eye accommodates itself to two-dimensional representation. The adding of sound and color aims at an increasing realism. New values are born with the new medium, and a new mode of imagination. (Giedion 1948, 42–43)

In a completely measurable world, where everything is mapped and people become part of the describable landscape in a human terrain system proposing apparently benign but almost total control, the imagination itself must be mechanized. A remarkably revealing passage in the conclusion to the *9/11 Commission Report* states that: "We believe the 9/11 attacks revealed four kinds of failures: in imagination, policy, capabilities, and management." In an even more remarkable elaboration, in section 11.1, titled "IMAGINATION," a new code is proposed: "Considering what was not done suggests possible ways to institutionalize imagination. [. . .] It is therefore crucial to find a way of routinizing, even bureaucratizing, the exercise of imagination."

4.

These meditations on war ("War is the father of all and king of all," Heraclitus; "We enter again and again the last days of our own history, for everywhere living productive forms in the evolution of forms fail, weaken, or grow monstrous, destroying the terms of their existence," Robert Duncan), always hinge on "conditions of mercy" and "acts of corruption." We cannot divorce ourselves from the technologies of reproduction and destruction in this widening war zone.

5.

In an interview, when asked about the role "resistance'" plays in his work, Salloum responded:

> As a general paradigm "resistance" could be thought of as a key, the underlying precept to the impetus of my work. There are many different forms of resistance, on the ground, in the political arena, in social and cultural relations/positionings and productions — and they all must play a role. In the work I've produced there is not only "resistance" being represented — for instance, the resistance to the occupation of South Lebanon by the Israeli Army, the resistance to the continuity of misrepresentation, and resistance to the use of Lebanon as a product/subject and "laboratory" for the West (in the testing of new & banned warfare technology, the "coverage" by writers, journalists, travelers and "experts," and as a case study for social/cultural studies) — but "resistance" is also being (re)produced structurally, formally, and ideologically in the pieces themselves albeit in a much different capacity. One way or another these productions are a type of resistance, a part of a greater movement, and though limited in its means it still plays a role. It correlates to other work on the ground or groundwork by engaging and one would hope mobilizing a viewer/reader through the agency that the work demands. (*Framework* 2002, 87–88)

"FOLLOW THE PERSON"

I am struck by the fact of being a contemporary, that we have traversed such parallel lines in such different media. My own methods to weave words into spaces they were unaccustomed to be in, to force the reader to move in relation to them:

> *In addition to the work that I was involved in as a translator and activist, I collected massive amounts of documentary material during the war, with the idea of eventually using it in some way as part of a text. The more time I spent with this documentary material, the more I realized that the materials that needed to be brought to bear on the events had to be the materials of culture itself, the materials that appear to remove art from life and confuse a certain rarefied aesthetic with the need to testify. When it came to my book from the warring factions, I wanted to place myself as author/narrator, and the text, in a specific time frame — the time in which the war took place and the text was written. So the first poem places the narrator on a specific date, in a specific place, and it ends on a particular date that happened to coincide with the sentencing of one of the generals responsible for the massacre at Srebrenica — an event at the center of the text but unspoken until the reference to the sentencing at the end of the book. I needed to confound the whole notion of a narrator, or a single self.*
>
> *At the same time, I was not writing about something that happened "over there." This has always been the problem of sojourns — one does not always look at the ground upon which one, or all of us, is standing. The whole question of American empire, of the obliteration and genocide of native peoples, for example, presented itself as a lens through which other reference had to be filtered. Other empires, Rome in particular, followed from this. And we can talk about the price of empire, but what about the dispossession of those who fought for it, the veterans? Coursing throughout everything is the simple question of transmission — how does memory survive? To what materials do we entrust it? Have we, in the cinematic and digital age, renounced claims to stable memory as materials we use*

to record this age implode and crumble more rapidly than any papyrus or tablet?

This led to meditations on film, on forms of propaganda, and the use of materials from newspapers. The more I thought about this, the more I felt that it would somehow be disrespectful, certainly to the dead if not to the living, to pretend that I, as an individual, could add anything to all that has been said or written about war, genocide, exile, memory, and loss. I felt that, by adding new words, I would become a polluter and obfuscate the directions my other work had taken me in, particularly the translation. The issue was not to "say something" or impose an order upon the world but to recalibrate the relationship of existing materials to new conditions and interpretations dictated by events, current or otherwise. I had to let events read themselves back into the texts. I had to become my own translator and a translator of the cultural materials that had been given me or that I had gone in search of. It was with that realization that I decided to generate the texts from word lists and phrases derived from my reading. Through this process, for example, words generated from Shelley's "Revolt of Islam" (1817) could address the massacre at Srebrenica in our time. The process is really the opposite of a chance operation. By using the words of others, I was opening up a way of taking greater responsibility for them than if they were "mine." Inhabiting the world means there is no "other" not already in us, no capacities outside the human that can be attributed to anything outside what we ourselves are individually and collectively capable of. (Alcalay 2012, 192–93)

The ground, groundwork.

The title of Robert Duncan's masterwork, composed of two books: *Ground Work: Before the War* and *Ground Work: In the Dark*. Before the War, though written at the height of the American War in Vietnam, takes the word "before" to mean "in front of," "as witness to," with the understanding as well that, as Duncan once put it: "my art too constantly rationalizes itself, seeking to perpetuate itself as a conventional society. [...] I am trying to keep alive our awareness of the dangers of my convictions." (125)

6.

The artists fumble, working their way through rooms and hallways, taking notes, trying to get to "the people" as they discuss "representation," only to hear:

"There isn't a word for this in Arabic."

7.

In Europe, even among the displaced, it's almost as if the "city" has already been abandoned in speech ("I've seen this city die, the city no longer exists"), because the level of resistance, at least among those being spoken to, has already accommodated itself to being an intruder within "fortress Europe." Over a bridge in the rain: "there's something about your body moving through space," but everything takes place in English ("we are in the position, in the position to be the subject").

There is a symbolic order ("values, habits, are a crucial element of life"). There is a merry-go-round, a carousel, of dream, desire, illusion, and activity: some can think and talk, some are just an image—"they have it, we are beyond it"—out of which conflicts are projected, those which are obscured, occluded, and controlled "domestically," and set into motion there, someplace else, where people are different, not like us.

("We are all hostages, taking part or resisting." "We lived in a fiction." "When we talk about these things, we are losing the possibility of interpretation.")

THESE SPEAK MORE GENERALLY — "Producing more illusions to survive" — (myself included, I recognize my voice-over here, I'm an "expert" of some kind): And THE SWEEP OF TRAINS THE

ELECTRIC LINES REFLECTION OF THE HORIZON IN TRANSIT (there is a yellow lighter on the table: Ilidža, it says, next to a package of Ronhill cigarettes). The old phrase: "DECLARE YOURSELF" comes up and there is no depth of field left in this dissolving Europe of MIST and RAIN, this "live post mortem" in which the old system was "an excuse for all our failures."

8.

Suddenly the instruments of war recede to the background, sweep across the bay. TV aerials? Radar towers? The assemblage holds back, hinting at mystery in a southern California tale documenting the undocumentable.

(Who is she? Did she go missing? Is that her the dogs are looking for? Where does the trail lead?) What is this referencing? I don't recall this scene ...

These are the visuals you choose to assemble, her face off-camera but her voice clear, certain, ever-present. The assemblage holds back ("the aphrodisiac and the blessing"), this is work and this is pleasure but there are hints of intimacy in the music, the voice, the gesture, and the song ("IF THAT'S ALL THERE IS, MY FRIEND, LET'S KEEP DANCING").

The clues are buried but she speaks of a terrain of struggle ("she didn't," her friend says/said/tells us, etc., "fight back from a sense of strength"), and the instruments of war, like the clarity of her voice, are ever-present ("I don't know where or how, but she had a shotgun, she wasn't fooling around"). The precipice of an education, learning to understand that everything you were supposed to want isn't you.

9.

Housepoem. Poemhouse. How many times had he heard this, his grandfather's story? About the adze. And the land. About being here, instead of there. Could there ever be an end to it? SPEAKING IN ARABIC (as if) beauty never ends: "I can still see

"FOLLOW THE PERSON"

them in my mind's eye, the pine trees that had been planted among the ruins").

The surfaces, while the voice is still speaking
LIKE FISH in the water before they're caught:

FREE, like flowers, like bloated bodies, the still life of a
clay oven, the bread and the winding sheet, the head of the adze.

"We took nothing with us."
"We drank from the gutters in the streets with the animals."

Whose speech is this? Which image?

MY WOOD:

> THIS IS A CAVE OUT OF WHICH
> I SEE THE RUINS AND THE
> SKY THE BLUE SKY

    cane

    hat

    shoe &

    sandal

Then (THE HOUSE) asks me about THE ARABS only to say:

> "tell those cowardly eyes about me"

> "should they ever sleep"

& when the sun disappears —

"tell those cowardly eyes about me"

"should they ever sleep"

AND TELL The Makers of Canada, of this "safe passage," that the laws of inheritance, of utensil and musket and rum and infectious blanket, still go to school, that our spirit is like a doorway, teaching us what is in front of us, what is still to come.

10.

About the resistance.

About those who stayed in their homes.

"I was all dressed up, waiting for you to come."

"My mother told me to sleep with my shoes on."

11.

"There isn't a word for this in Arabic."

But there are words.

For water.

For land.

12.

"Contact" brought disease: the ills of the Residential School. The funerals you weren't allowed to go to, the deaths you couldn't mourn, the "measures that would stay in place."

Being face to face with the enemy brings knowledge, an understanding of the terms of the struggle. How can the camera force you to come face to face with a consciousness you can't possibly begin to reach, steps you can only humbly strive to learn how you might begin walking in?

"If you wanted to go and visit a neighbor, they would shoot at you."

"The other day our daughter was going for a walk and they started to

shoot at her, she had to fall to the ground to avoid being hit."

"Last week two women were cultivating thyme, they shot and killed them both. Their only concern was the liberation of the land from the occupation. And the occupation is very very harsh."

13.

"They get tortured more because they have nothing to say."

14.

"This massacre was always in our memory."

15.

"I mean history books pretend that this is how things, events, happened — whereas there are many things that are not mentioned, that are not mentioned anywhere, but are present in the memory of the people."

16.

Tell me, your people, where are they? Did they use the stars to guide them in the night, or was there a planet visible then? Will you have a winding sheet to turn for them or will they end up in a place you'll never know?

Whoever sees these pictures will make
other pictures for themselves, but

"the people who resist, they
resist from within their image."

17.

The camera moves across buildings, across ruins, in a mix of signs and sky, feet walking, and cars driving. But the faces look at us, to question, to testify, to defy, to recollect, to be, insofar as that is possible, within the captive frame. This is a tension that both binds and releases: "Why have I agreed to have this conversation?" is an echo of the statement coming from a disembodied voice, from the camera, and the woman doesn't really answer to your satisfaction. You feel there is more, like when you ask about the flowers and she says: "I saw a shadow quickly pass by and then I noticed a rose in the middle of the empty cell which did not have either a blanket or a mattress." There is more, but instead of framing her as one thing or another, your camera allows her to speak, "of everything and nothing."

A Note on Sources

Throughout the piece there are quotations from Jayce Salloum's videos and other sources interspersed; rather than identifying individual speakers or writers, I have noted from which of Salloum's videotapes each quote comes and cite the other sources below.

The text is prefaced by two quotes; the first is by the American painter Adolph Gottlieb (1903–1974), taken from a note at an exhibition of his work, *The Pictographs of Adolph Gottlieb*, Brooklyn Museum, April 21–August 26, 1995. The second quote is from page 30 of a book referred to in several other sections of the piece, Siegfried Giedion's *Mechanization Takes Command: A Contribution to Anonymous History* (W.W. Norton, 1975).

"FOLLOW THE PERSON"

Section 1: from Jayce Salloum, *"...In the Absence of Heroes..." Warfare/A Case for Context,* 1984.

Section 2: Ian Jeffrey, *ReVisions: An Alternative History of Photography* (National Museum of Photography, Film & Television, 1999), 62.

Section 3: Giedion, *Mechanization Takes Command,* 47 and 42–43. Other quotes are from Salloum's *This is Not Beirut/There was and there was not,* c. 1995, and Salloum and Walid Raad's *Talaeen a Junuub/Up to the South,* 1993. See discussion of this passage of the 9/11 Commission Report in Ammiel Alcalay, *a little history,* ed. Fred Dewey (Re:public/UpSet Press, 2013), 130–33.

Section 4: Robert Duncan, *Bending the Bow* (New Directions, 1968), i.

Section 5: "Occupied Territories: Mapping the Transgressions of Cultural Terrain," an interview-essay with Salloum and Molly Hankwitz on some of Salloum's video works, *Framework* 43, no. 2 (2002): 85–103, specifically pages 87–88, and Ammiel Alcalay, "A Discussion with Benjamin Hollander," in *from the warring factions,* ed. Fred Dewey (Re:public/UpSet Press, 2012), 191–93. The other quote from Robert Duncan in this section is from his essay "Man's Fulfillment in Order and Strife," which appears in *Fictive Certainties: Essays* (New Directions, 1985), 125.

Section 6: *This is Not Beirut/There was and there was not,* 1994.

Section 7: Jayce Salloum, *untitled part 2: beauty and the east,* 2002, and *untitled part 4: terra incognita,* 2005.

Section 8: Jayce Salloum, Episode 1: *So Cal,* 1988, and *Once You've Shot the Gun You Can't Stop the Bullet,* 1988.

"LET ME SHOW YOU SOMETHING"

Section 9: Jayce Salloum, *untitled part 3a: occupied territories, 2001; untitled part 3b: (as if) beauty never ends…*, 2003; and *untitled part 4: terra incognita,* 2005.

Section 10: *Talaeen a Junuub/Up to the South,* 1993.

Section 11: *This is Not Beirut/There was and there was not,* 1994.

Section 12: *untitled part 4: terra incognita,* 2005, and *Talaeen a Junuub/Up to the South,* 1993.

Section 13: *Talaeen a Junuub/Up to the South,* 1993.

Section 14: Ibid.

Section 15: Ibid.

Section 16: *untitled part 3b: (as if) beauty never ends…,* 2003, and *Talaeen a Junuub/Up to the South,* 1993.

Section 17: Jayce Salloum, *untitled part 1: everything and nothing,* 2001.

3

"What I Found Out"

2009

Sometime around 1979, I remember driving out to a prison from Jerusalem with some friends. I don't know exactly why we went, but the windows were open in the small car and there were waves of dry heat beating against us that just became more and more oppressive the closer we got to the prison, located somewhere in the desert. There had been some disturbances in the neighborhood my friend lived in—people had blocked the streets off with burning tires and set the dumpsters on fire to keep the police out as protests mounted over the lack of housing and cuts in the subsidies on bread, milk, oil, flour, and sugar. One of the guys in the car was a junkie who had been active in the Black Panthers. I guess we must have been going out so he could visit someone, but I think there were a bunch of people that we spoke to standing outside the prison who were protesting something. Here everyone grew up together and knew each other—the guards, the prisoners, and those who'd come to see friends and family. Conditions were notoriously bad and the addict, Upright Son (which is how his name translated), told me in detail what he'd gone through when he'd been forced into solitary and had to kick cold turkey. Most of the prisoners had names like mine: Alfandari, Almosnino, Alhadef, Algazi, Altaras, Abulafia.

The next time I lived in Jerusalem, I found out a lot more about what the word torture meant. After the big prisoner exchange before the first intifada, I had the opportunity to meet a lot of people who'd spent many years in the Israeli prisons. Some of them continued to get harassed and were taken in routinely, under the so-called Emergency Regulations left over from the British Mandate which allowed for "administrative detention." We would wait for them in the yard near *Al-Moscobiya,* the Russian compound, right in the middle of Jerusalem, just a few hundred yards from the Central Post Office. After the uprising started, more and more people were taken in and they got younger and younger. Families would wait outside, hoping to get a glimpse of a son, a brother, or a husband, as they barely made their way from one building to another in leg shackles, held up and pushed along by their interrogators.

In 1991 I got a letter postmarked "Central Prison; Kuneitra, Morocco," dated June 24th. I had met Christine Daure-Serfaty some months before, when she had come to New York to accept a human rights award in her still imprisoned husband's name. Happy for the recognition but appalled at the institutional merchandising of pain and suffering she sensed in the proceedings, we immediately hit it off. She told me that the only visitors her husband might eventually receive had to be family relations. Because of our common background as Arab Jews descending from Spain, she suggested I pose as a long lost cousin, an American searching for "roots." I proceeded to write to Abraham, not quite knowing what to expect. By now an internationally known figure, Serfaty had been captured in 1972 and brutally tortured; in 1977 he was given a life sentence for "openly plotting to overthrow the monarchy," and "offences against state security." A mining engineer by profession, he had been active in the communist party and belonged to a clandestine Marxist group. By the time he wrote to me, his conditions had improved and the long letter (beginning "Dear Friend, Your letter of May 2nd gave me great pleasure. I am already familiar with your texts in *Middle East Report* and, moreover, I have long hoped to enter into contact with a younger, militant anti-Zionist Jew whose sensibility is representative of Oriental Jews maintaining some rapport with this ethnicity in relation to the State of Israel"), was typed out on thin paper and neatly pasted into an aerogramme. The Gulf War had only been officially over for a few months and Bosnia was on the verge of a siege that would last over three years.

Following the first intifada and the Gulf War, the almost total blockade on Arabic writing and culture in the United States, particularly as dictated through the liberal Zionist colored glasses of New York's literary-cultural mafia, began to slightly erode from the pressure of many years of activism around the issue of Palestine. The kinds of institutions and activities now considered normal and even expected — in film, music, translation, exhibits, and other forms — were unthinkable in the 1980s and exceptional through most of the 1990s. This kind of movement in such a relentlessly consumption-based society in which so many mechanisms of control have been internalized is always contradictory and paradoxical. Did Palestine and Iraq have to be under constant attack for the poetry of Adonis and Mahmoud Darwish to appear in the *New Yorker?* Have certain manifestations of Middle Eastern culture been embraced in order to avoid others?

The grand psy-ops dreamt up and practiced in the Cold War — the purpose of which were to sever people from experience and the consciousness of their experience — has had deep and devastating effects, both in the United States and elsewhere. Following World War II, poet Charles Olson wrote about the body, the actual physical body, as the last place of resistance:

> in this intricate structure are we based, now more certainly than ever (besieged, overcome), for its power is bone muscle-nerve blood brain a man, its fragile mortal force its old eternity, resistance.[1]

---

1 Charles Olson, *Collected Prose,* ed. Donald Allen and Benjamin Friedlander (University of California, 1997), 174.

"FOLLOW THE PERSON"

This is something prisoners, unfortunately, know all too well.

How can we who have not had such experience, make room for the consciousness of it? When former Moroccan political prisoner and poet Abdellatif Laâbi writes, "We will need a nakedness / that even our skin cannot distort," he offers us entry, through his suffering, back into the "infinite crumbling world" we are continually taught is out of our hands and no longer worth struggling for. When we remain casual in the face of former Syrian political prisoner, poet, and activist Faraj Bayrakdar "inventing an ink from tea and onion leaves" — to smuggle out poems from prison on cigarette papers — we sanction and participate in an indifference that can only come back to haunt us. But do we translate these texts simply to ease our conscience or to present and confront real formal, intellectual, political, philosophic, and ethical challenges?

The lack of personal relationships between North American intellectuals and their counterparts in the Middle East has made it that much easier for propaganda to tell the story. It has obliterated our primary line of defense, allowing the ensuing vacuum to fill up with lies and disinformation. The experts continually tell us, for example, that the Arab world has no Aleksander Solzhenitsyns or Václav Havels. The facts get in the way of such a claim, but they are not that easy to get a hold of. The number of writers, intellectuals, and political activists in the Middle East who have been censored, imprisoned, tortured, assassinated, or disappeared constitutes one of the great human sagas of our times, but there is no single place to go and find a cohesive narrative of these events. The need for an archaeology to excavate and represent this saga systematically is absolute and essential, and belongs in the realm of public health. But, just as importantly, such propaganda serves double-duty, also blocking access to the sources of our history, and a truer understanding of the structures that dictate our cultural politics.

At the same time, we need to reverse many of the prevailing assumptions. When one uses the discourse of human rights, for example, and thinks about the typical report on human rights, the first reaction is to be angry or shocked at the extent of the repression by the regime in question, rather than to think of it as an index of the enormous extent of *resistance* on the part of the people that *requires* such repression. How did we get to such a point? In addition to the obvious villain, the media machine and the political and economic forces driving it, conceptual and systematic failure and acquiescence must be laid at the doorstep of American intellectuals and their lack, not just of responsibility, but of response, on almost every human, creative, historical, and political level. And yet, the paradox and contradiction remain: In our post-NAFTA world, Americans feel they have a right to literatures from other parts of the world, much like they have a right to Chilean cherries in the middle of winter. In such circumstances, it may be wise to consider NOT translating certain things so as not to reproduce the process of getting something at "no" or "low" cost.

What is at stake are war mechanisms, primitive triggers to reorder the past to make it conform to the "logical necessity" of the present. Colonization takes place everywhere, even in time itself. There can be no liberty or liberation, nothing beyond an all-encompassing present that does not merely contain the past but dictates its meaning and limit. The totalitarian impulse behind "routinizing, even bureaucratizing, the exercise of imagination, " as outlined in the conclusion of the *9/11 Commission Report*, makes this very clear.

Against continual Orwellian scenarios usually presented by liberals and progressives, perhaps it would make more sense not to divorce something like the *9/11 Commission Report* and its recommendations from the general culture, to see it as following and not leading, as confirming what has already taken place these past thirty-five years in every realm of society since the end of the war in Vietnam, for which there can be no more revealing fact than the number of prisoners incarcerated in the United States. Thus, the "shock" of Abu Ghraib can only be experienced when the consciousness of the concrete realities and effects of such widespread domestic incarceration are held hostage, kept in some holding facility supposedly outside the realm of "our" experience. In *Prisons: Inside the New America,* poet and novelist David Matlin, who taught in the New York State prison system for many years, writes:

> This is a triumph generating barrenness and dread at the secret core of our daily lives so tangled we don't any longer know how exactly its touch rots everyone of us. The pictures from Abu Ghraib, swelled with perversion and self-satisfied hate, are only hints of our domestic abyss we have already perfected and begun to export. This is not a threshold looming before us as a People, it is a threshold we passed through long ago and we have been for at least two generations perfecting its ransoms.[2]

If there is ransom to be paid, then it is to free a consciousness held hostage and, for that, it is essential to explore and understand the mechanics of propaganda, along with the function of documentation and its role in the preservation and transmission of historical memory.

---

[2] David Matlin, *Prisons: Inside the New America: From Vernooykill Creek to Abu Ghraib* (North Atlantic, 2005), xxiii.

4

Relieving the National Debt:
W.D. Ehrhart & the Wages of Memory

2009

Few things are as determined as the time and place of your birth, the circumstances into which you might be born, and the relative distances you might need or want to move from those points. I was born in Boston in 1956, to parents who had come to the United States as refugee-immigrants just five years before, in 1951, having survived the wars of Europe. They came with great excitement, eager to be involved in new ways of life, to participate in the cultural renaissance that exploded in the 1950s, finding form in abstract painting, jazz, modern dance, and poetry. As opposed to my older brother, my age made me ineligible for the draft, which ended in January 1973, just a month before I would turn seventeen. Paradoxically, my brother's lethal allergy to eggs — something that nearly killed him several times — insured his 4F status, and the lucky privilege of not having to face the kind of momentous decision put before most eighteen-year-olds then.

The open political and cultural turbulence of those years, the constant activity evident everywhere in a city like Boston — from the underground press, the music you could hear, the clothes you wore, the demonstrations you might go to or just stumble into — was impossible to ignore and I already found myself immersed in and receptive to everything taking place around me at an early age, starting in my last years of grade school: 1968 and 1969. My father was an artist and the atmosphere around the house or the studio very often included family friends who were also artists or writers. There were plenty of books around, and most of them were very far from anything that might be construed as "mainstream." The still-obscure little magazines of the 1950s and 1960s — *Origin, Black Mountain Review, Yugen, The Floating Bear, Big Table, Evergreen,* and so many others — populated the bookshelves through which I freely wandered, as did the work of the so-called Beat generation or those closely identified with them.

I remember coming back again and again to a short essay I encountered by Charles Olson, most well known for his epic *The Maximus Poems* and *Call Me Ishmael,* his ground-breaking work on Herman Melville (who happened to be a family friend); it was a review of a book on Billy the Kid, and opened like this:

> It's this way. Here's this country with what accumulation it has — so many people having lived here millennia. Which ought to mean (people being active, more or less) an amount, you'd figure, of things done, and said, more or less as in other lands. And with some proportion of misery — for which read "reality," if you will wait a minute and not take "misery" as anything more than a characterization of unrelieved action or words.
>
> That is: what strikes one about the history of sd States both as it has been converted into story and as there are those who are always looking for it to reappear as art — what has hit me is, that it does stay, unrelieved. And thus loses what it was before it damn well was history, what urgency or laziness or misery it was to those who said and did what they did. Any transposition which doesn't have in it an expenditure at least the equal of what was spent, diminishes what was spent.

And this is loss, loss in the present, which is the only place history has context.[1]

I was caught by this, haunted then, over 40 years ago, and it remains a quote that I keep coming back to the truth of, as, to paraphrase Olson, it stands "more revealed." What I still find unique about it is the concept of "misery" being a state of "unrelieved" reality, and that, in order for history to become meaningful, to integrate itself into one's very consciousness (not to mention a more collective consciousness), there must be as great an effort in its presentation as there was in its very unfolding.

It is in the crux of this conundrum — between the burden of history, the burden of memory, and its coming to consciousness — that W.D. Ehrhart's enormous achievement as poet, memoirist, essayist, and creator of essential anthologies should be located. Within a literary culture that tends to follow the trends of technology (always looking for the latest formal innovation or theory), it is very difficult to find critical terms for the kind of historical burden and seemingly straightforward forms that characterize Ehrhart's work. Moreover, because he has established the context of his own history, through the early poems and memoirs drawing on his war experiences, when we come to later lyric poems, we are presented with an increased emotional charge precisely because of what we already know about how difficult a journey it was to achieve the clarity of such moments, as in this poem "Nothing Profound":

If you need a reason to care,
consider this feather I've found,
consider the sweetness of bare
young arms in sunlight, or the round
perfection of a ripe pear.[2]

---

[1] Charles Olson, *Collected Prose,* ed. Donald Allen and Benjamin Friedlander (University of California Press, 1997), 311.

[2] W.D. Ehrhart, *Beautiful Wreckage: New & Selected Poems* (Adastra Press, 1999), 222.

Thus, what might appear trite in another context suddenly forces us to reconsider the title: for most people, the feather or the pear is "nothing profound," but for Ehrhart, who has had the courage to explore the depths of self-loathing and human horror, these simple things are, indeed, most profound.

In our consumer culture, where we have stopped manufacturing almost everything, and have come to rely on labor that isn't ours, I would even say that our own history has taken on the character of our economy: we print and we print and we print, but there is so very little behind what a devious character on the Powderpuff Girls calls our "happy paper." How did we get to this state? As early as the 1940s, poet Muriel Rukeyser wrote:

> We are a people tending toward democracy at the level of hope; on another level, the economy of the nation, the empire of business within the republic, both include in their basic premise, the concept of perpetual warfare.[3]

While the concept of "perpetual warfare" has been around for a long time, most likely Rukeyser's source for this was a comment made by historian Charles A. Beard to his colleague Harry Elmer Barnes, stating that the foreign policy of both presidents Franklin Roosevelt and Harry Truman could best be characterized as "perpetual war for perpetual peace." Barnes, a major revisionist historian now mostly forgotten, maligned, and discredited, chose it as a title for a collection of essays questioning the motives for US involvement in World War II, following his work questioning US involvement in World War I. Notably, in homage to these sentiments and that historical tradition, Gore Vidal used this same title for his scathing post-9/11 essays, published in 2002.

Not being a small country with borders to defend or under intermittent siege or attack, the method through which perpetual warfare becomes naturalized in the United States must include both perverting the aspirations of youth, and their actual

---

3   Muriel Rukeyser, *The Life of Poetry* (Paris Press, 1996), 61.

physical displacement. In the headnote to a previously unpublished novella by Jack Kerouac unearthed from the archive, Todd Tietchen writes, "Kerouac's planning documents for *The Haunted Life* identify war as a primary catalyst of socio-historical change. In the case of World War II, Kerouac attributed the inevitability of such change to the 'great cross-migration' of an entire generation into the theaters of war, onto military bases, and into the centers of wartime production." As Kerouac himself writes, in one of the fragments on which the novella is based, dated April 12, 1944:

> War creates a situation synonymous to that of a great cross-migration. People who ordinarily were habitually suited to sedentary lives are quite suddenly wandering the earth. Soldiers are sent to all parts of the world, workingmen migrate to far places in their nation and in some cases to foreign lands, country boys sail stranger seas than did the Ancient Mariner. The virus of the war enters the veins of men, women, and children. [...] There is no way of computing the number of civilians who were forced to wander, refugees, workmen, and military auxiliaries alike. The whole panorama is staggering in its proportions.
>
> And when one considers the amount of national cross-migration in individual nations hard at war, the uprooting of families from regions where each had been settled for generations before, the situation grows to a proportion like that of a gigantic earth-shaking which scatters men and women helter-skelter, separating families and lovers and friends in all directions with no regard for traditional humanity and dignity. The picture presents a canvas of disrupted roots drifting like tumbleweeds in a thousand crossing winds. [...] And how haunting will be the memory of those who have lived through the great "cross-migration," the shaking of the earth.[4]

---

4   Jack Kerouac, *The Haunted Life and Other Writings*, ed. Todd Tietchen (Da Capo Books, 2014), 101–2, 109–11.

Given that getting the populace to want to send their children overseas to kill people they never even met isn't the easiest feat for a government to accomplish, we have to be cognizant of the enormous overt and covert machineries and mechanisms put into place in order to actually make this happen, something that has certainly been true since the First World War, and has only grown in intensity since then. Yet, despite widespread popular opinion against US involvement in both World Wars, and the need for politicians to maneuver the country into a certain fervor to attain its objective to engage, nothing quite like the mass anti-war movement of the 1960s and 1970s had been seen.

From common cause between elements of the old Right and elements of the new Left, an enormous resistance mounted: first and foremost by soldiers, but aided and abetted by parents, students, urban up-risers, and so many others. In writing about the heroic work of W.D. Ehrhart, one would hope that some or most of this would be self-evident. But in a country in which Ehrhart is not a household name, or even considered among the leading literary voices, one is better off not assuming anything. Having taught his work in a variety of contexts over the years — from seminars on contemporary American Poetry or Global Decolonization to Introduction to American Studies — it has become increasingly clear that his work resonates across many different subjects and approaches. More importantly, it both calls into question and illuminates — through the integrity of his experience and the force of his expression — both received knowledge and true blank spots. When students never exposed to such images see the very short surviving film clips of Dewey Canyon III, that extraordinary action in which veterans of the war in Vietnam chose, as a last resort, to liberate themselves by throwing their medals at the White House, and connect it to readings of Ehrhart's poems, essays, and memoirs, a whole new world opens up for them, a world they can hardly imagine actually existed.

I want to turn here to the role of poetry, that obvious catalyst for everything Ehrhart has written. During the American Civil War, for example, poetry was common currency. From the now more famous — Walt Whitman, Herman Melville, Emily Dickinson, Henry Wadsworth Longfellow, Bret Harte, William Cullen Bryant, Ralph Waldo Emerson, or Julia Ward Howe — to the countless unknown soldiers, their friends and families, poems were freely and constantly exchanged by letter, published in newspapers, and set to inspirational music. In Faith Barrett and Cristanne Miller's brilliant anthology *"Words for the Hour,"* they write that in the nineteenth century, "Americans not only heard poems at many civic events, but they also read poetry in broadsides, pamphlets, daily newspapers, and magazines, as well as in books and anthologies. [...] [P]oetry was seen as an integral part of American political culture."[5] This "explosion" of poetry is something Ehrhart himself notes about poetry from the era of the war in Vietnam; in the preface to *Unaccustomed Mercies: Soldier-Poets of the Vietnam War,* one of the groundbreaking anthologies that he edited, Ehrhart writes, "This vast body of poetry is a phenomenon unparalleled in American literature. No previous American war, with the possible exception of the American Civil War, has produced anything like it."[6]

There is no doubt that the more politically minded poets of the 1930s — someone like Langston Hughes, for example — strove to create an idiom that could function as a means of public communication, a form both containing and transmitting political, cultural, and social memory. But the advent of the Cold War pushed poetry underground or into the academy, creating what essayist, critic, and translator Eliot Weinberger has called "official verse culture." From that point on poetry became divided and institutionalized into what Robert Lowell called the "raw" and the "cooked" schools.[7] This is what Rukeyser would come to call, in her extraordinary series of lectures, delivered

---

5 Faith Barrett and Cristanne Miller, eds., *"Words for the Hour": A New Anthology of American Civil War Poetry* (University of Massachusetts Press, 2005), 2.
6 W.D. Ehrhart, ed., *Unaccustomed Mercy: Soldier-Poets of the Vietnam War* (Texas Tech University Press, 1989), 1.
7 The best comprehensive guide to some of these thorny issues can be found in Jed Rasula's extraordinary and encyclopedic *The American Poetry Wax*

in the 1940s and eventually published as *The Life of Poetry*, the "fear" of poetry. What I would call an inculcated pedagogy of distrust in our own common sense, in the witness of our intuitions, experiences, emotions, and consciousness, must begin early in order for the war mechanism to take root and operate. As Rukeyser wrote:

> The fear that cuts off poetry is profound: it plunges us deep. Far back to the edge of childhood. [...] Little children do not have this fear, they trust their emotions.
> But on the threshold of adolescence the walls are built. [...] Against the assaults of puberty, and in those silvery delicate seasons when all feeling casts about for confirmation. Then for the first time, you wonder "What should I be feeling?" instead of the true "What do you feel?"[8]

She goes on to speak about "repressive codes" that strike "deep at our emotional life." Breaking through these repressive codes was no easy feat. Certainly a key component in the persistence and reemergence of cultural transmission and its historical consciousness had to do with poets of the 1950s seeking models in those who had lived through the 1930s, as younger poets looked to the example of Hughes, Kenneth Patchen, Rukeyser, William Carlos Williams, Vincent Ferrini, and many others. Charlie Parker invented a new post-atomic language through bebop, captivating the writers who were listening: in his "History of Bop," Kerouac spoke of "America's inevitable Africa," something that could easily be related to the worldwide decolonization movement, and the return of an indigenous consciousness. In the Beat movement, so often written off as apolitical, human experience returns to the forefront, with a distinct and deeply subversive intent. In an interview with David Hadbawnik, poet David Meltzer says: "I've always considered the Beat Genera-

---

Museum: Reality Effects, 1940–1990 (National Council of Teachers of English, 1996).
8 Rukeyser, *The Life of Poetry*, 15–16.

tion as a dissident movement, a kind of resistance movement, anti-materialist, pro-civil rights, early poetic ecology, a whole bunch of things, and that it came out of a very complex postwar American culture."[9] And Michael McClure, one of the readers at the famous Six Gallery reading where Allen Ginsberg first read *Howl* in public, describes the times:

> We were locked in the Cold War and the first Asian debacle — the Korean War. My self-image of those years was of finding myself — young, high, a little crazed, needing a haircut, in an elevator with burly, crew-cutted, square-jawed eminences, staring at me like I was misplaced cannon fodder. We hated the war and the inhumanity and the coldness. The country had the feeling of martial law.[10]

But after the collective experience undergone through the public reading of *Howl,* McClure writes of "knowing at the deepest level that a barrier had been broken, that a human voice and body had been hurled against the harsh wall of America and its supporting armies and navies and academies and institutions and ownership systems and power-support bases."[11] Wally Hedrick, one of the organizers of the Six Gallery reading, had been an infantryman in Korea, and began a series of black paintings protesting the French and encroaching American involvements in Indochina. What McClure describes, of course, becomes greatly amplified in the unprecedented role that poetry takes on among the American poet-soldiers of the Vietnam War era, but these connections are seldom articulated or traced. And, to return to the subject at hand, we must also consider the extraordinary ways in which W.D. Ehrhart has overcome this "fear of poetry" precisely through the exposure of both his own history, his com-

---

[9] David Meltzer, interview by David Hadbawnik, March 2010, archived at: https://web.archive.org/web/20240723032354/http://www.bigbridge.org/BB14/2010_diprima/DiPrima_Meltzer_Interview.HTM.

[10] Michael McClure, *Scratching the Beat Surface: Essays on New Vision from Blake to Kerouac* (Penguin, 1994), 12.

[11] Ibid., 15.

ing to consciousness about that history, and his willingness to explore the most difficult emotional aspects of that process.

I am mapping this circuitous route — from my own personal background to Charles Olson, Muriel Rukeyser, the American Civil War, the Beats, and the work of poet-soldiers — to make the point that our history has been atomized, made illegible, as if there were neither connection nor consequence between one era or another, between one phenomenon and another. We have been made to think that the work of Ehrhart can somehow be relegated to a particular historical event or experience, to the war in Vietnam as a discrete event, detaching it from the collective burden of that war and all its myriad personal and political consequences that have rippled throughout our society and the world ever since. This would be like saying that Melville's *Moby Dick* is only about whaling, and since we no longer whale, there is really no need to consider what else that book might mean. But there is another literary and cultural history that it is up to us to map and describe, a history in which Ehrhart's work would be as central as the *Autobiography of Frederick Douglass,* as central as the slave narratives and the writings of the abolitionists, as central as the massive legacy of this continent's Indigenous peoples or the *Autobiography of Malcolm X*. And it is central because, by personally taking on the burden of the nation's history, a history for which he actually volunteered, Ehrhart has provided those who didn't or won't take it up with some relief.

In the preface to *Vietnam-Perkasie: A Combat Marine Memoir,* one of Ehrhart's most deceptive and important works, H. Bruce Franklin pinpoints one of the truly important qualities of Ehrhart's work, his "potent combination of personal experience and historical understanding." As or even more importantly, Franklin emphasizes the profundity of Ehrhart's courage, and its relationship to historical understanding:

> *Vietnam-Perkasie* features one characteristic of Ehrhart's writing that distinguishes it from most, though not all, literature by Vietnam veterans (or anybody else): he reveals things about his own actions that very few of us are brave enough to

disclose. As he relentlessly probes the moral significance of these actions in Vietnam, he begins to display their historical significance. This leads to what is most distinctive about *Vietnam-Perkasie,* Ehrhart's ability to shape the autobiographical memoir into his own special vehicle for exploring history through personal experience.[12]

By making his own experience exemplary, and daring to disclose the things most of us would do almost anything to never reveal, Ehrhart provides a vehicle — through the narrative imagination, through the story of his own experiences — that can offload some of that compressed volatility, some of that impacted and self or outwardly directed violence that continues to erupt "randomly" throughout our society.

Ehrhart's transformative abilities in this regard, in both prose and poetry, are remarkable. One text that I teach whenever I have the opportunity, and that I return to again and again as a true masterpiece, is his "forensic" essay "The United States Screw & Bolt Company." In the space of fifteen pages, including footnotes, Ehrhart presents a series of juxtaposed biographical facts, moving between policy makers and those forced to carry out those policies, the soldiers whose lives — if they survived — would always be marked by their participation as bearers of messages created in Washington and written on paper or exclaimed in speeches, but delivered via bombs, bayonets, zippo lighters, agent Orange, and myriad other means of destruction. Without resorting to any commentary, any historical, political, economic, sociological, anthropological, critical-theoretical, or other disciplinary source, Ehrhart lays out as accurate a picture of power relations in the United States as we have.

What comes across loud and clear in this text, and in so much of Ehrhart's work, is something expressed by another former comrade in arms, Tom Hawkins, one of the veterans included in Ehrhart and Jan Barry's anthology *Demilitarized Zones: Veter-*

---

12 H. Bruce Franklin, "Preface," in W.D. Ehrhart, *Vietnam-Perkasie: A Combat Marine Memoir* (University of Massachusetts Press, 1995), x.

ans After Vietnam, when Hawkins writes of "the unprecedented magnitude of betrayal — the common disowning and dissociation of responsibility."[13] This sense of betrayal and dissociation has, indeed, become one of the things we hold most in common as citizens of this republic, and it remains unrelieved, unspoken, unexpressed, left to seethe like Langston Hughes's "dream deferred." For Ehrhart, and many others whose writing emerged as poet-soldiers, poetry provided a path, a way back into what Olson called "the human universe." In his landmark anthology, *The Vietnam War in American Stories, Songs, and Poems*, H. Bruce Franklin writes:

> When Jan Barry, one of the earliest of these veteran poets and a leading figure in promulgating veteran poetry, speaks to students in Vietnam courses, he describes his working-class youth in upstate New York when "the last thing I would ever think of being was a poet." What he wanted to be was a career man in the U.S. Army, and as for poetry, that was something just for "sissies." But what he, along with many others, discovered in Vietnam was that "poetry saved my life."[14]

In this context, the function of poetry — first and foremost — is to reopen lines of recognition to oneself, and then to form the basis of resistance rooted in the integrity of one's own experience — personal, intuitive, emotional, imaginative, historical, economic, and political — even as that experience becomes exemplary, and neither a commodity nor a possession. In a literary culture largely built on the nepotism of prizes, awards, fashion, the professional life, and a turbo-charged will towards pyrotechnical innovation, this is, indeed, a bitter pill to swallow. More difficult in fact, is the idea that readers might not need to search for ever more obscure critical or theoretical terms

---

13 Jan Barry and W.D. Ehrhart eds., *Demilitarized Zones: Veterans After Vietnam* (East River Anthology, 1976), ix.
14 H. Bruce Franklin, ed., *The Vietnam War in American Stories, Songs, and Poems* (Bedford Books of St. Martin's Press, 1996), 222.

to obfuscate meaning but, rather, reach ever deeper into the recesses of their own experiences and consciousness to see just how near or far they might be from the poem in front of them.

By looking at Ehrhart's most powerful work, we might also be confronted with the horrors of looking at ourselves as others might see us, others whom we have tried to obliterate from the face of the earth. Here, as in Ehrhart's landmark poem "Making the Children Behave," all the poet can offer is the fact of his own realization that he comes not to bear culture or civilization but to wreak havoc, wanton destruction, and death:

> Do they think of me now
> in those strange Asian villages
> where nothing ever seemed
> quite human
> but myself
> and my few grim friends
> moving through them
> hunched
> in lines?
>
> When they tell stories to their children
> of the evil
> that awaits misbehavior,
> is it me they conjure?[15]

By displacing himself into the specters of fear projected at children whose parents or grandparents he once tried to kill, Ehrhart is displacing the power he once wielded, and handing it in trust to the emotional imagination of children who recognize in him an enemy. In this act, Ehrhart resists and refuses the stories we have been told and insists on his own experiences, and the emotional and political truths behind those experiences. At the same time, he faces head on "the fear that cuts off

---

15 W.D. Ehrhart, ed., *Carrying the Darkness: The Poetry of the Vietnam War* (Texas Tech University Press, 1989), 97.

poetry," and the "repressive codes" that Rukeyser wrote strike "deep at our emotional life." The courage of this transposition is a triumph of imagination. In some sense, it is finally ourselves that we must imagine and imagine away, since, as poet Diane di Prima writes,

> the war that matters is the war against the imagination
> all other wars are subsumed in it[16]

---

16 Diane di Prima, *Revolutionary Letters* (City Lights Books, 2021), 104–7.

5

"The Body is a House"

2010

The title of this piece is also a line from an apparently incomplete text by Charles Olson that Kate Morgan and I found in the archive at the University of Connecticut, Storrs, dated 1955. The paradoxical thing about an archive is that it is a place where revealing things can be hidden, a place that protects materials that expose the unknown.

The idea of the body and the house appears earlier, in Olson's essential statement from 1949, "The Resistance," written in light of the then-most recent and technologically brutal ways to dismember and dispose of human bodies during the Second World War. When the body has been reduced to "so much fat for soap, superphosphate for soil," Olson writes that a man is forced to arrive "at his own physiology," and concludes that the body is the answer, the only site of resistance left, "this house that moves, breathes, acts."

But if the body is a house, where do we live? What can a place mean?

We carry in our bodies memories whose physical traces have been destroyed in our constantly changing environment.

I carry the presence of Olson's eyes gripping me across the table as he gives me some penny candy during a visit when I was a child in Gloucester, circa 1962 or 1963.

"FOLLOW THE PERSON"

In Olson's childhood in Worcester, Massachusetts, when his father gave him the book of Mathew Brady's photographs at the age of six (1916) that so affected him, he would have soon realized that there were still Civil War veterans in town. What became of the Grand Army of the Republic Hall at 55 Pearl Street in 1912, a meeting place for Union veterans that was originally built in 1876, and lasted through the 1930s, serving veterans from the First World War? Surely this grand building would have taken up some space in Olson's childhood imagery.

This childhood, with birth in 1910, where Olson physiologically was formed — as Robert Duncan points out — nursing, standing, walking, and talking before the First World War, was also a time in which the past had a future.

The ancientness of the world, the pastness of the past, formed vivid markers for people growing up in the new, twentieth century. The musician Sun Ra, for example, followed the discoveries of King Tut's tomb avidly as a child growing up in the 1920s in Birmingham, Alabama, just as a young Olson followed the discoveries of ancient America through the excavations establishing the existence of Folsom Man, dating back to at least 10,000 BC.

Olson would write "that the archaeological discoveries of the past centuries have supplied, directly from the ground, substantive & narrative physicality to previously discursive language & thought."

In "Fish Lab," Morgan writes of her experience as an archaeologist, working in downtown Manhattan in 1980:

> We wash and we wash and we wash keeping our house of history. We, the scurrying maids of lore gabbing and splashing and scrubbing each and every one of these literally tons of oyster shells and bricks. Enjoying perfect moments when, how unexpectedly, a wampum bead floats to the surface of the muddy basin water. Wondering if it was ever meant to make it to here, rolling silently in the cracked palm of your hand. Or is it a travesty, this digging, this cleansing of the oldest people here? Dare we trespass all the corrosion, the

formlessness? Or sometimes just simply overwhelmed by the sheer number of things. Or is it the pieces that are the transgressors? They march in to be numbered, counted. They come to become you, until as much of the rust and shit that you brush off becomes as much of the inertness that grows inside. Inside here. Inside now. Inside me. Ai! Ai! Ai! Nipson Anomemata Monan Opsin, Wash not only my transgressions, but also my face! Clean me. Tell me a story to get through all this history. So, the poet answers "ISTORIN" — in other words, "tell yourself." That's what was said in the beginning.

"Our house of history." What is the body's artifact? Is it only made known through disruption or pain, a tumor, a growth, a bruise, a cut? Or through agility, alertness, intuition? Morgan tells me it is the immune system, that place in ourselves under more and more duress...

Do we have fewer memories when we are younger or do they take up more space in us then because we don't have as many?

Are breaks in the accumulation the thing we call memories?

In "A Poem Beginning With A Line By Pindar," Robert Duncan writes:

Finders Keepers we sang
           when we were children   or were taught to sing
    before our histories began

If "the body is a house" and you think of yourself as a place, what kinds of movement happen in that place and how do you account for its shape? Is this what Olson was getting at in "Proprioception," when he wrote that "the soul is proprioceptive" — "proprius-ception / 'one's own'-ception" — & the need "to have a third term, so that movement or action is 'home.' Neither the Unconscious nor Projection (here used to remove the false opposition of 'Conscious'; 'consciousness' is self) have a home unless the DEPTH implicit in physical being — built-in space-time specifics, and moving (by movement of 'its own') — is asserted, or found out as such."

Does history begin with song or image, with sensation or vision? Our history, I mean what we can remember or sense —

When I see the black & white footage of Fort Square & Gloucester I feel the unremitting velocity at which we've been propelled out of one world into another unforgiving and relentlessly mediated world...

Maximus to Gloucester, Letter 27 [withheld]: "I come back to the geography of it... no bare incoming / of novel abstract form... the imposing / of all those antecedent predecessions... all that I no longer am, yet am... I have this sense, / that I am one / with my skin / Plus this — plus this: that forever the geography / which leans in / on me I compel / backwards... to yield, to / change..."

Diane di Prima, in her lectures on Olson, says,

1) the body is proposed as the ground

As heart-beat and breath are the counterpoint in us
          we lay listening to in the dark, as children
   "What if it stops?"

this body stuff — it is the first time it is so patently there —

So when the relationships between places and the space in ourselves, in our body/house, are severed, the heart stops, the breath is held.

In *Wisdom Sits In Places,* the anthropologist Keith Basso examines the importance of places in Apache conceptions of history:

> Answering the question "What happened here?," it deals in the main with single events, and because these are tied to places within Apache territory, it is pointedly local and unfailingly episodic. It is also extremely personal, consistently subjective, and therefore highly variable among those who work

to produce it. For these and other reasons, it is history without authorities — all narrated place-worlds, provided they seem plausible, are considered equally valid — and the idea of compiling "definitive accounts" is rejected out of hand as unfeasible and undesirable. Weakly empirical, thinly chronological, and rarely written down, Western Apache history as practiced by Apaches advances no theories, tests no hypotheses, and offers no general models. What it does instead, and likely has done for centuries, is fashion possible worlds, give them expressive shape, and present them for contemplation as images of the past that can deepen and enlarge awareness of the present.

In his lectures on Olson, the British poet Jeremy Prynne said: "Myth is the telling of the story of where you are. [...] Mythography: the writing of where one is."

In the ancient Arabic form of the *qaṣīda,* the poet stops at the ruins of a particular campsite and recognizes traces of the beloved: the poet is a *turjumān,* a translator, the poet is *turjumān al-ashwāq,* the translator of desires, and his route, as in the poetry of Ibn al-'Arabi, are "stations of desire." The *qaṣīda* has to occur in a place, and when traces of the beloved are recognized, we are led to remembrance, to *dhikr.* Sometimes a phantom of the beloved appears, the *khayal,* a word that later comes to mean imagination.

The philosopher Ibn Sinna (Avicenna), whom Olson read through the interpretations of Henry Corbin, would later come to characterize a term derived from *khayal, takhyīl,* ("a mental process by which the poet can cause mimetic representations to be imagined, effective & creative"), as "an acceptance."

In the mythography in which Olson's *Maximus* creates a moral topography, a place we can learn how to walk in, we are shown, as Diane di Prima points out:

2) that the work proceeds by its own laws:
"he can go by no other track than the one the poem under hand declares for itself" opens the door to various specula-

tions and notions of the "dictated" poem. And Duncan's concept of "obedience" to the poem, if it does not grow out of Charles's sentence, proceeds from a like base.

> staying in the poem (the experience)
> not "memory of"
> not "emotion recollected in tranquility" etc.

> This is no easy indulgence, for the poem is not all-inclusive
>   it "includes" only what is itself
>   &
>   is thus particular

> Pound, and others, all the way back to Wyatt
> may well have experienced this "obedience"
> this following where the poem leads
> but Olson was the first to propose it as a

LAW OF POETIC COMPOSITION

Charles Olson talks of the "conventions logic had forced on syntax" and there are also the ones syntax has forced on thought

As is obvious by now, we are the inheritors of a syntax formed by logics other than our own:

And later, di Prima goes on to say:

> In composition by field, nothing is excluded a priori
> our materials are determined by the particularity of the event
> (the poem itself)
> & herein lies the challenge, or one of them —
> to adhere to
> this singularity (uniqueness)
> w/out allowing the attention
>   to wander, to be pulled off, distracted

>   by the Guardians of the Threshold
>
> those keepers of the New (our self-initiation
>   which every poem is)
>   the darkness of our self-initiation
>
> as there are postures of attention (readiness)
> unique to each of us

Posture, stance, where one is in relation to WHERE, then, becomes crucial — the distances, so the distances are —
As Don Byrd writes,

> Olson spoke of this quality in terms of innocence, of taking the words up innocently, so they are not references, not already ravaged by consciousness or grammar or logic or mimesis or style or meaning, so meaning and form are not prior to them, but their consequence, as a result of what happens to them in their environment.
>
> Words and syllables for Olson are molecular or cellular, events on non-Euclidean surfaces, which have the advantage precisely that one can decide for oneself how close or distant things are from other things.

This terrain on which we can walk is a map INCLUDING our being, "not the time of primal chaos, but just after it — the first moment of creative selection, which is called in evolutionary biology 'preadaptation,' when the creature selects, say, for the components of an eye without knowledge of sight or for the components of a wing without knowledge of flight...breath, not yet rhythm, but the medium of rhythm, from whence comes image, knowing, and the construct."

If words are cellular, then the accumulation of an understanding of them occurs both in an instant and a lifetime, each possibility containing and informed by the other. When Robert Duncan wrote, "The end of masterpieces...the beginning of testimony," we are in the presence of a writing that would resist administration, just as a victim of torture would resist the logic of torture and dwell in the body, no matter how scarred, since, as Kate Morgan writes, it is "our house of history."

SOURCES:

Materials from the Charles Olson Research Collection are housed in the Archives & Special Collections at the Thomas J. Dodd Research Center, University of Connecticut Libraries at Storrs, and used with their permission.

Charles Olson's "The Resistance" and "Proprioception" can be most easily found in *Collected Prose,* ed. Donald Allen and Benjamin Friedlander (University of California Press, 1997); "Letter 27" appears in *The Maximus Poems,* ed. George F. Butterick (University of California Press, 1983).

Kate Tarlow Morgan's "Fish Lab," can be found in her *Circles & Boundaries* (Factory School, 2011), 183–204.

Robert Duncan's "A Poem with a Line Beginning by Pindar" can be found in his *The Opening of the Field* (Grove Press, 1960). Other key ideas of Duncan's considered in my piece can be found in *Fictive Certainties: Essays* (New Directions, 1985), particularly in "The Truth and Life of Myth," "Ideas of the Meaning of Form," "Man's Fulfillment in Order and Strife," and "Changing Perspectives in Reading Whitman."

Diane di Prima's Lectures on Olson were originally given to me by her before eventually being published, partially, by *Lost & Found* as Diane di Prima, *"Old Father, Old Artificer": Charles Olson Memorial Lecture,* ed. Ammiel Alcalay and Ana Božičević, *Lost & Found,* Series III, Spring 2012 (Center for the Humanities, 2012).

Keith H. Basso, from *Wisdom Sits in Places: Landscape and Language Among the Western Apache* (University of New Mexico Press, 1996), 32.

Jeremy Prynne's "Lectures on Maximus" were delivered at Simon Fraser University on July 27, 1971; transcribed by Tom McGauley and published in *Iron* (October 1971), and reprinted in Minutes of the Charles Olson Society 28 (April 1999). They are also available at: https://charlesolson.org/Files/Prynnelecture1.htm.

Michael Sells provides an excellent explication of these concepts, from which some of my ideas are drawn, in his introduction to *Stations of Desire: Love Elegies from Ibn 'Arabi and New Poems* (Ibis Editions, 2000).

A discussion of Ibn Sinna's concept of imagination can be found in chapter two of my *After Jews & Arabs: Remaking Levantine Culture* (University of Minnesota Press, 1993).

Don Byrd's essay "an actual earth of value to / construct one" was prepared for the first *OlsonNow* event at the St. Marks Poetry Project on December 3, 2005, and remains unpublished. Available at: https://writing.upenn.edu/epc/authors/olson/blog/byrd1.pdf.

II

OUT OF THE SCHOOLS AND
INTO THE ARCHIVES

6

Interview with David Hadbawnik

2014

DAVID HADBAWNIK: First, some background: How long has the *Lost & Found* series been around, and what is its mission?

AMMIEL ALCALAY: We're going into our fifth year and the missions are multiple: the essence of it, I think, has to do with learning how I found myself in a line of particular transmission, a particular tradition, and figuring out how such a process might be presented as a possibility within an institutional educational setting. Of course, the odds are against you, particularly since institutional goals are getting more and more narrow, and as you get further along, specialization and professionalization kick in, making it even more challenging.

Some years ago, I helped create a Human Rights Program for undergraduates at Queens College and the key to that project was the decision to work with graphic arts students. The idea was not to bring the subject in from left field, but to integrate it with what people were already learning. In this case, each event, a memorial lecture, was dedicated to someone who'd been killed in a situation of political urgency and each student had to learn about the person and the situation and create a poster to announce the lecture. The results were extraordinary.

In the case of *Lost & Found,* when I began teaching graduate students who were mainly involved in contemporary things, I found that, as someone academically trained as a medievalist, there were tremendous gaps in how the students were thinking about things, through no real fault of their own. In addition, we found that our students were working so hard, between teaching and studying, that there were too few opportunities for extended research leading to publication prior to embarking on a thesis. So the idea was to bring that kind of research and hands on work into the setting of a seminar.

A lot of the work crystallized through long conversations with Aoibheann Sweeney, then Director of the Center for the Humanities at the Graduate Center, CUNY, and by thinking through how we could use this great public institution in new ways. One of the original concepts was what we called "The Living Archive," and involved bringing in elder, non-affiliated working artists to meet with young scholars, organize public events and find ways in which this interaction would be of mutual benefit. For example, it was as important to bring our young researchers OUT of the academy and into these artistic communities, to create new relationships and synergies, as it was to bring the artists into the university. Given that we're in CUNY, the biggest urban public university in the country, the university really is part of the community. Through this initiative we were able to have *Lost & Found* Fellows such as David Henderson, Diane di Prima, Margaret Randall, and David Meltzer, and events with the late Amiri Baraka or upcoming with Ed Sanders.

The mission has grown in many ways: our students/editors have curated exhibits, published books through *Lost & Found Elsewhere,* and been called in by various constituencies to share their knowledge.

DH: Why should we care about poets' archives? There have, famously, been some literary estates resistant to allowing access to and publication of archival materials (thinking of Louis Zukofsky and James Joyce, to name a couple); presumably the argument is that everything that was intended for publication has been published, and poking around in the archives is an invasion of what should be little more than a curiosity.

AA: We should care a lot about poets' archives. In most cases, as far as the mid-to-late twentieth century artists that *Lost & Found* has used as a focal point, we are talking about an inverted pyramid, with many major writers having more unpublished than published work. Take Diane di Prima, for example. Our efforts with Diane have centered on so-called "extra-poetic" work: lectures, essays, etc. When we finish working on what will surely be a multi-volume collection, the nature of our knowledge about poetics from this period will completely change. Our work with Michael Rumaker helped prompt a massive revival that was already partly underway but which has seen reprints of half a dozen books over the past three or four years. The correspondence between Robert Duncan and Pauline Kael will reveal a formative friendship that is of great historical importance. Even very well known writers like Muriel Rukeyser or Langston Hughes have layers and layers of work to be explored. One of our students recovered Rukeyser's unpublished novel about the Spanish Civil War, *Savage Coast,* written prior to either Ernest Hemingway or George Orwell's accounts. We're working on some Langston Hughes material, diaries and photographs from his trip to Central Asia, and the student working on this project happens to speak Uzbek and is tracing translations of Hughes into Uzbek from the period as well as friendships with Uzbek poets who were disappeared by Joseph Stalin. There are certainly another dozen volumes in Amiri Baraka's archives. And this is not even to mention correspondence. The correspondence of Ed Dorn and Baraka, published by the University of New Mexico Press and edited by one of our former students and *Lost & Found* editors, reveals a relationship that gives us a completely different version of late 1950s, early 1960s political and cultural history. The same is true with the collected letters of John Wieners, a recently completed project. Not to mention the discovery made of Harlem Renaissance poet Helene Johnson's late poems, appearing in our last series, or the teaching materials of Adrienne Rich. Needless to say, I could go on at length!

DH: What are some of the more surprising finds that have turned up since the series began? Have there been some materials unearthed in poets' archives that fundamentally changed the way you and other critics might think about the poet?

AA: Many of the examples I've just mentioned would provide a response to your question. But let me get more into the micro level here: one of the mottos of *Lost & Found* has been to "follow the person." In other words, students trained on anthologies have a tendency to think in terms of "schools," and that there might be deference or antagonism between these formations. And then they encounter letters and they see who is talking about whom, or they read some of the original magazines and can't understand why people from seemingly different worlds appear in the same publication.

So, what has interested me more than anything, besides the dramatic discoveries, is the creation of dense networks that can truly reconfigure our historical conceptualization of things, making everything more dense and complicated. For instance, we have an incredible project for the next series on Jean Sénac, an openly queer Algerian poet who was involved in the Algerian revolution and was assassinated in 1973. Sénac started a little magazine in 1954, at the same time that little magazines in the US started, *Four Winds,* for example, co-edited in Gloucester, Massachusetts, by poet and former labor organizer and factory worker Vincent Ferrini, subject of one of our Series IV chapbooks. Sénac was also head of the Algerian writers union and had a radio show on which he featured shows about revolutionary poets from around the world: these included shows on Allen Ginsberg, Bob Kaufman, Amiri Baraka, Gregory Corso, etc. Now we have another project on Kathy Acker. In the archive, our editor found a very hard to find first edition of Jack Hirschman's translation of Algerian poet Ait Djafar's amazing poem "The Wail of the Arab Beggar in the Casbah," first published in 1954 in J.P. Sartre's magazine *Les Temp Modernes*. This became a very important text for Sénac for his manifesto, the text we'll be publishing, *The Sun Under the Weapons*. And in the margins Kathy Acker has various notes about Algerian revolutionaries. I could give you twenty more examples like this; although this is less the kind of dramatic discovery than the Rukeyser novel, in the long run, I think this is the kind of work that presents the evidence for a fundamentally different literary, cultural, and political history, and that, really, I daresay, is what most excites us.

DH: There is a movement afoot in older literature to digitize archival material — manuscripts, illuminations, early print texts, etc. To what extent do you see that happening with twentieth century poetic materials, and how is it complicated by copyright issues? What is the role of *L & F* amidst the increasing digitization of archival materials?

AA: We've been militantly print- and object-oriented for many different reasons, none of them having to do with nostalgia. To begin with, for the pedagogy involved, the stages involved in creating a print object, as well as the different constituencies involved, present stages of learning that are not replaceable in digital media. Granted, there are very different processes involved in the creation of digital editions, and these are also of extreme value. But for our purposes, the print object remains central. On the other hand, as you know, many of the writers we're concerned with sold their papers in piecemeal fashion, in order to pay the bills or survive. Thus, to work on someone like Diane di Prima really entails research in at least half a dozen locations all over the country. In our larger vision, we would like to create digital pathways between these archives, to reunite this diasporic grouping, because I think that is one of the central reasons why it has been so hard to look at the work of these writers more coherently, and not as individual parts of a grouping or school.

DH: Describe the role of student editors working with you at CUNY. How does this kind of research and editing intersect with their scholarly focus? To what extent do they dictate the direction of the series, vis-à-vis upcoming projects, etc.?

AA: The student editors are, in a word, awesome! I can't even begin to say how knocked out I've been by the kind of work they've done, the kinds of relationships they've developed to people connected with their subjects or, in some cases, if the subjects are alive, to the subjects themselves. This is a thrilling process to watch. The work can be daunting in that these younger researchers may be taking on a text by a writer whom they have adored for a long time and this may be a text that is completely unburdened by any anterior critical commentary. So there is daring involved, and a rapid onset of mature thinking. In many cases a *Lost & Found* project has become a dissertation; this was the case with the Rukeyser novel or the journals of Philip Whalen, the collected letters of Wieners, the Dorn/Baraka correspondence, and a number of others in the pipeline. I am thrilled that we've come around to legitimizing contemporary textual scholarship as a worthy academic endeavor because the learning curve, the skill set, and actual usefulness of the work, I think, often far surpass many standard dissertations, particularly on contemporary subjects. As far as the direction of the projects go, my role has really been to infect people with the bug and let them take it in new directions.

DH: Could you talk a little bit more about your medievalist training and how it has informed your understanding of twentieth-century poetics and, more specifically, the archival mission of *Lost & Found*? On a related note — as you know from my own contribution to *L & F, Jack Spicer's Beowulf* — I'm keenly interested in medieval inflections as well. In a sense, this speaks to what you mentioned earlier, the way in which archival research really broadens and alters our view of some of these poets and the "New American Poetry" generation, not only in terms of undiscovered works, but the hidden roots of influence and tradition that might be elided if one simply looks at previously published material. So in that vein it's been an explicit mission for some of us — Dan Remein, Sean Reynolds, and me — to reorient the image of Jack Spicer to include these medievalist roots.

AA: My own training was pretty hybrid. I was a pretty colossal fuck up in high school, it was also 1969–1973, and I didn't go to school much. My grades were awful and I went to work after high school and college seemed very distant; it was always "shows great promise," "has lots of talent," "can't organize," etc. At some point I'd been taking classes with Gilbert Sorrentino, this would be 1975 or so, and he suggested I sink my teeth into languages.

I ended up enrolling at City College as a "night student," School of General Studies, with the trick then being that you could take anything and just pay by the credit. And I took two courses that really turned my head around. One was called "Science in Antiquity," taught by a wonderful guy named Mr. Hennion who seemed like some kind of lapsed Jesuit. But he also seemed to know everything, and I loved that; we started with Egyptian and Babylonian math and worked our way through the Pre-Socratics. I still have my notebook from that course and I reproduced a few pages in my book *neither wit nor gold*. The other class was intensive Latin with a linguist by the name of Louis Heller, I think there's a sound change law named after him. That was both thrilling and terrifying because we met four times a week and you were constantly on the spot to decline something or recite our "sententiae" and translate them. But after a semester of that, I was able to read Cicero and the following year I was in a tutorial with one other student and we read the *Aeneid*. And that remains, unquestionably, one of the formative reading experiences I've ever had.

At a certain point I began pursuing things that, ultimately, derived from an interest in my own family background, that of a Sephardic family with roots in the Balkans and, of course, Spain and al-Andalus prior to that. In some sense, it fit in very well with a desire to get away from a Eurocentric model of things.

"FOLLOW THE PERSON"

I began studying Arabic on my own, then Hebrew. I ended up spending two years in Jerusalem and immersed myself in Arabic and Hebrew philosophy and poetry, really spanning from the inception of Islam through the various expulsions from Spain. I was totally hooked on a kind of old-time philological approach to things but I brought with it my own immersion in the American poetry that I grew up with and around. It was an unusual combo — my politics made it pretty impossible for me to go the route of traditional Jewish Studies, and Middle East/Arabic stuff was almost completely based in the social sciences. So I somehow had to construct my own curriculum.

Back in New York circa 1980 I floundered around a bit and after looking at an admissions application for Columbia that I took out of my mailbox, ripped into shreds, and threw into a trash can, I headed to 42nd Street to see if I could visit Allen Mandelbaum at the Graduate Center. The stars must have been very well aligned because I simply knocked on the door and he took me into his office, an office I would spend many, many hours in subsequently, and we talked for about two hours. It turned out that he had grown up in a Hebrew-speaking home, that he knew the medieval poetry very well, had even translated some of it, but was also hip to Ezra Pound, William Carlos Williams, Charles Olson, and North African writers like Mouloud Mammeri. He walked me down to the Comparative Literature office and simply told them to figure out how I could be admitted. From the present perspective, this is almost unimaginable — though I've done it a few times with new students! I don't even remember formally applying, though I must have.

Anyways, Allen's approach was incredible: We read generations of scholarship and I did Romance philology (Spanish, Old French, and Italian), and pursued the Arabic/Hebrew stuff on my own. Frederic Goldin was there too, and he was incredible; interestingly, he had connections to people like Paul Blackburn and George Economou, other poets who had done important medieval work. It all just seemed to make sense. I then ended up spending about five years back in Jerusalem where the bulk of the work that went into *After Jews & Arabs* was done. When I was there, I worked with one of the truly great scholars of medieval Hebrew poetry, Dan Pagis, also a great poet, and that just seemed to corroborate things.

I could go on, but that's already a pretty long response. For me, I'm not sure if it's the archive itself as much as the fact that older material has generations of scholarship attached to it and, while that can be a burden, it's also very humbling, and I think that's a great corrective. You also have to deal with interpretations coming from very different perspectives, in different languages, motivated in completely different ways. Reading itself is layered and very complex. So I think that when I started teaching contemporary work, I wanted to impress upon students ideas about transmission, ideas that are much more obvious and out in the open with older material. And that one might need, for instance, to reach back into the origins of a discipline or a discourse to understand how to find one's place in it. In that sense, one of the things that is incredibly exciting about *Lost & Found* is that it presents an opportunity to move the proverbial Spicerian furniture around quite a bit because actual scholarship on writers of the recent past is still very much in its infancy and there is a lot that can be said and done to establish some principles and groundwork.

DH: I wonder if you could describe in more detail the process of how a typical *Lost & Found* edition gets made. What are the steps, from a practical standpoint? Do student-editors begin with archival research and then turn up something worth publishing, or do you and the editors already have a sense of what's out there in certain archives? How do you work with the editors to shape the material, and with the estates and archives to deal with permissions and so on? And how do you decide what to publish and what to leave out? I can imagine that for every edition, there is a great deal of material that remains unpublished.

AA: They're all pretty different and our process is constantly changing. One of the early projects, the Frank O'Hara/Kenneth Koch letters edited by Josh Schneiderman, emerged from a class in Textual Scholarship taught by the great scholar and our Textual Editor, the medievalist David Greetham. Besides the intelligence of the editing and the ancillary materials, the great accomplishment there was for Josh to impress upon Maureen O'Hara, Frank's sister and Literary Executor, the seriousness of his intent and his love for the subject. This was a trial he passed with flying colors and it presented a model for an "ethics of scholarship" that is very central to what we do. In other words, permissions are generally not something we think about after, but something that is front and center, part of the whole approach. Who are the heirs? Can we involve them? How do we bring them on board? What kinds of sensitivities might need to be considered? It was very moving to have Pablo Conrad, Adrienne Rich's son, speak at the launch of Series IV, and to have Pauline Kael's daughter, Gina James, in the audience. In the extraordinary uncovering of Harlem Renaissance poet Helene Johnson's later poems by Emily Claman, we had constant and full cooperation from Johnson's daughter, Abigail McGrath. Muriel Rukeyser's son William has been incredibly helpful. The idea here is to instill in our students a sense of community and continuity. Seth Stewart, whose brilliant work on John Wieners has resulted in the collected letters (as his dissertation), as well as selected journals (published by City Lights), has found himself part of an extended group of John's friends who have become like family.

All kinds of things happen: Wendy Tronrud went to the Bancroft last year to look at some Gwendolyn Brooks material and found the holdings a little disappointing, less than what she thought might have been there. I suggested she look at the archive of Ted Joans and she got totally immersed in it. Bradley Lubin loved the work of Pauline Kael but had only a peripheral sense of Robert Duncan until he took a few classes with me and realized how formative their friendship was. He immersed himself in their correspondence and prepared a selection that we published in the new Series. In a seminar I suggested that everyone listen to Robert Duncan's Olson Memorial lectures. A group calling itself "the Duncaneers" soon organized themselves and transcribed the lectures, which we published alongside your and Sean Spicer's project in Series II. That has become part of an effort to publish all of the Olson Memorial lectures, given at Buffalo, because they seemed to me a kind of "dead sea scrolls" of North American poetics, a lost link for those who didn't happen to be there to hear them.

We're now in our second year of direct funding for *Lost & Found* research stipends and that will present a whole new set of circumstances as we're offering "exploratory" grants for people to just get their feet wet, without any definite project in mind. Then we have stipends for project completion and, finally, stipends for former editors to be mentors. This was the idea of Kyle Waugh, the extraordinary editor of the Skeat-like variorum edition of Ed Dorn's *Abilene! Abilene!* So the project grows in different directions and with the Adrienne Rich teaching materials project, we're trying to create a network across the CUNY system to involve poet-teachers at the community college and undergrad levels to engage in the classroom and through public events with our own institutional history. At the same time, there is an ongoing process of coming to understand what we ourselves have already produced, and how one thing feeds upon and leads to another. This has led to various projects.

DH: I also wonder if you could expand on your point about *Lost & Found* projects blossoming into dissertations. As a PhD student at University at Buffalo, I'm aware of a long tradition of this kind of work — Robbie Dewhurst is engaged in something like this now as he completes his project on John Wieners. Often, as PhD students in this hypercompetitive market, we're told not to do a project that involves publishing an archival edition, because it isn't recognizably "scholarly" enough. On the other hand, such an edition has the advantage of being useful, even vital, for critics and readers alike. To summarize the perception: Editing falls between the cracks of creative and scholarly work, and it doesn't reflect academic rigor the same way as a project that develops and pursues a critical-theoretical concept. Do CUNY students encounter any resistance of that kind, either in the dissertation process or once they go on the academic market? Do you, as a thesis adviser, help guard against this by making sure that students include a strong critical element to their editing projects, or do you see attitudes towards this kind of work changing in academia?

AA: For a variety of reasons, I happen to supervise an insane number of dissertations and, as an administrator, I'm on the committee that ends up reading all the dissertations at the end of each year. Given the size of our program, that's lots of reading and trends become more evident. One of the early textual dissertations I was involved in as a committee member was actually a translation project in Comparative Literature. The student, Lucy McNair, had created an edition of Algerian writer Mouloud Feraoun's landmark book *The Poor Man's Son*. The book, as Feraoun had written it in French, never came out as he intended, since even the liberal and sympathetic editors of the day couldn't conceive that a colonial subject like Feraoun would have the self-consciousness to write the text as he had intended and they dumbed it down. At any rate, Lucy established the text through archival work and then translated it, and the book was actually already published and in hand at the time of her defense! The first one that came directly out of *Lost & Found* was Claudia Moreno Pisano's edition of the Baraka/Dorn letters, recently published by the University of New Mexico Press.

There have been others: Brian Unger's edition of Philip Whalen's journals; Seth Stewart's edition of the Wieners letters that I mentioned; Rowena Kennedy-Espstein's edition of Rukeyser's novel *Savage Coast*; and another great, upcoming project by Kai Krienke on the Algerian poet Jean Sénac that includes a major textual component. As you say, this kind of editing and textual scholarship often seems to fall through the cracks between creative and scholarly work. On the other hand, as I was working on various chapbook projects with *Lost & Found* editors, I found that their learning curve and skill set, in being forced to think through certain things sometimes as mundane as permissions and acknowledgments, often outpaced many dissertations. More importantly, the need for exactitude as opposed to speculation, to make sure that we get things right, imposes a kind of rigor that is all too often missing in many "idea"- or "theory"-based dissertations.

I think the results have actually been great; students are publishing books and getting jobs. There has really been no resistance in the program or the university. On the contrary, these efforts to bring works to the public have been applauded and supported institutionally in very strong ways. Having said that, yes, I also do make sure that the framing of all these works involves rigorous scholarship. Some of it might appear a little old fashioned and run against the theoretical grain but I think there is a sea change occurring and that this kind of work will be seen to be more and more valuable and valued.

DH: Finally, a related question: I'm struck by your insistence on the physical archive, the material print process. So often we hear that Digital Humanities is the answer to declining enrollment and budgets in the university. I wonder if you could talk a little more about what a researcher gains by taking the trouble to visit a physical archive, such as we have at Buffalo and, as you mention, as exist now in many university libraries. Why shouldn't we just wait until it's all been digitized?

AA: I'll preface this question by saying that, paradoxically, I think the support we've gotten for this kind of textual scholarship is very related to some trends in the Digital Humanities but that a certain conflation takes place at some point in which anything digital is seen as the New Jerusalem. I mean, yes, Educational Digitization, like the ATM, may ultimately lead to less people in the workplace and more people serving and being served by the machine, so it's no wonder that administrators and policy-makers embrace it. But that embrace may actually run contrary to some of our best DH scholars, many of whom are also hard-nosed text people and really useful thinkers. Of course there has and continues to be great digital scholarship, through the creation of access to materials and the creation of important editions and approaches to textual materials, so I might be considered a nut case but I still think the book is a superior reading technology than the screen which, while allowing hypertext and various other incredible tools, forces sequential movement. You can scroll but it's very hard to flip. This is similar to the problem of the demise of good bookstores, whether new or used, and the proliferation of e-texts as opposed to books in the stacks. When you wander through the physical world of objects as opposed to the hypertextual world of links and lists, I still think it's easier to find things you're not looking for. I mean, of course you find all kinds of interesting things noodling around on the internet but I still think we're left right where we were when Olson defined what he then called the "postmodern." In a letter to Robert Creeley, dated August 9, 1951, Olson wrote:

> The EXPANSION of peoples, materials and sensations that the AGE OF QUANTITY involves itself in, DEMAND a heightening of that servant of clarity, the CRITICAL FUNCTION, wherever: that is, the above increases in the quantity of experience is also an increase in the sources of confusion, and so, to cut them down requires more labor than previously [...] that the job now, is to be at once archaic and culture-wise — that they are indivisible.[1]

Clearly, these are things Olson had on his mind for a long time, as in this letter to anthropologist Ruth Benedict, from 1946:

> It is my feeling that *the record of fact* is become of first importance for us lost in a sea of question. [...] In New History, the act of the observer, if his personality is of count, is before, in the collection of the material. This is where we will cut the knot. [...] I think if you burn the facts long and hard enough

---

1   *Charles Olson & Robert Creeley: The Complete Correspondence*, vol. 7, ed. George F. Butterick (Black Sparrow Press, 1987), 75.

in yourself as crucible, you'll come to the few facts that matter, and then fact can be fable again.[2]

I think a lot of people have been rehearsing the elements of this problem in many ways since then but I don't know of anyone who has as dramatically cut to the chase and come to a useful conclusion, placing fact and fable next to each other, as necessary companions.

All of what I'm saying here may appear wildly contradictory, but I think that's fine. This is not a case of nostalgia or burying one's head in the sand but thinking about the circumstances of encounters and relationships between people and physical objects in the world. Obviously computers and all these other devices are physical objects but their sensory qualities are rather limited so I think, yes, actually handling materials, going to places, is an irreplaceable experience, even though the materials themselves have become institutionalized, you know, "for their own good," to be preserved, so all of it is fraught with contradiction.

---

2 Charles Olson, *Selected Letters,* ed. Ralph Maud (University of California Press, 2000), 58.

7

Peter Anastas: A Walker in the City

2013

The organic integration of newly acquired sights and sounds into the very fabric of one's being and behavior is a complex and intimate process that perhaps comes as close to defining what it means be human, and inhabit a human universe, as anything that comes to mind. The journey can be as near as your hands pushing at the floor to stand up or as far as you can go once you've learned. In 1988, while living in Jerusalem and searching for a past I wasn't fully aware I already possessed, I discovered that it began in a place:

> My Mediterranean began on the Atlantic coast, first frontier of the New World, in a fishing city called Gloucester settled by Portuguese immigrants. Whenever I was sad, I would ask my mother to take me up to the Church of the fisherman, high on the hill, majestic in blue and stucco, with its two open bells ringing in the tide. Gloucester also meant the Greeks: cool drinks at the Anastas luncheonette, seedless grapes hanging abundantly off the white arches across from the movie theater at the Ketchopoulos Market.[1]

---

[1] Ammiel Alcalay, *Memories of Our Future* (City Lights Books, 1999), 27.

From this very poignant and primal memory, my text veered into things much more recent, things that I was attempting to fit into a pattern in order to prove a point rather than simply be. This quite profound difference—between ideology and existence—is at the heart of all of Peter Anastas's work, and particularly so in this collection, culled from many years of newspaper columns written in and about the city of Gloucester.

In this day and age, the very fact of having a newspaper column, of having the freedom to write about what is on one's mind, to a particular audience in a particular place, has become almost unimaginable. But that has not always been the case, as Anastas writes of the "ascendancy of print journalism" in the mid-1950s, when he began working at *The Gloucester Times,* and "its editors were well read and superbly educated." Even though a few of these columns spill past the year 2000, the great majority of them were written between 1978 and 1990. In other words, a few years after the end of the American war in Vietnam and before the Gulf War, when US policy-makers still respected the populace enough to know that the only wars they could wage had to be covert wars. That means that the bulk of what is depicted in *A Walker in the City* took place in the past century, a century that is, clearly, past.

How are we to contend with this rather startling but altogether ordinary bit of chronology? For one thing, the demise of print culture, the descent of print journalism—through the Trojan horse of technology and efficiency—is something we haven't even begun to address. It is as if the machinery of the recent past has come to inhabit us, but like phantom limbs strewn about every which way with no map or guide to chart to whom they once belonged. As I've written elsewhere, nothing has come to replace the complex, material nexus of relations that formed the basis of immediate human and vocational interaction, from paper-making and printing, to trucks and delivery, from design and shipping to the space of encounter at a newsstand or streetcorner. In the scheme of human time, that epoch of print journalism was merely a blip, but a significant one that has shaped our more recent ways of structuring society, of processing information that is supposed to pertain to us.

But as the fish go, so goes paper: We enter a bank and are served cash (if we're lucky enough to have any) by a machine that asks, magnanimously but with some underlying tone of guilt, whether we want to "go green." Such a gigantic lie, given to us as our daily dose of mystification: We actually are made to believe that not printing the tiny slip of paper will somehow "save" our "environment," at the same time that it obscures our ability to imagine how the dispensing machine itself might be disposed of, where its toxic remnants might find their resting place and curse the earth or air they will end up in for decades, if not centuries to come. It is towards the continual layered exposure of such logical detail that Peter Anastas has wielded his pen lo these many years, asking us to think about what is in front of our very noses, what is under our feet, what scents come into our nostrils, what sounds prevail or have disappeared. This is a constant mapping, a mapping of the ordinary as it etches the texture of a place into our very nerves and soul, creating our accents, our gestures, our memories, and our ability to safeguard the world and its secular institutions, its civic life, the household economy writ large that must always start from where we are. And because the ordinary is so firmly grounded within us, the violence necessary to unseat it, to unmoor us from the familiar, must be great indeed but also subtle, pervasive, and relentless. Thus, the battles fought on much broader ground, of apparent international geopolitical significance, are not very different from those battles fought in a place like Gloucester, in Gloucester itself.

We seem to have come full circle: In the late Palestinian national poet Mahmoud Darwish's masterpiece, *Memory for Forgetfulness: August, Beirut, 1982,* he writes about coming to Beirut as a six-year old refugee from Palestine. In perhaps one of his most radical gestures, Darwish departs from the national story to both probe and recollect his own childhood, to find memories that only forgetfulness can create:

"FOLLOW THE PERSON"

I came to Beirut thirty-four years ago. I was six years old then. They put a cap on my head and left me in Al-Burj Square. It had a streetcar, and I rode the streetcar. It ran on two parallel lines made of iron. The streetcar went up I didn't know where. It ran on two iron lines. It moved forward. I couldn't tell what made this big, noisy toy move: the lines of iron laid on the ground or the wheels that rolled. I looked out the window of the streetcar. I saw many buildings and many windows, with many eyes peering out. I saw many trees. The streetcar was moving, the buildings were moving, and the trees were moving. Everything around the streetcar was moving as it moved. The streetcar came back to where they'd put the cap on my head. My grandfather took me up eagerly. He put me in a car, and we went to Damur. Damur was smaller, and more beautiful than Beirut because the sea there was grander. But it didn't have a streetcar. *Take me to the streetcar!* So they took me to the streetcar. I don't remember anything of Damur except the sea and the banana plantations. How big the banana leaves were! How big they were! And the red flowers climbing the walls of the houses.

When I came back to Beirut ten years ago, the first thing I did was stop a taxi and say to the driver: "Take me to Damur." I had come from Cairo and was searching for the small footsteps of a boy who had taken steps larger than himself, not in keeping with his age and greater than his stride. What was I searching for? The footsteps, or the boy? Or for the folks who had crossed a rocky wilderness, only to reach that which they didn't find, just as Cavafy never found his Ithaca? The sea was in place, pushing against Damur to make it bigger. And I had grown up. I had become a poet searching for the boy that used to be in him, whom he had left behind some place and forgotten. The poet had grown older and didn't permit the forgotten boy to grow up.[2]

---

[2] Mahmoud Darwish, *Memory for Forgetfulness*, trans. Ibrahim Muhawi (University of California Press, 1995), 86–87.

By insisting on the indelible markers of memory, Darwish is not only consecrating a personal experience but positing a political reality. The very contradiction here—of the grown poet trapping the boy in a frozen past while still fighting to regain consciousness of that boy's actual memory—reenacts a more profound union than that of simple homecoming, the "nostos" of the exile that gives us "nostalgia," our adoptive word for sentiments of the past. This past, however, is made entirely of detail: particular tastes, voices no longer audible or alive, shades of light that have been obscured, the sound of birds or other animals no longer there, the faces of buildings that have disappeared, paths that have been paved over, and streets once as familiar as one's own skin that have become unrecognizable.

In an extraordinarily prescient address, delivered in 1940, the great geographer Carl Sauer wrote:

> Year by year the sweeping hands of modern industry and commerce brush away more and more of what is old. Traditions die with the old people; documents are destroyed; weather, storm, and flood erase the physical remnants; science and market standardization destroy old crops. [...] The terrific impact of the modern western world, however, does not repeal the old truth that the history of man has been markedly pluralistic, and that there are no general laws of society, but only cultural assents. We deal not with Culture but with cultures, except so far as we delude ourselves into thinking the world made over in our own image.[3]

In his postscript, Anastas freely admits the elegiac nature of his work, that he is, in fact, actively lamenting a sense of irreparable loss. But *A Walker in the City* also provides the kind of assent that Sauer describes, opening up—through intricate accounts and imagery—those places of the past lodged within us, treas-

---

3   Carl O. Sauer, "Foreword to Historical Geography," in *Land & Life: A Selection from the Writings of Carl Ortwin Sauer*, ed. John Leighly (University of California Press, 1963), 378.

ures whose energy can fuel the imagination to think otherwise, to seek other structures and other venues for expression than those we are now given. In this way, the very activation of memory can become a political act, a form of resistance whose language, form, and texture is both completely unique and part of a commons owned by all and none at the same time. In such a world, the boundaries between what we see and what we imagine become quite porous as, like the author of this book, we too become walkers in a city so real we can feel it.

8

"Out of the Schools and into the Archives"

2014

On the evening of December 12, 2014, I attended an extraordinary gathering celebrating the life of painter Jane Freilicher at the Poetry Project in New York, an event intended to mark her ninetieth birthday. She had planned to come and partake in the festivities, to watch old films of her unearthed from various archives, and be in the company of old friends like John Ashbery, Alex Katz, and so many others. But she died on December 9th, just three days before the event. The crowd at the Poetry Project was young and old, filled with friends and admirers whose associations spanned the gamut of artistic lineages dating back to the mid-twentieth century and well into the twenty-first, from Black Mountain College to the Jack Kerouac School of Disembodied Poetics at Naropa University, with much in between.

Ralph Maud, a name most likely less recognizable than that of Freilicher, passed on in Vancouver at the age of eighty-five the day before, on December 8th. Born in Yorkshire, Maud's scholarship began with work on Dylan Thomas but an encounter with Charles Olson at SUNY Buffalo in the early 1960s left him forever altered. He went on to become the most important scholar of Olson's work and then, with a move to Vancouver in 1965 (as a founding faculty member of the new Simon Fraser

University), took Olson's dictum of studying the local to heart, eventually producing scholarship on First Nation peoples of British Columbia, particularly the Salish.

On December 10th, a day after the death of Jane Freilicher, poet, novelist, editor, publisher, and environmentalist James Koller passed on. One of the last of his generation to continually crisscross the North American continent in the spirit of earlier luminaries, Koller is probably the name least recognizable in this particular mortal cluster. A glance at the finding aid for his papers, housed at the Thomas J. Dodd Center, University of Connecticut, Storrs (where one can also find the enormous Olson Archive along with significant holdings by such writers as Bill Berkson, Tom Clark, Diane di Prima, Edward Dorn, Joel Oppenheimer, Allen Polite, Tom Raworth, Michael Rumaker, Ed Sanders, and Aram Saroyan), reveals Koller's correspondents, a roster that includes Richard Brautigan, Robert Creeley, Larry Eigner, Anselm Hollo, Joanne Kyger, Michael McClure, Duncan McNaughton, Eric Mottram, Jerome Rothenberg, Irving Rosenthal, Gary Snyder, John Taggart, Janine Pommy Vega, Anne Waldman, and Philip Whalen. The exchanges with each of these luminaries, some lasting for years, provide a completely unique perspective into a particular world of intersecting relationships and soundings that probes the very depths of the multiple layers that constitute our world of letters, ideas, poetics, and politics: our history.

I mention these recent deaths not just to acknowledge the passing of these figures but also to emphasize the fact that any single person or relationship mentioned in these three short paragraphs can open into a whole field of new research that would almost immediately contradict the ways this history has been codified and transmitted, usually in readily digestible and atomized categories that are easy to identify but more often than not hide more than they reveal. When I first started teaching graduate seminars in twentieth-century North American poetry, poetics, literary history, and cultural politics, I found that working with students primarily attuned to things contemporary proved to be challenging in ways I hadn't quite anticipated. My own academic training was primarily as a medievalist, in which the palimpsestic nature of the accrual of texts, languages, influences, and erasures was simply a given in the course of study, and "thickness" of description and context were expected. But this was certainly not the case with students primarily concentrating on the present or more recent past.

To begin with, many of the students had come to know the "non-canonical" twentieth-century poets through anthologies and, even when studying particular writers further, still tended to identify them according to a "school" or movement. Never having encountered the much denser terrain of little magazines and small press publishing from which figures associated with the Objectivists, Beats, Black Mountain, San Francisco Renaissance, New York School, Black Arts Movement, or other configurations actually emerged, students were continually surprised — when I brought in stacks of books and magazines — to see writers they couldn't imagine having *anything* at all in common between covers of the same publication. This surprise came about, of course, through no fault of the students, because the kind of rummaging through used-book stores, where you might actually discover or encounter something you weren't looking for, has become an activity confined to very few select locales. The order of things has almost been reversed in the digital age: it's possible to find almost anything, but only if you know what you're looking for. The archival encounter, on the other hand, can present — under the right circumstances — a much less mediated experience in which the pursuit of particular things (names, dates, titles, and incidents), can explode a whole host of assumptions and received knowledge, creating a completely new set of relations.

While many, for example, would be familiar with Donald M. Allen's landmark anthology *The New American Poetry 1945–1960*, published in 1960 when Allen was still an editor at Grove Press, there is much less familiarity with Allen's subsequent trajectory as editor and small-press publisher through Four Seasons Foundation and Grey Fox Press, one of the most vital records of major strains of North American poetics in the decades following publication of *The New American Poetry*. This was particularly true for his Writing series that published essential texts across decades, from Olson's *Proprioception* to essay collections by Dorn, Whalen, and many others. In 1960 Allen's anthology had finally made available work by poets that had previously circulated almost underground, in most cases through small-press editions of several hundred copies or, in some instances, as carbon copy typescripts, something one can see referenced in the voluminous correspondence between Denise Levertov and Robert Duncan, in which a "new book" of the 1950s refers to a carbon copy mailed from reader to reader. The anthology was, in many ways, made possible by changes in print technology, allowing LeRoi Jones (later Amiri Baraka) and Hettie Jones to create *Yugen*, cheaply printed and quickly distributed, the first little magazine to consolidate all the poetic outliers flung across the country. In fact, Jones/Baraka held the copyright to Olson's seminal text *Projective Verse*, with cover and design by Matsumi "Mike" Kanemitsu, in the pamphlet edition he published in 1959.

This explosion of work immediately took hold of a new generation of readers, making available works that had mainly circulated among people who almost all knew each other, or of each other. In its wake came *The Floating Bear*, initiated by Diane di Prima, a mimeographed and stapled newsletter that set a new standard for speed of dissemination, enabling a major figure like Olson to get new work out to his known readers within a few weeks. While the Allen anthology irremediably changed the cultural landscape, it also fixed certain views, certainly regarding the geographies of activity and influence. Terms that existed in some form or were used more loosely got solidified, as readers were often much less discriminating than Allen himself in pointing out the porous nature of his arrangement: thus labels like the Beats, Black Mountain, the New York School, and the San Francisco Renaissance became much more monolithic than they actually were. A comment in class from one of my students remains indelible: "I can't understand why it's called 'The New York School,'" he said. "These people are never in New York at the same time, all they write about is how much they miss each other and how far away they are from their friends." Such a conclusion could only come after having spent countless hours in the Berg Collection at the New York Public Library, poring over letters written between key figures of the time such as Frank O'Hara, Kenneth Koch, John Ashbery, and others.

Thus was born one of the first and still primary principles of *Lost & Found: The CUNY Poetics Document Initiative:* "Follow the person." In other words, forget about what "school" or movement you think this or that poet belongs to; instead, actually go and look at the magazines they first published in, see who they appeared with, note down all the names you don't recognize; look at letters, journals or unpublished notes to see who they paid attention to, ignored, made fun of, attacked, loved; try to map out to what and whom their attentions were drawn. Now into its fifth year [at this writing], with an annual set of chapbooks and an affinity group of book publications under the *Lost & Found Elsewhere* rubric, the fundamental aim of the project — in addition to training students in the principles of textual scholarship — has been to encounter our history anew and wrest its vital materials away from a kind of tyranny that has continually worked to diminish the political and liberatory impact of our ability to inhabit and dwell within those materials.

We should never lose sight of the fact that this great period of cultural activity — by artists in various forms and media: musicians, painters, dancers, poets — took place at the height of the Cold War, and in a place of isolation so acute that, as Gary Snyder once remarked, "you would hitchhike a thousand miles to have a conversation with a friend." As the administration of knowledge grew, with the expansion of universities and the military-industrial complex, artists struggled to redefine the parameters of knowledge, but completely outside the framework of official institutions and structures. Without enough money for long distance phone calls or frequent travel, the most vital work of thinking in the United States following the Second World War took place through correspondence, in letters, a venue that was also still fairly well protected from surveillance during *one* of the ages of J. Edgar Hoover and *the* age of

Senator Joseph McCarthy. While we have undeniably inherited the structures of the National Security State, we seldom stop to examine just how deeply its legacy taints our reception of the fairly immediate past.

Our adulation of the individual, tied to the destruction of any collectivity or commons, dictates that our cultural figures remain lonely, unmoored from friends, lovers, competitors, idols, or places of reference, unless some scandal or possibility of ideological hijacking might be involved. From our present vantage point, it takes more than some mental gymnastics to grasp the intensity of reaction, for example, of Jack Kerouac when he writes in a 1957 letter to Allen Ginsberg about how excited he is that Boston born John Wieners, newly arrived to San Francisco following the dissolution of Black Mountain College, wants to publish a few of his poems in a new magazine Wieners has launched called *Measure*. Or that Amiri Baraka became Wieners's legal guardian after a hospitalization. Needless to say, most readers will never have heard of these incidents or of *Measure*, a magazine lasting three issues over a span of five years. Ironically, while Wieners remained largely obscure in his lifetime, he was beloved by other poets and his survival depended on friendships, while Kerouac was turned into product, eaten alive by the relentless machinery of consumption. The return to materials that have been withdrawn, the creation of a world of beauty out of them, is a turn to what Olson called "the gold machine," interpreted by Canadian scholar Miriam Nichols as "an alchemical trope that makes actual things rise up as concretely *in situ* as possible, thus to trouble generic representations — to throw the disturbance of actuality into the universe of discourse."[1]

---

[1] From *"Mythopoeisis* in Charles Olson's Later *Maximus Poems:* The Importance of the Beautiful," unpublished paper by Miriam Nichols, 2014. In her *Radical Affections: Essays on the Poetics of Outside* (University of Alabama Press, 2010), Nichols, referring to Olson, writes: "Here is the poet as 'Gold Machine,' transmuting the lead of the everyday into the gold of a human commons"(61).

9

On Robert Creeley's "Contexts of Poetry"

2009

By all accounts the 1963 Vancouver Poetry Conference (actually a three-week summer course offered by the University of British Columbia and organized by UBC professor Warren Tallman and Robert Creeley), was a landmark event deeply effecting the participants and providing one of the rare opportunities for extended and collective exchange among such major poets as Charles Olson (1910–1970), Margaret Avison (1918–2007), Robert Duncan (1919–1988), Denise Levertov (1923–1997), Philip Whalen (1923–2002), Allen Ginsberg (1926–1997), and Robert Creeley (1926–2005). The reverberations reached Mexico, as seen in A. Fredric Franklyn's letter to Margaret Randall and Sergio Mondragon's important transnational magazine *El Corno Emplumado,* and the pulse would continue through to the landmark 1965 Berkeley Poetry Conference. While the Vancouver events have remained under examined, interest has grown, including production of *The Line Has Shattered,* a film by Canadian documentary filmmaker Robert McTavish.

In an unpublished account by Warren Tallman, uncovered through Canadian poet Aaron Vidaver's research,[1] Tallman stresses the actual physicality of the events, and the quality of speech the poets brought to bear upon the space they inhabited: "For [Robert Duncan] articulation is like terra firma. [...] As he warms to the reading an almost Orphic ground sense or swell enters, as though his voice is not so much in the midst of a room as in the midst of a life it knows." Recounting Ginsberg's reading Tallman writes that "he always broke off when the body presence wouldn't enter into the voice tone. When it did enter, the audience was caught, bowled over into corresponding awareness as though stunned to be so fully reminded of all the ways in which they had emotions, a physical being, presence." Tallman writes of Denise Levertov casting a "physical spell" that, for then twenty-three year old Daphne Marlatt, "was the first time I ever saw a woman hold a whole audience with the magic of her voice."

So contrary to what has become a fashionable distrust or misapprehension of voice and presence, Tallman stresses that "it would seem that we are entering an era in which the voice bridge is recognized as an actual dwelling locale. [...] Whether it is Duncan's 'torso-reverberations of a Grecian lyre,' Creeley's 'I will go on talking forever,' or Ginsberg's 'poem of life butchered out of their own bodies good to eat a thousand years,' the reversal is the same. Wisdoms, truths, experiences, memories, moralities, realities become not end points but food, meat, manure, lending nurture to that living tree of breath called speech."

The root of this thought points back to Olson's insistence, in face of the impossibility of relying on anything we might

---

[1] Important documentation of the 1963 Vancouver Poetry Conference was prepared by Aaron Vidaver in a special issue of the *Minutes of the Charles Olson Society* 30 (April 1999), available at: http://vidaver.files.wordpress.com/2009/09/1963-vancouver-poetry-conference-charles-olson-society-minutes-1999-guest-ed-aaron-vidaver.pdf. See also Aaron Vidaver, "Warren Tallman: 'Poets in Vancouver' (1963)," *vidaver.wordpress.com,* August 10, 2009, http://vidaver.wordpress.com/category/poetry-and-poetics/.

call "civilization" following the devastation of World War II, that resistance first takes place in the body, a passage referred to earlier: "In this intricate structure are we based, now more than ever (besieged, overthrown), for its power is bone muscle nerve blood brain a man, its fragile mortal force its old eternity, resistance."[2]

It is precisely here where Robert Creeley begins to consider "writing as a physical act" in this remarkable talk, and moves from the most mundane conditions his own consciousness of writing imposes upon his practice to a stunning and revelatory conclusion about radical historical changes in the very definition of the terms of reality. In a thorough and fully cogent explication of Creeley's talk, Turkish scholar Özge Özbek Akıman writes:

> Creeley's attention is on the process of cognition — reaching an awareness of the physical "habitat" of writing. […] The "writing man" is affected not only by the way he interacts with society but also by the way the skin of his hand touches the paper, or by the friction between the tip of his pen and the kind of sheet he is writing on. The process of "coming to know what I do" works the same way on both personal and social levels. Creeley lays the foundations of his argument on the physical qualities of the writing act, and goes on to imply that actuality is the only term within which the human being "knows."

She goes on to write:

> The changing terms of consciousness provide him with the grounds and tools to articulate the "senses of writing" in the way he does. This is the moment when the private is linked to the public. […] The mutual effect that the elements of the context have on each other might well be thought of as 'creative

---

2 Charles Olson, *Collected Prose*, ed. Donald Allen and Benjamin Friedlander (University of California Press, 1997), 174.

strife,' as a result of which new forms emerge. In a similar way creative strife is between, say, the habit of using 8 × 11 paper and the necessity of using a legal sized sheet caused by the fact that he was in Spain. On a different level, the same strife exists between the white and black consciousness. Creative strife manifests itself as the "uprising" of the "Negro reality" which forces the white mainstream consciousness to come to terms with its reality. In this sense, history is understood to be the constant strife between one order and another, the mutual disagreement among one subject and another leading to different forms of survival.[3]

The elements explored by Creeley in this talk are further articulated in his postscript, written five years after the Vancouver Conference, where he describes actual changes in his writing practice that parallel changes in consciousness and terms of reality. A key Creeley text in this transition is A Day Book, published in 1972, with the date "Tuesday, November 19, 1968" on the front cover and "Friday, June 11, 1971" on the back. It is during this period, during the composition of *A Day Book*, that the character "I" in Edward Dorn's masterpiece *Gunslinger* dies. When queried in an interview about the death of "I" ("I is dead, the poet said"),[4] Dorn refers to a line in which "I" becomes "the container of the thing it contains." Far from some metaphysical meditation, Dorn goes on to explain this as a reference to "using our returning dead as containers. Back then the CIA was sewing kilos of heroin inside the thorax of the cadavers of our returning dead from Vietnam, sewing it back up, and shipping the body back to Long Beach, San Francisco, and Chicago. These were the first containers of heroin. This was Air America. This was the first big off-the-books money."[5] In the wake of rebellion on all

---

3   Özge Özbek Akıman, "'Finding Out For Yourself,' Or Poets Re-Writing History" (PhD diss., Hacettepe University Graduate School of Social Sciences, 2009), 90–101.

4   Edward Dorn, *Gunslinger Book II* (Black Sparrow Press, 1969), 23.

5   Edward Dorn, *Ed Dorn Live: Lectures, Interviews, and Outtakes*, ed. Joseph Richey (University of Michigan Press, 2007), 24.

fronts — urban uprisings in 125 cities across the country, Vietnam veterans fighting against the war and hurling their medals at the White House, the formation of the Black Panthers and other liberation movements, student strikes, and a variety of other manifestations — there came an era of widespread repression in which the prison population would swell from 200,000 in the early 1970s, to well over 2 million presently.

The literary and aesthetic implications of these further changes in the terms of reality have barely begun to be examined. In a tour de force that has the audacity to examine Creeley's *A Day Book* in relation to George Jackson's *Soledad Brother*, a collection of letters written from prison and published in 1970, before Jackson was killed in 1971, Ramsey Scott writes:

> On the surface, comparing *A Day Book* to *Soledad Brother* appears random, or at best, the attempt to make something of the coincidental fact these contemporaneous works share a remarkably similar (one sheet of paper) constraint. This superficial similarity may soon be dwarfed by apparent differences: Creeley, the White New Englander, versus Jackson, the displaced African American; or perceived cultural importance: Creeley, the famous white poet, versus Jackson, the prison-bound Black radical. And yet, working through the ideological obstructions Jackson faces as he struggles to convince his parents of the radical structural changes necessary to correct America's inequities, one begins to recognize the system of values he challenges has been imprinted or embedded far below the surface of the language in which he writes, as if such institutions supply its very words and sentences, construct its rhetorical tools, and ultimately disable any oppositional arguments. [...] For Jackson, the utterly dehumanizing space of the prison suggests a narrative or revolution yet unwritten; for Creeley, American myths privileging the march of progress open onto old graves, uninhabited houses, human failure. The house — the space of the American domestic — is Creeley's cell; as both Creeley and Jackson begin to recognize, what expectations of punishment, what

senses of ownership or entitlement, what fantasies of possession or domination exist as violent abstractions in the bombing of Vietnam or the beating of prisoners, what the sum of these actions and events reflect is the unbroken grip of ideologies that begin in the seemingly banal spaces of America's single-family dwellings, that overwhelm or occlude any clear sense of what should be done.[6]

This brings us back to one of Creeley's favorite quotes by Olson: "we do what we know before we know what we do."[7] This becomes the space where experience, language, consciousness, and condition intersect and it is striking to see Daphne Marlatt's writing from the three-week seminar in Vancouver in this context. In many ways, Marlatt is already enacting — in the wide-ranging freedom of her journal entries — the space that Creeley is striving for in his talk. While Marlatt's work would go on to engage and explore the complexities of many such intersecting legacies — whether patriarchal, colonial, or linguistic, in a wide formal range of prose and poetry, while coming into further knowledge of herself as a lesbian — the roots of this exploration are in the Vancouver Conference: "As a young poet in the 1960s, I had the good fortune of meeting a number of poets whose work openly addressed the spiritual component in being human — Allen Ginsberg, Charles Olson, Robert Duncan, Denise Levertov, Margaret Avison, Robert Creeley were all there for one extraordinary summer school on poetry and poetics at UBC in 1963. That groundswell where language, psyche and political consciousness came together in a large vision of what it means to be awake and alive in the world shaped me as a writer."

---

6 Ramsey Scott, "In the Butcher Shop of Subjectivity: Autobiographical Works from the Black Liberation Movement, 1970–1987" (PhD diss., The Graduate Center of the City University of New York, 2009), 115–17.

7 Robert Creeley, *The Collected Essays of Robert Creeley* (University of California Press, 1989), 557.

10

On Diane di Prima's *R.D.'s H.D.*

2010

Diane di Prima's *R.D.'s H.D.*, published here for the first time, is an extraordinarily moving homage to a dear friend and a deep influence, as well as an illustration of a unique methodological approach to poetics. As to the formal nature of *R.D.'s H.D.*, di Prima herself has offered an explanation of some of the different processes she undergoes in preparing talks and lectures: "I think for me a lecture is something more formal, that I've written out in advance — sometimes put in a fair bit of research on, i.e., reread *Maximus* through twice before beginning to write the Buffalo talks: once straight through and then again, slowly, reading all of Butterick's 'Notes' as I went along. [...] The Shelley lectures at New College were written out in full before I gave them. [...] *R.D.'s H.D.* I wrote out longhand and read. So by these (rather vague) definitions I'd say it was a lecture."

R.D.'s H.D. was given as part of a series of lectures dedicated to Robert Duncan and organized by Aaron Shurin, poet and former student of Duncan's at New College in San Francisco. The lectures took place in 1989 at the San Pablo Avenue storefront of Small Press Distribution in Berkeley, then directed by Steve Dickison. The full title of the series was *Derivations: A Living Tradition*. The first group of lectures, on January 27th, featured Diane di Prima's *R.D.'s H.D.*, Duncan McNaughton's "Circulations of the Song: Robert Duncan and Rumi," and "Reading/

Writing, An Introduction to 'Derivations,' Robert Duncan and the Poetics of Influence," by Aaron Shurin. These were followed by a second set, on February 17th, with Thom Gunn, David Bromige, and Leslie Scalapino. On March 10th, the venue shifted to New College and a series called "Poetics of Instruction," with Michael Palmer, Susan Thackrey, David Levi Strauss, and John Thorpe.

The idea of sets of lectures followed a format that had been created in the Poetics Program at New College, a program that di Prima formed an essential part of. Through the work of poet Duncan McNaughton and sociologist Louis Patler, New College had, from the mid-1970s, become a hub of activity for poetry readings and associated events. In 1980, McNaughton and Patler formally instituted the Poetics Program, serving as codirectors, with an initial core faculty of Diane di Prima, Robert Duncan, and David Meltzer. Many taught in the program during this period, including Bill Berkson, Robert Grenier, Anselm Hollo, Michael Palmer, Leslie Scalapino, and Anne Waldman, with many others to follow in later periods. One of the unique elements of the Poetics Program, which was definitively *not* a program in writing, was the visiting lecture series. Three guest lecturers (as well as core faculty) were invited to give three lectures as part of a course, making up nine of a semester's class meetings. Giving three lectures ensured that guests were on hand for an extended period, providing both students and faculty ample time to exchange ideas and establish relationships. In a course on Emily Dickinson, for example, the guest lecturers were Robert Creeley, Beverly Dahlen, and Susan Howe. The Stein course included lectures by Lyn Hejinian and Philip Whalen; the Sappho course included Robin Blaser, Judy Grahn, and Jack Winkler, a classicist; the Whitman course included Ken Irby, Nathaniel Mackey, and Bernadette Mayer; while a course on the troubadours featured poet and medievalist George Economou, as well as Carl Grundberg, then an MA student, and scholar-translator Magda Bogin whose groundbreaking work on women troubadours was just gaining wider circulation. John

Clarke's essential *From Feathers To Iron: A Concourse of World Poetics* (1987) is based on his 1980 New College lecture series.

At a time of growing polarization that resulted in the so-called "poetry wars" of the 1980s, the aim of the Poetics Program, as Duncan McNaughton put it, was "to ventilate the scene," and keep the stage open for all kinds of poets, particularly through a weekly reading series that lasted ten years. Ironically, given the archival emphasis of the *Lost & Found* initiative, New College had a certain evanescence built into it: it was more involved in the creation of relationships that could resonate beyond the perimeters of its immediate activities than in the documentation or institutionalization of those activities. At the same time, remarkable teaching went on and many remarkable students, a number of whom di Prima refers to in her lecture, attended or were associated with the program. In an interview conducted by David Hadbawnik, himself a student of di Prima's, David Meltzer describes the program at New College:

[Diane] taught what she called the hidden roots of poetry, which again dealt with the mystical, the magical, and so on. And she taught sometimes two or three semesters on these subjects, and each semester would be a further and further unfolding. And Robert—ultimately it turned out we had all these poets teaching themselves, and learning from each other. It was an immensely interesting synthesis of poets and really gifted students. So many of them came to study with Robert. [...] I'm convinced, and I think Diane is too, the program kept him alive. [...] It was just the interchange with the students, and the energy. I remember the whole program would meet on a weekly basis, and each week would be devoted to a topic, and both students and a professor would give presentations on the topic, and then discussions. And Robert was dealing with his kidney problem, and he had to be in dialysis, and he had a bag attached. And so right in the middle, Robert would be chattering away about all these things, and he would notice that the bag was full, pull up his shirt, flop the bag on the table ... talking all the time, unplug, and then put in the new bag, without breaking a beat in what he was talking about. And so he taught us how to live, but also how to die. It was a gift, and a profound presence.[1]

The title of di Prima's signature year long course was "Hidden Religions in the Literature of Europe," and her occasional one semester courses were centered either around "Literature of the Grail," or Paracelsus, John Dee, and Giordano Bruno. Actually, Duncan was unaware of his illness until 1985, after collapsing from congestive heart failure that had been brought on by kidney failure. From then on he was on dialysis and, as di Prima describes, after some months of her driving him to a center for treatment, he was set up to administer it himself and would do so during class breaks, "usually sitting at a table and talking to students." She recalls that Duncan once told her that he even treated himself during intermission at the opera.

In addressing "the poetics of influence," di Prima elaborates on the "precision of lineage" among poets, and how this key idea has not been traced accurately enough or been given enough attention, other than by poets themselves. Perhaps this is as it should be, but New College's curricular initiative can draw very clear lines back to Black Mountain College (the early to mid 1950s, through the presence of Charles Olson, Robert Duncan, and Robert Creeley, along with their extraordinary students), and the various periods of activity at the State University of New York in Buffalo (often referred to as Black Mountain II), with Olson's brief but decisive two-year stay there beginning in 1963 (at the behest of Albert Cook, then chair of the English Department), and continuing with the appointments of John Clarke in 1964 and Robert Creeley in 1967.

At a crucial point between the dissolution of Black Mountain in 1956 and the influx to Buffalo in 1963, di Prima, with LeRoi Jones/Amiri Baraka, began a newsletter called *The Floating Bear*.

---

1 David Meltzer, interview by David Hadbawnik, March 2010, archived at: https://web.archive.org/web/20240723032354/http://www.bigbridge.org/BB14/2010_diprima/DiPrima_Meltzer_Interview.HTM.

One of *The Bear's* primary objectives was to speed up communication. As di Prima put it:

> Apart from getting hold of out-of-the way work and unpublished poets, our other major concern, at least for the first year or so, was speed: getting the new, exciting work into the hands of other writers as quickly as possible. I remember that the last time I saw Charles Olson in Gloucester, one of the things he talked about was how valuable *The Bear* had been to him in its early years because of the fact that he could get new work out that fast. He was very involved in speed, in communication. We got manuscripts from him pretty regularly in the early days of *The Bear*, and we'd usually get them into the very next issue. That meant that his work, his thoughts, would be in the hands of a few hundred writers within two or three weeks.[2]

The fact that seventeen issues of *The Bear* came out in its first year, 1961, was almost inconceivable to poets unused to immediate contact, separated from one another by geography and poverty. When one looks at the early years of Denise Levertov and Robert Duncan's voluminous correspondence, from the mid to late 1950s, much of it centers on the exchange of carbon copied poems or manuscripts. The idea that new work could circulate so quickly was truly revolutionary and certainly may have been one of the factors in making such places of congregation as Buffalo possible. di Prima would utilize these same principles of speed and immediacy in the later 1960s with her *Revolutionary Letters*, many of which were syndicated to over 200 underground newspapers by Liberation News Service. Here we can see another form of lineage: a direct line leading from an initiative like *The Floating Bear* to the underground press, breaking through the Cold War policy of communication as propaganda to the counterculture's call for communication as empower-

---

2 Laurence McGilvery, ed., *The Floating Bear: A Newsletter* (L. McGilvery, 1973), x.

ment, exploration, and kinship. One can follow other significant patterns of lineage in di Prima's co-founding of the New York Poets Theater in 1961, the Poets Press during that same period, her work with the Diggers in the Bay Area in the 1960s, her involvement with the formation of the Jack Kerouac School of Disembodied Poetics (founded by Allen Ginsberg and Anne Waldman in 1974), and her co-founding of the San Francisco Institute of Magical and Healing Arts in the 1980s.

It doesn't at all seem happenstance that di Prima's lecture locates itself so precisely, beginning with a dream she had on the morning Robert Duncan died, February 3, 1988, a dream she realizes was not her own but Robert's. As the "CODA" of the lecture goes back in time — to 1961, when di Prima made her first visit to the West Coast, and Michael McClure, with whom she was staying, invited Duncan over for breakfast so they could meet — we are given another leg of the journey. From there, we are taken to 1975, almost exactly midpoint in their twenty-seven-year relationship, when Duncan, now her "friend, master & initiate" gives her a tape of H.D. (Hilda Doolittle) reading. By having these moments frame her path through "the poetics of influence," and her profoundly poignant remarks on "the great works of old age," both fulfilled and truncated, it is almost as if di Prima is illustrating her own repossession of the dream that was Robert's, now fully dwelling in the vast terrain of this inheritance and taking upon herself the responsibilities of lineage and transmission.

In choosing to publish some of di Prima's lectures (which also include work on the Renaissance physician, botanist, alchemist, and astrologer Paracelsus; Elizabethan mathematician and astronomer John Dee; Shelley; Keats; H.D.; Olson, and many others), we want to begin making available work that has been largely inaccessible but which forms a bedrock source for that combination of research and poetics characterizing the thought of North American poetry in the twentieth, and now twenty-first centuries. di Prima's position in this realm is almost unique — as heir to and participant in what has been most important and vibrant in our culture during the period following the Second

ON DIANE DI PRIMA'S *R.D.'S H.D.*

World War, she has insisted on living with her work as record, document, and palimpsest, without rushing to codify it. This has cast her work in poetry and poetics very much in Duncan's terms, as described in his classic essay, "Man's Fulfillment in Order and Strife":

> [I]n writing I came to be concerned not with poems themselves but with the life of poems as part of the evolving and continuing work of a poetry I could never complete — a poetry that had begun long before I was born and that extended beyond my own work in it.[3]

Going against so many of the prevailing shifts in fashion, thought, or ideology, di Prima has steadfastly refused to relinquish possession over the mysteries, over openness to interpretation, and over the paradoxical complexities of plain language. One cannot overstate the importance of her insistence on these principles, since we have become so adept at approaching complex work through critical subjugation and specialized terminologies that attempt to control things that might defy control. di Prima's method, on the other hand, emphasizes and exercises continual layered readings over time: here the text becomes not a mirror but a well that can always be drawn from. Rather than the obfuscation created by blacking the back of a pane of glass to create a mirror, we are led to the layering and deepening of sources. By digging deep into this well — poetry, mythology, sacred texts — di Prima has enacted a bulwark against the technocracy of materialist reductions of human intention and will, particularly in relation to works of art. The poet Ed Dorn has offered an absolutely uncompromising and scathing statement regarding what he calls "the structuralist preference" of interpretation:

> [T]hese methodists detest authorship. They prefer to maintain authority in their own hands and to scoff at the worth-

---

3 Robert Duncan, *Fictive Certainties: Essays* (New Directions, 1985), 113.

lessness and ignorance of writers, in order to enact their own rites of explication or exploitation. In other words, authorship is an authority signal. Any one who chooses that interpretation of the function of words is, of course, quite anti-art.[4]

Di Prima's adherence to an interpretive practice that does not subsume the range of a writer's own intent is a most unfashionable position, one that clashes head on into every imaginable contemporary orthodoxy, whether aesthetic, poetic, theoretical or political, and one that has certainly made her work that much more difficult to subjugate to one doctrine or another. The fact that she has opted out of the poetry gravy train, as meager as it is, not yielding to the often dictatorial constraints of "communities" but finding her own company along the way, only adds to the lack of a "handle" one can grab onto in trying to "control" her work.

Beyond the crucial years in the Poetics Program at New College, she has taught largely outside the framework of the academic-university system, and most vitally to small, ongoing, and long-standing groups of students, in her own space. Study in these groups often consists of prolonged and in-depth work on texts by her master elders and near contemporaries. She has made of herself an example of this kind of study, continually going back to our classics: Pound, Olson, Duncan, H.D., and other texts sacred in so many ways, Keats and Shelley in particular. All the while, she has emphasized the need for students to study all the formal aspects of poetry. Continually revisiting the sometimes problematic nature of these classic texts, rather than labeling them in order to place them in some form of administrative detention or "protective" custody, is an enormous service. And this service is a weight, a burden di Prima carries on our behalf — in the act of writing, thinking, teaching — in order

---

4 Ed Dorn, "Reading for the Olson Lectures, March 1981, Lecture 2," *PennSound,* https://writing.upenn.edu/pennsound/x/Dorn.php.

to enact and demonstrate the commitment necessary in performing the rites of poetic passage.

In *R.D.'s H.D.*, using her remarkably disarming style, di Prima grounds her readings of Duncan in both the actual events of her life and the ongoing process of interpretation within the context of those events. The key, though, is that her readings are also events in her life. In that sense, interpretation itself, the act of being with a text makes, in Duncan's terms, a certain kind of living possible and, as Meltzer points out, a certain kind of dying. Encountering di Prima's lectures, one feels very much in the midst of primary forces, as if one is finally native to the world in which the writer and the reader's engagement with a text actually exist. This, in itself, is a remarkable achievement, since the whole thrust of life in the modern state has been to sever common sense and experience from the often draconian demands the state would exact from us. Though performed with great subtlety, this quite radical shift changes the nature of both the kind of knowledge brought to bear upon her investigation and the knowledge one, as a reader, can glean from such an encounter. But it is still up to each one of us to make something of that knowledge and that encounter.

11

Confluences

2011

As *Lost & Found* completes its second series, this transcription project signals a new departure. With a mix of graduate students having different interests, some with background in the so-called "New Americans" and others without, we embarked upon an auspicious endeavor: collectively editing two of Diane di Prima's lectures (also in this series, *The Mysteries of Vision: Some Notes on H.D., and R.D.'S H.D*), in preparation for her arrival. Not having been on the East Coast for a number of years, di Prima's visit was itself an event, and included appearing in class, readings (the Graduate Center, Bowery Poetry Club, Living Theater), and her presence at *Olson 100* in Gloucester, a centenary celebration of the continuing literary, civic, and political legacy of Charles Olson.

A lot was happening: Several students (Bradley Lubin and Kyle Waugh) went to Gloucester to experience the latest manifestation of this legacy first hand. Kate Tarlow Morgan (later a guest in class) and I performed a piece in Gloucester called "Blue Suit," partially based on a day spent in a bookstore in New York with Robert Duncan in the mid-1970s. Fred Dewey, an early interlocutor and supporter of *Lost & Found* and *The Living Archives* project, was also a speaker. Henry Ferrini, one of the key organizers of Olson 100, had ended his remarkable documentary *Polis Is This: Charles Olson and the Persistence of Place*, with a scene filmed some years earlier at my Graduate Center seminar on Olson.

Meanwhile, di Prima's presence was a catalyst, propelling students in various directions: Megan Paslawski discovered the work of Michael Rumaker, a student of Olson's at Black Mountain College, and a featured guest at the Gloucester events. Seth Stewart rapidly moved from long-standing work in the eighteenth and nineteenth centuries to an intense engagement with the work of John Wieners, helping lead to movement in the possible resolution of the Wieners Estate. Gabrielle Kappes began exploring the Gregory Corso archives. Meira Levinson, trained in classical Hebrew texts, began to discover radical Jewish figures like Wallace Berman, Jack Hirschman, David Meltzer, and Stuart Perkoff. Ana Božičević explored the possibilities of translating di Prima into Croatian. Kyle Waugh went to Storrs to continue his work on Ed Dorn, Stan Brakhage, and others. Becca Klaver found a long forgotten essay by Alice Notley. Brian Unger continued work on the Philip Whalen archive, but came back in time to give di Prima a ride to visit her daughter in New Jersey. Rowena Kennedy-Epstein, while completing work on "Barcelona: 1936" for the series, discovered Muriel Rukeyser's unpublished Spanish Civil War novel at the Library of Congress and quickly got the blessing of William Rukeyser, Muriel's son, to edit the text for publication. She appeared, along with di Prima and others, at a tribute to Rukeyser organized by Aoibheann Sweeney from the Center for the Humanities. Lindsey Freer continued transcribing Ed Dorn's *Olson Memorial Lectures*. And work by Trace Peterson (on Gil Ott), John Harkey (on Lorine Niedecker), and Jen Russo (on Hannah Wiener) continued.

Surely there was more but at a certain point a quite magical confluence of energy and camaraderie took over: On the heels of work on di Prima's lectures, we began reading more Robert Duncan, as well as listening to audio on Penn Sound and at the Naropa Archives, and the idea to transcribe a Duncan lecture emerged. A "Duncan Committee" formed but quickly found itself dubbed, by Kyle Waugh, the "Duncaneers." With the presence of events in Gloucester palpable in the room, the decision to start with one of the Olson Memorial Lectures seemed not only natural but inevitable.

Histories

According to Michael Basinski, Curator at The University at Buffalo's essential Poetry Collection, the chronology of the Olson Memorial Lectures is as follows:

> In the late 1970s, the David Gray Chair of Poetry and Letters was established in the Department of English. It was named after David Gray, a nineteenth century Buffalo poet, essayist and travel writer, whose generous family was well known and respected for its philanthropy. Robert Creeley was the first scholar/poet to occupy the Gray Chair and as the Gray Chair he established The Charles Olson Memorial Lectures. A poet in the tradition of Charles Olson was selected each year to deliver three lectures loosely relating to Charles Olson poetic ideas or themes explored by Olson. Each poet also gave a poetry reading. The series continued for eleven years. Charles Bernstein followed Creeley as Gray Chair. Steve McCaffrey is the current Gray Chair. Robert Creeley subsequently assumed the Samuel P. Capen Chair of Poetry at the University at Buffalo, where he served the University, the Department of English and Buffalo poetry community at the pleasure of the President of the University at Buffalo, William R. Greiner. Those poets that delivered Olson lectures were:
>
> 1979 Robert Duncan
> 1980 Michael McClure
> 1981 Ed Dorn
> 1982 Joel Oppenheimer
> 1983 Ed Sanders
> 1984 Philip Whalen
> 1985 Diane di Prima
> 1986 Tom Clark

1987 Robin Blaser
1988 Allen Ginsberg
1989 Duncan McNaughton

Thanks to the auspices of Penn Sound, we have a number of these lectures available in audio format (Duncan, Dorn, and Blaser). Michael McClure's lectures formed the basis of his essential *Scratching the Beat Surface: Essays on New Vision from Blake to Kerouac* (Penguin, 1994), and we have transcripts of Diane di Prima's lectures. As mentioned above, work is also being done to transcribe Dorn's lectures. These quite fugitive performances seem to us a key to understanding a crucial transition or break in the transmission of North American poetics and thought so rooted not just in Olson but in the energies, interests, and possibilities he activated. Much remains to be done to simply understand what happened to those energies. For example, it would be useful to consider the neglected role of John Clarke (as emphasized by Michael Boughn, poet and co-editor, with Victor Coleman, of Duncan's *H.D. Book*), since Clarke had essentially taken on Olson's teaching duties at Buffalo in 1964, following the death of Olson's wife Betty in a car accident. Outside of a dedicated group of readers and interpreters, Clarke has essentially remained far off even the margins of contemporary poetry and poetics, though he both prefigures, anticipates, and diverges from so much of what would take place during the period these lectures were given. While having audio available is an extraordinary thing, it is our intention—to the extent possible—to make more of the Olson Memorial Lectures available as texts, as aids for reference, teaching, and for the pleasures and illumination offered by the printed word. The choice to start with Duncan comes as the *Collected Writings of Robert Duncan* (University of California) finally begin to appear, and opens the possibility for preparing a larger collection of Duncan's transcribed lectures, something that would provide yet another facet to his extraordinary work and continuing presence.

The Lecture: Background

Invited to deliver the first Charles Olson Memorial Lectures, Robert Duncan gave four lectures in Buffalo, from March 20th to March 29th, 1979. Our decision to work on the fourth lecture derives mainly from the fact that it is here that Duncan most directly addresses Olson, particularly through a tour de force reading/interpretation of Olson's "MAXIMUS FROM DOGTOWN I," and Olson's relationship to a site, a *temenos,* a concept that came right at the beginning of their friendship, in 1947, when Olson asked Duncan:

> "Do you know what *temenos* is?" "Do you know — Have you, have you, have *you* come across, like one poet after another, how the dreams take place in *your* work?" "Have you come across this — have you begun to be, to know the magic of *temenos?*" "Do you know what it means to take a — to cultivate a locality — to have a *precinct* — know what it is to make a precinct?"

These concepts are central in Duncan's thinking about Olson and begin far beyond most mundane considerations of the "local" or "place" through which Olson's work is often characterized. From the Greek word "to cut," *temenos* is, according to the eleventh edition of the *Encyclopedia Britannica,* "the term in archaeology given to a piece of land that forms the enclosure of a temple, or sanctuary," and has come to mean the territory or receptacle of a deity or divinity. The term also holds great weight in the thought of Carl Jung, whom Olson was a close reader of. Despite the far-ranging, associative nature of Duncan's lecture, there is certainly a plan, and much of what comes as a revelation in this fourth lecture is hinted at or prefigured in the previous lectures.

Ironically, Duncan begins the first lecture by mentioning how reassured he is to know that tapes disintegrate and there will be no record left of his ramblings. Luckily, this has not been the case, and these lectures were preserved through tapes made

"FOLLOW THE PERSON"

by Robert Creeley. One of Duncan's central concerns is addressing "the idea of a serious poetry," and the need to "awaken our coexistence to how primary poetry is" when we engage a universe in which "each of us is an event." There are lures in experience that lead us *into* the universe, that, literally, move us: He speaks of falling in love, of the rhythm of language, and of his "conversion" through Olson's "Projective Verse" to a realization that poetry and language take place in and through an actual human body.

In relation to this, Duncan is quite suspicious of terms that are becoming more and more prevalent: "I have a feeling," he says, that "contemporary poetry has massive techniques, post-structuralism, for copying, and copping out on what I'm talking about — they're absolutely sure that if you could describe it as a set of structures — it would be *merely* language?" Such conceptions in which language subjugates experience, Duncan emphasizes, evade the idea that "we have a universe that is both in communication" and "in travail." "The universe speaks to us," Duncan says, "and yet we feel it needs a hearing." This becomes part of a long exploration of "soundings," and how poets have transmitted these soundings to the point they become images, "world-mind-images," but "when the universe fails to speak to us, we've lost language." At some point, about thirty-five minutes into the lecture, Duncan excitedly says: "Now I'm going to work." This travail, pointed to as "a theogony of poetry," is the core of Duncan's poetics and his ability to lead us through a revelatory arrival of an understanding of the faith guiding Olson's quest, just as he himself is coming to realize and articulate it. This becomes part of the cumulative transmission that is the serious business of poetry.

Interspersed throughout are Duncan's ideas on communion and the commons; on the insight that there are no "primitive" languages; on choosing one's ancestors (as William Blake chose John Milton); on the poet's relation to the "tremendum" and the domain of the sacred; on the sense of presences beyond the knowable and that, in the reception of poetry, in the hearing of it, "you do not hear the content, you hear what you know";

and on Olson's idea of a "further nature" and its intimate and historical relationship to the idea of a "nation that is not a race." Of course, this provides the barest outline and is interspersed throughout with comments on Ezra Pound, William Carlos Williams, H.D., D.H. Lawrence, James Joyce, Wordsworth, Dante, the troubadours, Heraclitus, Hesiod, Homer, and many others; most if not all of whom reappear or are "recalled" (another key Duncan concept), in the fourth lecture, allowing Duncan to demonstrate, as he says, that these are not really lectures but poetic "operations."

Responses

Many responses of the group to Duncan's work were, naturally, rooted in the actual process of listening and transcribing. As Megan Paslawski put it:

> I first understood Duncan's scrappy command of tone when he began to speak again after the recitation of Olson's poem. He is assured, but excitable. Nasal, but charming. Quick-witted, but comfortable with unfinished thoughts. His lecture demonstrates that memorialization should be an art of vitality and not a soporific designed to dull our grief. Duncan refuses to sum up Olson and instead ends his lecture when he runs out of time, with a joke that only half comes off but has so many parts that I marvel at the brain that thought to assemble them. It is a reasonable stopping place in a tribute to a poet, as Duncan argues that poets "don't get to show anything until actually the whole nature of your dying, of your going back into all the pieces, and being taken back, has ended that absolute isolate vector that you are" (1:24). Left to trace Olson's pieces, Duncan of course finds them in Gloucester, but his poetic sense prevents him from presenting these pieces as part of a completed puzzle. Instead he gives us a scholarship whose intelligence acknowledges the place of stammering, of nervous laughter, and incomplete pronouncements.

Similarly, Rachael Wilson describes how Duncan's performance is also a demonstration of the subject of his lecture:

> Listening to Robert Duncan one is struck by the *immediacy* of a voice that urgently, almost frantically modulates, intones, mimics, cries, pitches up, whips down, whispers, shouts, whines, pants, trembles, and fills the room. As Duncan's voice brims and cracks under its own ebullience — his stutters describing a mind racing to catch up with itself — it seems fitting that the lecture be addressed to the topic of "the world felt as a presence." In the space of an hour and a half, Duncan doesn't just describe the world felt as presence. Instead, he sediments and cements his words into a world which is carried by a voice — an urgency in the voice — that presses itself on the listener and makes its presence felt. Composing by field, Duncan drives language through its music — through its rhythms, its melodies, and its pitch — from one province to the next, over a connected terrain that spreads as far and wide as the reach of Olson's giant-sized stature, or his "central fact to man born in America," which is space. In so doing, Duncan's lecture provides a powerful example of a projective-verse style that through its attention to the sonic embodiment of language, forges a world felt as presence.

In his commentary, Kyle Waugh gets to the heart of one of Duncan's most unique qualities: a dialectical process of thinking that always goes beyond the dialectical, that gums up the works of systematized thinking while never ignoring the importance of systems:

> Like the page's "field" upon which Olson proposed the poem to be enacted, in Duncan's hands the lecture becomes a domain in which multiple and adjacent constellations of ideas intermingle, held aloft by the energy and dexterity of his rapid-fire attention. Here is a mind with a mind for interfering with itself, for incorporating its own distortions and malapropisms as fodder for further discussion. In ways that

a term like "discursive" doesn't even begin to cover, Duncan's inexhaustibly reflexive mode of intellectual discovery-by-way-of-total-externalization achieves a keen and exact play-by-play record of the motions of his *thinking*, not the stable foundations of codified thought.

Central to Duncan's poetics is this conviction, that everything contains its opposite, engenders its own undoing, and takes its form and substance from that which it is not. Duncan reminds us, for instance, that Pangaea's promise of one world is forever broken and reconstituted by tectonics. And according to Duncan, in the most "awe-full" experiences of poetry, we don't feel the singular emotive power of an individual, but the individual's peculiar potential as a conduit of an agency that's communal. When presence comes through, language is the myelin, the armor of experience Duncan compares to an exoskeleton we continually break out of in order to reinvent ourselves. And here we have the privilege of encountering this molting of Duncan himself, whose lambent iridescence is yet to ossify in polished sentences, or measured poems. These "awe-full" moments of "first intensity" are occasions upon which Duncan illuminates the collective nature of our experience, not the privatized eloquence of a single self. For Duncan, like Olson, the poem delivers us "into a further nature," a *temenos*, a precinct. We discover the essence of ourselves at the extremes of our experience, where we convert the unfamiliar, "the unknown," into "the knowable," in a poetic process Duncan's subject named "projective." The projective poet goes out to know the world's interior — I think of Tennyson's Ulysses warning his men as they approach the lotus-eaters' isle: "'Courage,' he said, and pointed toward the land." The projective mission means you're a part of whatever wreckage you pick through, and thus is always unfinished — "undone business," Maximus calls it, talking to himself, as he feels the bombardment of weather and sea on the edge of a continent adrift, gazing back toward the Old World. The purpose of knowledge is to acknowledge the tonnage of what one cannot know. "But the known?" Maximus asks himself: "This, I have had to be given, / A life, love, and from one man / the world." In this magnificent oratory, the empowering nature of that kind of gift begins to take shape; here Duncan instructs us to find our Gloucester anywhere, anywhere we feel the call to dig our place. Go beyond yourself, press the edge to know the heart. Anything will fit if one makes a place for it.

In Meira Levinson's response, we get a further sense of the effects of the actual process of transcription. In light of the fact that she was a newcomer to both Duncan and Olson's work, her comments are particularly useful:

In the process of working on this transcription, I listened to this hour and a half of Duncan speaking over, over, and over again — and each time I re-listened, I understood something new. Duncan's enthusiasm, his kinetic energy — the actual speed of his speech and associative connections, his wry humor, and his candid personal reflections of his own experience reading and writing poetry — all of these qualities are contagious. Duncan's articulation of poetry as feeling, as the "changes taking place in our own bodies when we are moved out of the rhythms of our speech and excited by a music moving through the language"; the idea that poetry and language are creations in and of themselves, that poetry "spreads...a ground of, of *possible* engendering of meaning"; the idea of a precinct and presence, and Olson discovering that in Gloucester; and the concept of the poet as an agent in the transmission of something beyond himself, and as simply a part of that larger — transmission, lineage, and community — are all just a few of the tenets of poetry that Duncan conveys through this lecture. Yet he does more than simply state these ideas, more than place them in context of previous and contemporary poets — he makes them *felt*. In a similar manner to the very rhythmic process he identifies in poetry itself, Duncan's speech — his emphasis on certain words, his specific analogies, and the way in which he vocalizes these points — makes these poetic elements felt and true in a way different than do written words.

In a similar vein, the points at which Duncan develops or changes his thoughts *as he's speaking* are exciting as moments of history in and of themselves — moments of Duncan hitting illumination via verbalization, in the here and now of the lecture. The speed at which Duncan speaks and tries to convey his ideas — his half-uttered thoughts as he jumps from image to image, idea to idea, and from one way of articulating a concept to another — is indicative of a mind at work at a remarkable velocity, a velocity that clearly exceeds, in some instances, vocalization. All of the elements to this lecture can be gleaned, to a certain extent, from either just listening to the recording or just reading the transcription. There is, however, an enormous benefit to the juxtaposition of the two, and to the mixed-media experience. Part of this benefit is pragmatic — the transcription helps clarify moments of inaudibility, and helps contextualize and reference the content. Yet, there is a value to simply seeing Duncan's words on the page, and to moving between hearing his voice, his unique emphasis and manner of speech, and seeing the visual presentation of the words we chose to italicize or capitalize or punctuate or separate with dashes. Through the availability and juxtaposition of the audio and visual presentations of this lecture, readers can find their own connections to, and make their own meanings of, Duncan's words, voice, and personality.

Finally, Bradley Lubin sums up the rationale, value, and possible inadequacy of this project:

> What follows is our audio-to-text translation of Robert Duncan's fourth lecture in the first Charles Olson Memorial Lecture series. From the outset, our foremost question (and difficulty) in transcribing Duncan's recorded utterances was how best to *represent* an occasion that, being of a different generation, few of us were even alive to attend. Working

from the audio, Duncan's lecturing style posed a distinct set of challenges: how to capture the poet's unbridled energy and staccato rhythms? the impression that what's being said possesses an intrinsic extemporaneous quality? the transporting feeling his voice gives of actually "being there"? Even at an inexorable remove from the Buffalo event, when listening to Duncan, one gets the sense of beholding the impossible: an unfolding of a master poet's insights and epiphanies in realtime; the sensation of something continuously and mysteriously coming into being.

As the first transcript of a spoken event in the *Lost & Found* initiative, Duncan's lecture is a unique addition to the series: where other projects have resuscitated valuable extra-literary materials, we have endeavored to create a musical score that might be read as an accompaniment to the original audio, an imaginative re-creation of the historic lecture for those who couldn't be there. If you were one of the lucky members of the audience in 1979 to have witnessed RD in the theater of his classroom, we invite you to complement and challenge our interpretation of the event. What we give you here is a new context for assessing one of Duncan's lectures on Olson, a text-based document that we hope will bring well-deserved attention to one of the most vital and trenchant evaluations of Charles Olson.

In our decision to strive for verisimilitude (pauses, audience laughter, leaving in repetition of words, other forms of throat-clearing), our aim was to approximate the "sound of Duncan" in text and edge towards the music and dance of his speech. We encourage you to listen to the original lecture on *Penn Sound* against our transcript.[1]

---

1 Robert Duncan, "Charles Olson Memorial Lecture, Fourth Lecture," *PennSound,* http://media.sas.upenn.edu/pennsound/authors/Duncan/Duncan-Robert_Fourth-Lecture_Charles-Olson-Memorial-Lectures.mp3.

12

"the whole thing has no meaning if it is not signed"

with Megan Paslawski, 2012

The August 1944 issue of Dwight Macdonald's magazine *Politics* featured "The Homosexual in Society," a short but momentous article by poet Robert Duncan. He was twenty-five when he published the article, just a year older than Michael Rumaker would be in 1955 when Duncan served as his outside examiner at Black Mountain College.

Just a few months before the appearance of Duncan's article, in May 1944, Charles Olson resigned from his position at the Office of War Information. His resignation certainly bore structural knowledge of deep policy changes that would lead the United States to assume not just the mantle but the practice of imperial might. In taking on the role of global steward and policeman, government sponsored cultural policy would go hand in hand with economic and military policy. The very framework of knowledge would alter radically with the growth of the university and the culture industry in the Cold War.

In August of 1945, less than two weeks after atomic bombs were dropped on Hiroshima and Nagasaki, Olson changed the narrative of *Call Me Ishmael*, his groundbreaking study of Melville, to focus on the tragic story of the whale-ship Essex, and how the crew resorted to cannibalism after going astray. Having left party politics, Olson now sought a new base of knowledge and experience from which to explore what Duncan would later call "the underbelly of the nation."

It was that very "underbelly" that Rumaker was born into in 1932, but he would, as unlikely as it might have seemed for someone of his means and background, end up at a prime location for the base of this new knowledge, Black Mountain College, where Olson would be Rector and Duncan would teach. He was one of nine children in a working-class Catholic family trying to make ends meet during the depression. Rumaker's mother, as he wrote in *Black Mountain Days,* "helped pay for her keep and my getting born by peeling potatoes in the kitchen of the Retreat, a maternity home for poor married women of 'good moral standing.'" The circumstances of this childhood would loom large in Rumaker's most ambitious novel *Pagan Days* (1999), narrated in the first person by Mickey Lithwak, age six at the beginning of the book and only nine by the end of it. Between the poles of this fantastically open calling forth of his own queer beginnings and his earliest stories (written at Black Mountain in the mid-1950s and shrouded in the depths of unconscious impulse), Rumaker's work would distinguish itself by what Duncan later characterized as, "a writing that matters, that feeds a hunger for depth of experience and that will make new demands upon our understanding of human life."

Few writers in this country have explored the politics of memory as profoundly as Rumaker. Yet, this later writing, in many ways, was born from silence. After the appearance of *The Butterfly* in 1962 (a novel based on Rumaker's two year stay at Rockland Psychiatric Center and his subsequent relationship with Yoko Ono), and *Gringos and Other Stories* in 1967, ten years would pass until the publication of *A Day and a Night at the Baths,* a groundbreaking portrait of pre-AIDS gay life that Allen Ginsberg said allowed him to see through Rumaker's "eyes and feel thru his body." While Rumaker fought the demons of addiction through the late '60s and early '70s, Robert Duncan declared — in 1968 — that he wouldn't publish a new collection for fifteen years. By the time Rumaker started working on his portrait of Duncan in San Francisco, Duncan was a poet of major stature that few knew about and even fewer were able to read, given that he had deliberately chosen to remove himself from the careerist gravy-train. By circulating his work among friends or only through small editions, Duncan was able to block out the noise and listen closely to what poetry might summon forth from him.

While critics have been quick to see Rumaker's memoir as being more about himself than Duncan, such superficial readings completely miss the deeper implications of the book. In retrospect, it seems that Rumaker's decision to work on a portrait of Duncan (a project eventually leading to his landmark memoir *Black Mountain Days*), had something to do with repaying a debt, with keeping a pledge to those mentors and friends whose memories of him helped him to survive. But like all great writing, this debt was not simply to individuals, no matter how cherished they might be, but to the act of writing itself, to the historical and political process of exploring how identity is formed through perception of oneself and of oneself through others, in specific times and places, through specific forms, and in the context of very specific oppression. And it is this multifaceted process of liberation that is so richly displayed in *Robert Duncan in San Francisco*. Moreover, in Rumaker's portrait of San Francisco, we see a city that is inhabited and permeated by Duncan's spirit, despite the fact that "it was indeed a police city." Back on the east coast after a year and a half in San Francisco, Rumaker writes Duncan about some poems of his that appeared in *Measure*, the magazine edited by Boston poet John Wieners, another queer Black Mountain student who had temporarily migrated west: "Your 'Propositions' in *Measure* is ... I can't find the word. I'm thrilled, and moved. You're the richest man in San Francisco." That richness also had to do with Duncan's exemplary and open life, his construction of a protective domestic space in which the freedom that he brought into the outer world could be practiced.

As someone unable to fully inhabit his own queer skin for so long, Rumaker's encounters with Duncan on his home ground, deeply ensconced as he was in a domestic partnership with the great artist Jess Collins, would take years to sink in: "I didn't know the secret then: the more open, the more protected you are." It is this very precept that Duncan had stated so clearly, way back in 1944, when he castigated the notion of group allegiance and its consequences. To hold the "devotion to human freedom, toward the liberation of human love," he wrote, "every written word, every spoken word, every action, every purpose must be examined and considered. The old fears, the old specialties will be there, mocking and tempting; the old protective associations will be there, offering for a surrender of one's humanity congratulations upon one's special nature and value. It must always be recognized that those who have surrendered their humanity, are not less than oneself."

Such thinking, though, as Duncan wrote back in 1944 in response to Dwight Macdonald's well-founded trepidation for Duncan's public future were he to publish "The Homosexual in Society," must be backed up by openness: "it is only by my committing myself openly that the belief and the desire of others for an open and free discussion of homosexual problems may be encouraged ... *the whole thing has no meaning if it is not signed.*"

This kind of conviction would temper Duncan's sometime contrary politics through the 1960s, as when he described the humanity of the police charging demonstrators at a march on the Pentagon where he had been scheduled to speak: "Two of the faces I find immovable with hatred for what I am. What have they been told I am? But the third wavers in the commanding panic and pleads with his eyes, Retreat, retreat, do not make me have to encounter you." It is then that Duncan realizes he must refuse an audience that would want what they think he can give them:

> In the face of an overwhelming audience waiting for me to dare move them, I would speak to those alike in soul, I know not who or where they are. But I have only the language of our commonness, alive with them as well as me, the speech of the audience in its refusal in which I would come into that

confidence. The poem in which my heart beats speaks like to unlike, kind to unkind. The line of the poem itself confronts me where I must volunteer my love, and I saw, long before this war, wrath move in that music that troubles me.

It is the acceptance of such contradictory motivation that has made Duncan's work, like Rumaker's, extremely difficult to mobilize on behalf of any single identity and so, perhaps, that much more difficult for the critical establishment to assess. The appearance of Duncan's *H.D. Book,* along with Lisa Jarnot's biography and the first volume of Duncan's *Collected Poems,* parallels the republication of key works by Rumaker: this book, *Black Mountain Days, A Day and a Night at the Baths, Selected Letters,* and Leverett T. Smith's *Eroticizing the Nation: Michael Rumaker's Fiction,* all point to a revival of interest and the possibility for these essential writers to once again circulate more widely and re-inhabit the common currency of significant historical and literary achievement. Our aim in presenting this new edition of Michael Rumaker's *Robert Duncan in San Francisco* is to provide a new context for the work, both through an interview we conducted with Rumaker in February 2012, and the publication of selected correspondence between him and Duncan, to illustrate an evolving relationship that reveals so much about life, and particularly queer life, at the height of the Cold War. These new and newly gathered materials allow us to think outside the historical categories that have been handed down to us, whether of schools or identities, and follow the persons, to see where their journeys have taken them.

13

Letters to & from Joanne Kyger

2011

> "There is more political energy in friendship than in ideology."
> — Edward Dahlberg

I.

Each year of *Lost & Found* has been characterized by events that chart a particular mood or trajectory. As we began work on this series in Fall 2011, a student movement — at the Graduate Center and the City University of New York as a whole — took shape and grew rapidly. Students, faculty, and staff organized and demonstrated together against budget cuts, rising tuition, and a host of other issues. Their protests soon joined with those of nurses, transit workers, and other union members and filled the streets with a sense of life and purpose that had long been absent, outside, in the public realm. Less than a week after the trashing of the library at Zuccotti Square in lower Manhattan, a number of our students were arrested. What stood out most then and in the months following was the evident sense of care and friendship amongst those involved. As students began taking greater charge of their education, themes that had been present in their work became more and more pronounced. Given that students participating in *Lost & Found* were themselves often drawn from textual scholarship to political activity (or vice versa), the boundaries between texts and events became more porous, even when a project did not seem overtly political.

Two projects long in the making, John Harkey's edition of Lorine Niedecker's *Homemade Poems* and Anne Donlon's work on Langston Hughes, Nancy Cunard, and Louise Thompson during the Spanish Civil War, explore friendship and politics from very different perspectives. For Niedecker, living in rural Wisconsin, correspondence with other poets was a lifeline, and her act of creating homemade books as gifts was also a forceful statement about the kind of life she had chosen to live, and the perspective on the world that choice of life afforded. Harkey's work included not just trips to the textual archive but to the archive of Niedecker's workaday life, on Black Hawk Island in Wisconsin. For Hughes, Cunard, and Thompson, the urgency of their political activity was sustained, as Donlon writes, "by friendship and poetry." Here the wall between the text and the world was even more dramatically breached through Donlon's discovery of a picture taken of Hughes in Madrid in 1937; in pursuing the provenance of the photograph, another student, Mariana Soto, was led to a first-hand encounter with ninety-four-year-old Julio Mayo Souza, master photographer and Spanish Civil War veteran, now living in Mexico.

The other projects create a prism of personal, poetic, and political documentary, charting an intimate and intricate history that remains largely unwritten outside the very materials presented. Michael Rumaker's extraordinarily courageous and moving journey into the full embrace of his queer humanity is flawlessly documented by Megan Paslawski's edition of his *Selected Letters,* just as she and Rumaker have found a certain bond across their fifty-year age difference. Edward Dorn's complex relationship to his teacher and mentor Charles Olson is brilliantly interpreted by Lindsey Freer as she traces how Dorn hones Olson's legacy to face the challenges of very new conditions in the world, all the while referring to friends who sustain this travail. Seth Stewart's prodigious exploration of John Wieners brought him into a circle of friends of various ages directly involved in Wieners's life and dedicated to sustaining his artistic and human legacy after his death. And as Ana Božičević continues to lovingly trace the thought of Diane di Prima in one of her Olson *Memorial Lectures,* following her journey from Gloucester west in 1968 to form part of the "new Pleistocene," Božičević finds di Prima's words drifting from the text into her very dreams as she hears di Prima say: "We danced the dream, and then the dream exploded." In all of these letters and documents, people appear and reappear, in critical or carefree times, with humor and the pathos of "pain and suffering," the "formula," as Wieners so unforgettably wrote, "all great art is made of."

II.

Part of the pedagogy underlying *Lost & Found: The CUNY Poetic Documents Initiative* has been to create or reenact conditions of connectedness — between students, with the materials, and with those still living connected to the materials. This sets the stage for exploring the transmission of ideas and how they operate within the framework of friendship. If we accept claims about friendship's "political energy," how might that relate to our organization of historical data, to our consideration of any given time writers share? In the fall seminar in which *Lost & Found* projects are incubated, we examined a group of writers all born in the same year, to see if they might, in very different ways, be responding to the conditions of a particular time. We chose 1934 as the birth year and looked at the work of Amiri Baraka, Ted Berrigan, Ray Bremser, Beverly Dahlen, Diane di Prima, Henry Dumas, George Economou, Anselm Hollo, Hettie Jones, Audre Lorde, John Rechy, A.B. Spellman, George Stanley, John Wieners, and, of course, Joanne Kyger. A number of these writers were friends or had close and intimate relationships. As we searched for descriptive terms — particularly in reading Baraka's *System of Dante's Hell,* di Prima's *Dinners and Nightmares,* and the stories of Henry Dumas and Kyger's first book, *The Tapestry and the Web* — feelings of submersion, the subterranean, and the underworld all came up. Following an old schema of Robert Duncan's, in which he traced the dates of various writers' key developmental stages (nursing, standing, walking, and talking), we realized, as Mariana Soto pointed out in class, that the 1934 generation would have been walking and talking by the time of the Spanish Civil War.

As these discussions took place, we were in the process of arranging for Kyger to come and visit the Graduate Center for the launch of Series III. We began to think about a project with her that could be undertaken at fairly short notice. After perusing the list of correspondents in the Joanne Kyger Papers finding aid at the University of California, San Diego, we made a wish list and set out to get the letters. The letter that immediately stood out for us, included in this selection, was written to Michael Rumaker in 1959. After mentioning that, "Through the past months I have had dreams of war and destruction," Kyger writes:

> I fell into Hell for 6 hours, and the taste of what I had previously experienced for periods of moments or minutes, the horror of disassociation from the self, was now prolonged… I realized later how frightened I was of myself and how completely & utterly Ignorant. Ah well, it is most difficult. But it seems to be the problem that all of us face in our generation. And we either try to face it or we don't, or we can't. Duncan shakes his head, sympathetically enough, but says "his time" never had this problem, he can't understand it…

This passage, tucked away in a letter between friends, very quickly opened a possible sight line onto complex questions of transmission with which we were grappling and what, in a poem, Kyger has called, "the architecture of your lineage."

As a poet embracing multiple lineages and traditions ("your teachers / like Robert Duncan for me   gave me some glue   for the heart / Beats   which gave confidence / and competition / to the   Images   of Perfection"), Kyger's work explores and inhabits the process of memory forming in and of the present. "Me is memory" she writes in "Visit to Maya Land," and again "Now the memory is mine" in "Day after Ted Berrigan's Memorial Reading." Her alertness to the ever-changing phenomena of both mind and things (air, light, animals, people, trees, thought) recalls Duncan's call to "break up orders, to loosen the bindings of my own conversions, for my art too constantly rationalizes itself, seeking to perpetuate itself as a conventional society. I am trying to keep alive our awareness of the dangers of my convictions." For Kyger there is a constant and ongoing recognition that relying on received perception and memory is never enough, that such binds must be loosened through observation, vigilance, awareness, and active thought. It would be hard to think of another writer of her generation who has so steadfastly practiced this consciousness, almost as if her work provides an ever-present antidote — both playful and relentlessly focused — to the proliferation of both poetic and perceptual hot air, always bringing things and thought back into a phenomenal world that defies definition.

Coming into her lineage more directly when leaving the University of California, Santa Barbara to live in San Francisco's North Beach in 1957, Kyger found herself, as she describes in her introduction to these letters, at the confluence of an extraordinarily rich and vibrant scene. Like a kaleidoscope turning to reflect this or that quality of light or color, these letters provide a unique perspective on this key period. The velocity of nuclear warfare had recalibrated itself to target the living fiber of common civic life through "urban renewal," as neighborhoods like Bunker Hill in Los Angeles fell to the wrecking ball. A person seeking the suppressed wisdom of the earth and the human spirit was turned into a "beatnik," fodder for Madison Avenue ad-men, isolating and magnifying images that could be manipulated at will and turned into consumer categories. Charlie Parker, Jack Kerouac, and so many others not as well known were themselves consumed by this machinery. At the same time, with great political foresight and courage, Robert Duncan and his life partner Jess Collins built a fortress of domesticity in which to practice a freedom that could be brought into a world only too prepared to deny it. As Kyger recalls: "Robert Duncan was especially important to me when I was young as he presented the 'religion' of the household."

By the early 1960s, when the bulk of the letters included in this collection had been written, Joanne Kyger, Michael Rumaker, John Wieners, and George Stanley were all still in their twenties. The question of whether or not poets could create a new republic was still moot, not yet visible until Olson's filibuster that inspired some and angered others at the 1965 Berkeley Poetry Conference, and Bob Dylan's choice, just two days later, to go electric at Newport, with similar results. Amidst literary gossip, there is striking tenderness woven into these letters, a sense of common cause, and an unswerving allegiance to the work of writing and what it might yield in a world largely gone mad and detached from sources of its own sustenance. Poet David Meltzer writes: "History is not only written by the winners but also the survivors." While certainly a survivor, to call Joanne Kyger simply that would surely be a misnomer because in her choice of ways to live and write she has flourished where many have failed. And to not call what is contained in these letters history would also surely be a misnomer, even if it means that we need, as Kyger writes, to constantly remember:

>   that's your life...
>   in a past   that keeps happening
> ahead of you

As the archive keeps getting rearranged, new facets come to light, particularly as different selves are reflected through the prism of friendship. And just as importantly, "your life" exists in a phenomenal world whose passing moments constitute a living archive, where the borders between text and event no longer exist. Here, as Kyger also writes:

>   the evening sky
>   looks pretty clear
>
>   that
>   was a history
> just happened

14

"Querido Pablito"/"Julissimo querido": Paul Blackburn & Julio Cortázar's Selected Correspondence, 1958–1971

with Jacqui Cornetta, Alison Macomber, and Alexander Soria, 2017

Following the lead of our *Lost & Found* mission statement, a concern with "figures central to and associated with the New American Poetry," has meant, from the beginning, a willingness to "follow the person"[1] and see where the leads take us. Our forays into translation and worlds not seemingly associated with "New American Poetry" came early, have led far afield, and continue: selections from Margaret Randall's *El Corno Emplumado / The Plumed Horn;* various projects centered on the Spanish Civil War; Jack Spicer's translation of *Beowulf;* Jean Sénac's *The Sun Under the Weapons; Poems, Photos & Notebooks from Turkestan* by Langston Hughes; Bobbie Louise Hawkins on Colette; an upcoming project on Muriel Rukeyser's Rimbaud translations; and now *"Querido Pablito"/"Julissimo querido": Selected Correspondence, 1958–1971*. In these last two instances,

---

1 For example, in a letter to Cortázar dated October 25, 1968, Blackburn mentions the legendary journalist and sportswriter George Kimball (1943–2011), who had many friendships with poets, including Edward Dorn, and who happened to be at the launch of the first Series of *Lost & Found* in 2010.

all the editors are themselves working translators, a neglected and highly undervalued vocation in the US, where the assumption of control and dominance bestowed by the imperial language permeates the culture at every level. As we explore North American poet and translator, Paul Blackburn, and Argentinian novelist and translator, Julio Cortázar's relationship, issues of trust, friendship, faith, and love — enacted through translation — emerge, surface, and become intertwined to forge new routes of transmission and exchange.

Despite being woefully out of fashion, Ezra Pound remains the touchstone for engagement with translation as a prerequisite for writing poetry in the modern era and it should come as no surprise that Blackburn's encounter with Pound was decisive. After getting out of the Army and reenrolling in college, Blackburn began corresponding with Pound, even hitchhiking to visit him at St. Elizabeths Hospital in Washington, DC in the late 1940s, where Pound was incarcerated following his capture and imprisonment in Pisa, Italy, on charges of treason for which he never stood trial. Through Pound, Blackburn soon found himself in touch with Robert Creeley (then living in Mallorca), Denise Levertov, Charles Olson, and many others, all poets he corresponded with voluminously before his first letter to Cortázar in 1958. In his letters to Blackburn, Pound never blames students for their ignorance but their teachers, railing against academic convention. He urges the younger poet to find the books that matter, to familiarize himself with printing techniques, to put out the books that he and his contemporaries need to write and read. These imperatives and energies imparted by Pound inspired a generation of writers who took things into their own hands, creating little magazines and presses that still remain far outside the purview of mainstream literary culture.

This directive also meant discovering and reinventing the past and other traditions, not simply accepting what had been handed down, for it was Pound too who inspired further study of Provençal, and the troubadour poetic tradition. Speaking with David Ossman in *The Sullen Art* (1963), a pioneering book of interviews with North American poets, Blackburn said:

"QUERIDO PABLITO"/ "JULISSIMO QUERIDO"

"What got me started on Provencal was reading squibs of it in the Cantos and not being able to understand it, which annoyed me. It hadn't been taught at Wisconsin since the 30's, so I found Professor Bottke, the medievalist out there, who offered to tutor me in it.... That started me. I'd been studying mostly English literature, with French as a minor, along with Greek and Latin and Anglo-Saxon — all that jazz." Pound looked on with approval, remarking in an early letter to Blackburn that it is "EXcellent that the PB shd/ be learnin his purrfession." Such learning, though, had purpose for a poet. As Pound put it in another letter to Blackburn: "merely retrospective philology LACKS vitality." In other words, the reason for all this study was to renew and reshape one's own language and poetics, reaching to the very parameters of what might be imagined or knowable.

But for Blackburn, it went further: As Cortázar notes in a letter from 1959, Blackburn's work went "beyond professional," and became "personal," to the point that, by 1961, Blackburn became "the absolute pilot" of Cortázar's "soul in the States." This adds another dimension to Pound's approach to the "purrfession." Aside from actual business dealings — of which there are many in this correspondence — the understanding of one another's internal literary language is engaged, from inquiry to feeling. Pound's sense that one doesn't necessarily need to be a fluent speaker in order to be a translator crystallizes in Blackburn's journey as Cortázar's agent, translator, and friend, beginning from the first letter in which Blackburn emphasizes his ability, knowledge, vocation, and good will by writing: "no soy grammatico pero poeta." Cortázar's response — and continued responses — display his "remarkable English," eventually leading to one of the final letters of this collection, when Cortázar writes to mutual friend, poet and novelist Toby Olson, after hearing of Blackburn's death: "Ah Toby, is so tough and my English is so bad, forgive me." It is almost as if Blackburn's death severs Cortázar's own ability to access the kind of English that had been linked to a particular body in the world, continually reinforced by the exchange that made further striving in language, thought, and across borders possible, for it was that trust, originally, that made Cortázar even want to "appear" in the US, as expressed in a 1958 letter where he writes to Blackburn: "A long time has passed since I last felt the desire to publish something in the United States."

Through their correspondence, Blackburn and Cortázar create a space in which they are not faultless experts of language but play freely, moving in and out of Spanish, English, and sometimes French, for the sake of the closeness it brings to friend and collaborator across an ocean. The vulnerability they allow themselves leads to a language created "entre los dos," between those languages they have at hand, at times filled with beautifully off grammatical constructions, rooted in their consideration for a world larger than their own and to the centrality of language and poetics. In the linguistic climate of the US during those years (and ours), where language is so often regarded as a rather invisible monolith, not a pliable and permeable vehicle, the unique world they inhabit and create is particularly significant. In the US, one learns a language for tourism, for business, but not to travel to the fluid place between languages where conceptions of the world are suspended and brought into question. This narrow understanding of language — where it is treated as a problem of logic — cuts off possibility of welcoming anything other than one vantage point into the arena, an especially dangerous threat with American English. The relationship built through Blackburn and Cortázar's letters reveal the interstices that open up between two languages, in translation. It is not just a carrying over, but predicated on a contact that shapes and is shaped by that connection which, in turn, is based on trust, admiration, and love, for it is language that allows for and enriches their friendship.

Blackburn and Cortázar are translators, after all, and their fascination with and dedication to language is evidenced everywhere in their correspondence. While Blackburn's work spanned the medieval and modern, Cortázar's most important work was on Edgar Allan Poe, a translation that Peruvian novelist Mario Vargas Llosa called "among the masterpieces of contemporary literature in the Spanish language." Likewise, the translation

"QUERIDO PABLITO"/ "JULISSIMO QUERIDO"

work of mutual friend Edith Aron, Gregory Rabassa, and Cortázar's wife of many years, Aurora Bernárdez, undergirds many exchanges in the letters.[2] And while Blackburn worked both as Cortázar's literary agent and sometimes translator, Cortázar adored Blackburn's poetry and worked on his own translations into Spanish, continually expressing his admiration: "Ante todo, gracias por los dos poemas. Me hicieron pensar en la China, no sé por qué, supongo que ciertos poemas chinos (que he leído en traducciones) tienen esa misma brevedad, esa síntesis rápida y esencial que se apodera de lo que vale — como la gaviota del pez — y deja sin decir todo lo secundario."[3]

They immensely enjoyed working through snags in the translation process together, and there are numerous drafts filled with notes in the archival materials. In a 1959 letter from Cortázar, he offers various suggestions for work on *Cronopios and Famas,* before summing up all his edits: "ENOUGH ENOUGH ENOUGH!!! I've run out!!! Wow! Triple wow! Poor Paul, how bored you must be. But you wanted my critiques, and now you have them. But they are really nothing more than mere details. The rest is MAGNIFICENT. The more I read it, the more I like it." For many, the world of *cronopios* and *famas* soon became a meta-language to describe the world, but for Blackburn and Cortázar it remained an intimate mode of communicating their closeness and distance.

Cortázar's *Historias de cronopios y de famas,* published in 1962, released the curious landscape of three interactive beings, *cronopios, famas,* and *esperanzas,* to the public. In his descrip-

---

2 In a letter to Blackburn from Rabassa, for example, the possibility of a whole new world opens up: "Have you been translating any poetry lately? I was thinking the other day when I was reading some of them that you ought to hone up your Portuguese and do some Brazilians. I was thinking of Joao Cabral de Melo Neto, who is superb, and also that Carlos Drummond de Andrade is in need of rescue..."

3 "First of all, thank you for the two poems. They made me think of China, I don't know why, I suppose certain Chinese poems (which I've read in translation) have that same brevity, that swift and essential synthesis that takes a hold of what matters — as the gull with the fish — and leaves everything inessential unsaid" (2 de noviembre 1959).

tions of them, Cortázar abandoned developing much detail regarding their physical attributes but, instead, recorded their interactions and attitudes in their irregular, mundane environment. *Cronopios* — loosely defined as naïve, idealistic, disorganized, sensitive, and shy — differ from *famas,* those highly organized and judgmental beings and, likewise, from *esperanzas,* who are dull and unimaginative. But Cortázar and Blackburn already discuss *cronopios, famas,* and *esperanzas* in their first letters to each other some four years prior, in 1958, and when Blackburn asks Cortázar about the true origin of "cronopios" and other key phrases, he responds: "How can I know? I was in the Théatre des Champs Elysées, listening to some jazz ... and the cronopios arrived.[4] They just arrived, body and soul. Bailar tregua y bailar catala can't be translated ... For me, it's simply a phrase with a certain magic, a sort of 'runic rhyme' in Poe's sense ... I think our philological enquiry is delightful and quite true in the poetic sense of Truth, which is the ONLY sense of Truth. (I am speaking like Shelley, I'm afraid) ... I really like your explication of what a cronopio is. What happens with a glass of beer is exactly that. Of course! Perfect! I also like that you left the names of the cronopios, famas and esperanzas without translating them. Your very right in what you say."

The pair believed that, in fact, their friendship was the truest and most inimitable of all cronopio-friendships. As Cortázar wrote to Toby Olson in the same letter quoted above, his "brother" Paul was "a wonderful friend, he was the first and most wonderful of *cronopios,* who he loved, who he made live in English." This unique and encoded bond provided a place for language to erupt in animation, absurdity, humor, and wit. After sending what then seemed like a sizeable check to his friend, Blackburn writes, in a 1965 letter: "It doesn't seem right or decorous for a little Cronopio to make so much money, but a *crono-*

---

[4] See Cortázar's text, "Louis enormísimo cronopio," describing the evening he spent listening to Louis Armstrong; in *La vuelta al día en ochento mundos,* vol. 2 (Siglo XXI Editores, 1968), 13; also translated into English by Thomas Christensen as *Around the Day in Eighty Worlds* (North Point Press, 1986).

pio can never become a fama, true?" In order to transcend their transatlantic boundaries, Blackburn and Cortázar often placed *cronopios* in each other's respective environment. As Blackburn made his way through the translation, Cortázar wrote how his *cronopios* "have become acclimated to New York, and are happily strolling about and going into the bars of Christopher Street." In a 1959 letter, he thanks Blackburn for "scattering his cronopios in cafés on 9th Avenue. They ate all of the hamburgers, I imagine, and then forgot to pay. Lamentable conduct for cronopios in New York." At one point, Blackburn suggests that Cortázar visit one of his favorite bodegas while spending time in Spain, recounting that: "When you bought a litro de conac, they always gave you una copita de vino dulce y una tapa, on the house, as we say ... Only cronopios know of it." Throughout the course of their letters, Cortázar wrote from Paris, Vienna, Saignon, and Buenos Aires, while detailing visits to places like Uganda, Galicia, Andalucía, Teheran, Cuba, and Peru, as Blackburn continued to cultivate the domestic spirit of his fellow "Village cronopios" in New York City.

Far from a simple display of wit, these exchanges were set against the backdrop of the concept of "alienation," foisted onto the US as a Cold War extension of existentialism and meant to supplant the deeper revolts of Bebop and the Beats. The struggle was to rediscover and retain the familiar, to actually exist in the world and become part of what Charles Olson defined as the "human universe," a place in the larger cosmos where one might no longer be estranged from that which is most familiar. For Cortázar, then, it was never an ideological stance, but the candor and outrageousness of "our Allen" that captured his imagination, as when Allen Ginsberg declared himself, to the amazement of those present at a press conference in Havana in 1965, a "maricón y chupapijas."[5] Thus, the circle of writers and artists and musicians close to Blackburn immediately become part of Cortázar's world, through anecdotes, publications, and their unique exchange of tapes in which actual voices and notes

---

5   "a faggot and a cocksucker."

could be heard across the distance, always keeping in mind the economy of the time: While Cortázar traveled for work, the mail remained their lifeline, since the cost of long distance calls was prohibitive and the luxury of personal visits a rarity.

Their relationship shines through each collaboration and exchange as does their conviction to letting language live on, in many languages and many places. Their own vocabulary in the letters, which shifts so playfully and naturally between different languages, creates a terrain so often lacking in conceptions of language acquisition. There are moments where things don't come through (Blackburn's "horse-stable full of Mexicans" which perplexes Cortázar in their first exchange), but this is precisely what translation can do, to allow things to be muddled up and reconfigured through a relationship (language to language, translator to translator, person to person), which trusts communication is possible across borders and political climates. Ultimately, the work they endeavor together always entails a "we," even when years later Cortázar proposes that Blackburn no longer serve as his agent, so he might consolidate all publication matters to one agent throughout the world. Upon Blackburn's understanding agreement to this proposal, Cortázar answers, "It made me so happy to receive your letter, Pablito. I already knew it, but what a beautiful thing to be reminded of the friend I have in you. Your response is what I hoped for, but you have such a clean way of saying things that my eyes filled up with tears. I'm an idiot, but I'm happy to be one, to have a heart that doesn't get old and to marvel at finding solidarity and goodness in the people I love. Well, stop it. But I had to say that to you and to hug you tight" (September 4, 1970).

In choosing our title, we present the reader who does not know Spanish with the facts of endearment that are part and parcel of a culture and mode of relation. Being the elder of the two, Cortázar is in his full right to refer to Paul as "Pablito," little Paul, in an endearing and not diminutive sense. And in referring to Julio as "Julissimo," Julio the maximal, Blackburn extends all admiration to his friend without losing any of his own stature in the process. In presenting this collection of the portrayal of a friendship, we want to emphasize the initiative taken by Paul Blackburn: To bring the world of Julio Cortázar across all the obstacles that one language, culture, economy, and political system might present to another — and by so doing to create a completely new place of form and thought — is a conscious and far-reaching intervention whose implications still reverberate.

II.

While a good portion of the letters between Blackburn and Cortázar from the first period (1958–1962) are concerned with more mundane "business" matters — translation questions, contractual issues, publication plans, and the transfer of money — the magic between them is felt immediately and continues as their long-distance friendship develops. In what almost seems like an incident from a Cortázar novel, a *Hopscotch*-like skipping of chapters, the first letters between them cross each other. Thus, they both write to each other first, and this typifies their relationship: Each comes first for the other. The letter below, written in French from Paris on March 20, 1958, precedes the Blackburn letter of March 26 opening our selection:

> Dear Blackburn:
> Edith Aron suggested I write to you, she has told me that you like my cronopios and would like to receive a copy. I am sending it to you with great pleasure (in a *GRAND LUXURY* edition ... You'll see!) ... All this goes from cronopio to cronopio, since I have no doubt you are one. If you decide to translate something of mine to English, it will make me very happy, and my cronopios will speak a new language. As of now they only know Spanish and German.

The initial connection between Blackburn and Cortázar appears to come through Edith Aron, another Argentinian living in Paris and an extraordinary translator whose own first meeting with Cortázar also seems to have come out of a novel. It is she after whom the character La Maga in *Hopscotch* is modeled, something she wrote about later in life in *55 Rayuelas,* a book written in homage to her endearing but sometimes vexed relationship with Cortázar.⁶ Blackburn may in turn have found Aron through his connection to Cid Corman, poet and founder of *Origin,* one of the most important and influential little magazines of the 1950s. And it was through Aron that Corman met the German poet Paul Celan in Paris since she, apparently, had gotten Celan a job at UNESCO, the same organization for which Cortázar worked as a freelance translator.⁷

By July 1958 Blackburn placed a few translations in *New World Writing* and sent Cortázar the first of many checks that would cross the Atlantic by mail or wire. Cortázar writes, "All this I owe to you and am very grateful," despite also writing that, "A long time has passed since I last felt the desire to publish something in the United States." Clearly, Cortázar's trust in Blackburn completely changed this, as they embarked, from these early letters, on an adventure that would have a deep impact on the literary culture of the period.

Throughout the correspondence there are wide gaps in letters from Blackburn, though judging by Cortázar's letters we know he received letters that have gone missing. From the beginning, Cortázar responds enthusiastically to Blackburn's poetry, and deeply appreciates Blackburn's initiative to translate and try to place his work. In a letter from Vienna that typically switches between Spanish and English, sometimes mid-sentence, Cortázar writes:

> From Paris they sent me your letter Therefore, do not be surprised if I was so slow in answering you. But, what happened with our last correspondence? I am sure that I wrote you on

---

6 See Juan Cruz, "Edith Aron, su propia 'maga,'" *El País,* April 19, 2007, https://elpais.com/diario/2007/04/20/cultura/1177020004_850215.html, and Juana Libedinsky, "Edith Aron: La maga de Julio Cortázar," *La Nacion,* March 7, 2004, https://www.lanacion.com.ar/lifestyle/edith-aron-la-maga-de-julio-cortazar-nid577957/.

7 See Gregory Dunne, *Quiet Accomplishment: Remembering Cid Corman* (Ekstasis Editions, 2014).

the "The Dissolving Fabric". Was my letter dissolved while crossing the ocean blue? I pity the fish that swallowed it. Next time I'll send my mail in a bottle. I feel bad that I don't have it here with me in Vienna, to reread and to tell you what I think of it. Nevertheless, in my memories are things that I like enormously. You have a way, that's very much yours of transmitting your poetry. I also read your poem in the gorgeous edition of "Jargon", that you sent for the New Year, which I really am thankful for. My friends were left amazed with the design and layout of that book. Of course, in those days we were going about reading poems by Allen Ginsberg and others...

Paul, I'm so glad and proud about your translating and placing my stories and things. You can't imagine the joy that it gives me, because I know that it's something that interests you personally before professionally. From poet to poet, and from friend to friend, and that happens rarely in the literary market. So it is my pleasure to accept your proposal and from now on you can consider yourself my AGENT. Hallo, Mr. Agent! How do you do Mr. Agent? It sounds kind of strange, no? What is an Agent? What is an Author? If an Author sees an Agent/coming through the rye...!!! (March 27, 1959)

And in another letter, Cortázar's enthusiasm for Blackburn's translations is infectious: "Paul, your translation is tremendous. I read it over twice, taking note of the observations I must give you, which are really just mere details. You have captured the spirit of the thing, the manner of writing I used for the cronopios, which is now magnificent in the English" (June 29, 1959).

Cortázar is always eager to hear Blackburn's opinion on things he might feel Blackburn is closer to. In a March 27, 1960 letter, Cortázar writes: "The story about Charlie Parker ('El perseguidor') is driving everyone crazy. Have you read it? I'm interested to know how you, an American, would react to it, face to face with a subject that refers to jazz and things close to your heart." And throughout, as with the Jargon publication sent overseas (an important small press associated with Black

Mountain College, founded by poet Jonathan Williams), Blackburn introduces Cortázar to the work of poets and artists he is close to: The possibility of Robert Duncan's partner the artist Jess doing illustrations for *Cronopias and Famas* is mentioned in a 1961 letter; George Economou, Robert Kelly, Rochelle Owens, Jerome Rothenberg, Carolee Schneeman, Armand Schwerner, Charles Stein, and others all come up and are avidly inquired about. In a letter from February 21, 1961, Cortázar writes: "Kelly has sent me the second issue of TROBAR, which has some quite magnificent things. Your poem is very difficult for me, but I feel the MAGIC, tremendous magic. I don't like that you put the periods separate from the words, I don't know why you do that. Do you want the reader to take a long pause or what? Please explain. I'm so dumb." In addition to books that Blackburn sends, in the same letter, Cortázar also orders books:

> So you lost my list of books, you obnoxious cronopio. Never mind, I had a double. Here it is:
>
> Ezra Pound – ABC of Writing [*sic*]
> Dylan Thomas. – Quite Early one Morning.
> Ferlinghetti. – A Coney Island of the Mind.
> NEW DIRECTIONS 16
> NEW DIRECTIONS 11 (Giant)
> Ferlinghetti. – Her
> Harry Levin (?). – James Joyce
> Ezra Pound. – The Confucian (?) Odes
> Gregory Corso. – The Happy Building [*sic*] of Death (or something like it, I don't understand much
> Denise Levertov – With The [*sic*] Eyes at the Backs [*sic*] of our Heads

Encounters with poets across the Atlantic are made even more palpable through Blackburn's tapes, featuring readings, music, and ambient sound, and eagerly awaited by Cortázar on the other side: "Me, crammed into a store on Champ de Mars, and you speaking near a window where you can hear the sounds of

"QUERIDO PABLITO"/ "JULISSIMO QUERIDO"

New York... I think the age of magic has just begun, not in the time of Hermes Trismegisto. Everything is magic, it's incredible that that roll of brown tape holds two hours of your voice, of your breath" (March 27, 1960).

Though there is always a sense of intimacy in the letters, they seldom get into personal details. Yet, the feeling of trust — established almost immediately — is woven throughout the correspondence, as in this 1959 Cortázar response to a letter that must have referred to Blackburn's relationship to his first wife, Winifred Grey McCarthy: "Thank you for the trust that you showed me in the paragraph about you and Freddie. I don't know much about your personal life, except for what I learned about from Edith, but I wish you the best of luck in your escape. You deserve to be happy, gran cronopio. And it's very difficult, damn it." By 1961, in a letter from Paris dated July 28, Cortázar declares: "By this time I reckon you got my letter explaining that you're the absolute pilot of my soul in the States." And there is immediate enthusiasm in sharing important news with "Querido Pablito," as in a letter from Vienna, dated September 9, 1961: "Last week I finished RAYUELA (HOPSCOTCH, you know). It is, I humbly believe, a very beautiful thing."

While Cortázar's involvement with Cuba has been well documented, letters about it often have a wistful feel, knowing he'll be so close to possibly visiting the US to see Blackburn but also knowing that he can't. In letter from December 16, 1962, Cortázar writes:

> Yes, I would like so much that old mother Unesco sent us on a good-will tour around the States, but... Things are rather upside down, for it is my old pal Fidel Castro who is inviting me to join the jury for their annual literary contest. So, as the invitation has been extended to Aurora (they must know that we are such an inseparable pair) we shall fly to La Habana on the 10 or 12 January. The invitation was so unexpected that I have not fully realized yet what is going to mean to me. All this years I have been longing to go to Cuba to have a direct experience of what is happening there, and suddenly... there

> we go! The damned pity of it is that, under the circumstances, I wont be able to make a stopover in New York. They take you by plane to Prague, and from there they snatch you directly to Cuba. Return, same. I have not lost all hopes, anyway, and once I'll be in Havana, I'll try any possible traffic combination to come back to Paris via USA. But I'm not confident at all.

The letter brings other news as well, news about a film project, news about friends, and news about politics, in the typically understated way in which a demonstration, a concern, or an event gets mentioned: "In the meanwhile, things happened that I am sure you will glad to know about. Luis Buñuel asked me to give him the rights to film 'Las Ménades', a short-story belonging to 'Final del juego' (the little yellow book printed in Mexico in '56). I have always tremendously admired Buñuel, so I was as happy as a polecat, admitting these bumptious felines to be happy, which I doubt... I will write to Kelly, of course, and ask for 'The cronopios in America.' Now I have to prepare the trip to Cuba, but I promise a letter from Havana and — who knows? maybe a personal call. Now, Paul, I'm sending you bucketfuls of canopies, y también." And, after his signature, "I knew from you the General Strike for Peace. The French papers were silent about it. No wonder, since all the American news come through American news agencies."

The second period (1963–1966), begins with a long letter by Cortázar describing his first visit to Cuba, just some months before the assassination of John F. Kennedy, and ends with protests against escalation of the war in Vietnam and a *cronopio* story by Blackburn. In between, Blackburn mentions the arrest of Lenny Bruce at a nearby café while Cortázar recounts a story about Allen Ginsberg in Havana, his travels around the world, fixing up a "ranchito" in the countryside, and all manner of news continues to be exchanged.

"QUERIDO PABLITO"/ "JULISSIMO QUERIDO"

In a letter from July 15, 1963, Cortázar writes: "I also saw EL CORNO EMPLUMADO from Mexico.[8] These journals that you and your friends collaborate on are very well done, and I think there is a decent sized readership for them. So much better than the typical boring 'literary magazines', read only by old ladies at tea time." There is Cortázar's meeting ("I met Joyce Johnson in Paris, and we had a very nice chat") (March 23, 1964), that Sara Blackburn recounts rather differently in her response: "Your remark about your meeting with her makes it sound as if you sat and stared at one another for a long half-hour, each silently cursing out the Blackburns. I hope not! Anyway, our apologies; we don't intend to send you every wayward Parisian visitor" (March 26, 1964). But Cortázar immediately writes: "I hope to meet Carolee Schneeman, if she arrives in Paris by the end of July. If she's your friend, I'm sure that I'll like her very much" (May 21, 1964). And Sara Blackburn becomes more of a presence in this period as letters are written to both Paul and her and she continues a separate correspondence with Cortázar about publishing issues.

The subject of Gregory Rabassa's translation of *Hopscotch* comes up again and again: "I already sent Rabassa 100 annotated pages of RAYUELA. I hope they will be useful for his work. What a hellish job he has ahead of him, poor soul" (May 21, 1964). And then in August: "Rabassa: Why, this person has disappeared altogether! Before leaving Paris in May, I took all my courage and sent him about 100 pages of RAYUELA with marginal notes to help his work. I asked him to write back telling me if my comments were of any help. It seems they weren't, because he didn't write. Perhaps he went to swim to Bermuda. Anyways, if you contact him, tell him I'm waiting for his news." And in another letter: "I'm revising my new stories and I want to start a new book. But Rabassa doesn't let me, because this caring man is sending me tons of translations that I barely have

---

8 See *Lost & Found*, Series II, Spring 2011, *From El Corno Emplumado / The Plumed Horn: Selections,* edited by Margaret Randall and Sergio Mondragón. In addition, a full run of the magazine has been digitized at: http://opendoor.northwestern.edu/archive/collections/show/5.

time to finish a batch, before then pops another, and so on. It's like the plagues in the Old Testament. A blessed plague, by the way, because the translation is jolly good." The complexities of the novel seem to require comic relief: "A very infinite cronopio from Buenos Aires has invented a machine which helps to read RAYUELA. You press button A, and out pops the right chapter. There are 5 different buttons. The last is for setting on fire the whole machine. There is a super-luxe model, with bed and bar." And friends appear, to assuage the distances: "Octavio Paz was here last week and we talked of you, and listened, Paul's voice reading poems. It was a great evening."

In between politics ("These days we are very worried and saddened by the story of the marines discharged in Santo Domingo. How do you think Latin America can trust the United States? LE MONDE published a telegram from the AP, from Washington, revealing that in 1962, Kennedy blocked an attempt to poison a shipment of Cuban sugar headed for the USSR. Did you know that? Machiavelli pas mort. I'm imagining everything Castro is going to say in his next speech..."), Cortázar is concerned about his friend's situation: "I got your letter and I felt sad about this job hunting of yours" (May 1, 1965). And in between that are opinions about writers: "I have a notion that Bellow, after all, is an excellent, perhaps a very good second-rate writer. Gombrowicz deserved the prize much more than Bellow, he's a revolutionary artist" (May 17, 1965). And "Here in Paris everyone is very excited about Leroy Jones' work...everything explodes from the first sentence, so some effects are lost which might have more success if done differently. But the piece that happens in the subway is very good, really, and the idea is brilliant." (December 14, 1965). Politics again appears, in the form of news about a 1965 march on Washington attended by Blackburn: "Your description of the big protest meeting was very helpful for me, because of course the newspapers, here, told the news in their way, and we know how that goes. Tell Chuck Stein that someday I'd like to talk with him about simultaneities and coincidences" (December 14, 1965).

"QUERIDO PABLITO"/ "JULISSIMO QUERIDO"

There are fewer letters preserved from this period (1967–1971), as both Blackburn and Cortázar find themselves going through major changes in their lives. Blackburn's marriage to Sara Golden ends in 1967 and he meets and then marries Joan Diane Miller, with son Carlos T. born in 1969, to Cortázar's great joy at his friend's new found happiness: "Send me a photo of Carlos, I want to see if he looks like Joan (which I hope) or you (which I fear!!!!)." In 1968, Cortázar separates from Aurora Bernárdez, whom he had been with since 1953, and becomes involved with Lithuanian writer, editor, translator, and filmmaker Ugne Karvelis. The war in Vietnam rages on, disagreements with actions taken by the Cuban government come up, friends appear and reappear. As Cortázar writes in May, 1967: "Yesterday I read a declaration by McNamara in Le Monde, where he calmly said that the U.S. would drop 50 'small' bombs over 50 urban centers in China, which would exterminate FIFTY MILLION PEOPLE, without including another TWENTY-FIVE MILLION technicians, civil servants, etc. Oh what a lovely time we're living!" And again in July: "I heard last night that MacNamara is thinking of sending another 100,000 men to Vietnam. Nice news, as usual." When Blackburn is far away, his friends talk about him: "I met Margaret Randall, of course, and José Iglesias, and we spoke much of you. The people were terrific and they were quite steadfast in their work on questions of revolutionary culture — [...] Write to me in India, at Octavio's (136 Gold Links, New Delhi)" (January 21, 1968).

There is a different sense of urgency in some of Cortázar's letters: "So, my debt is so immense, that to pay it I ought to mortgage my soul. The snag is that nobody would give a damn for it, so the only thing I can do is batter once more the old typewriter (it has 30 years of use, and millions of pages have gone under its rubber roll). And also, Pablito, I'll keep writing in Spanish because I have many things to tell you and English is a hellish language for this poor 'Argentine'" (May 11, 1967). But Blackburn's illness and the rapid demise of his health loom large and come quick. While at first treating his friend's then unknown condition with his usual inimitable humor, Cortázar's concerns mount quickly, to the point that he plans the purchase of medicine from Europe, unavailable in the US. As had always been the case with Blackburn, employment, money, and time to write were central issues. He finds a steadier teaching job, at State University of New York, Cortland, just before his health begins to decline. The final extraordinarily moving letters are by Cortázar to Joan Blackburn and poet, novelist, and mutual friend Toby Olson. The first, written to Joan on August 20, 1971, breaks the news of Blackburn's true condition, and the others are written after learning of his dear friend's death shortly thereafter. And the last letter, written in English and addressed to Joan, is from Paris, dated October 6, 1971:

Dear Joan,

I just learned it by a letter Toby Olson sent me. What could I say that you don't know already? I'll always miss Paul's friendship, loyalty, his letters, his laugh, his voice. I've lost such a friend that no language can give or convey what I feel. And you, young and tender Joan, what can I tell you now? Kiss Carlos for me, Joan, and be sure that Julio will always be there for you and he. To be your friend is a consolation. I love you both as I loved Paul,

Julio

15

Of Suckers and Gulls

2012

Now an archaic word, gull was first used (at least according to the *Oxford English Dictionary*), by Thomas Nashe in 1594: "Liues there anie such slowe yce-braind beefe-witted gull," and denoted a "dupe, simpleton, or fool." Sucker, however, seems a particularly American word, emerging, apparently, during the Gold Rush, to denote a "greenhorn" or a "simpleton," though its primary meaning was still "a young mammal before it is weaned," or "a child at the breast." In one of Charles Olson's favorite dictionaries, *Webster's 2nd Edition,* definition 2b of sucker is, "One who is sucked, or bled or victimized; hence, one easily duped or gulled." In one of my own favorite word-books, *March's Thesaurus Dictionary* (first published in 1901), the word "sucker," as we now commonly use it, only appears in the 1925 supplement of "words which became known to the public during the World War period," and is defined as, "An easily deceived person." Here we seem to be in the realm of the Midwestern comic genius George Ade (1866–1944), a world of rubes where someone's always got the goods on you. The phrase "sucker punch," according to varied sources, was only fully popularized by the boxer Jack Dempsey in the late 1940s. One can only imagine what Ken Warren might make of this symbiotic relationship between sustenance — the very act of feeding at the breast — and deception. But perhaps, in fact, this is the very theme that runs between the lines of these essays.

As for Captain Poetry, those in the know will recognize a nod to the "superhero" figure created by Canadian poet bpNichol, first published by the much neglected bill bissette, through his blewointment press in 1970. And no doubt 1970 is a watershed moment, given the death of Charles Olson, and his centrality to the issues at stake here. At a lecture given in Buffalo (a major site, along with Lakewood and Cleveland, for the imaginary out of which the ethos of Warren's writing emerges, if we remember that ethos originally meant "lair" or "haunt"), the great poet Ed Dorn comments:

> In Olson's time, and I take it really that 1970 was a, without making such a large claim for an actual transaction for a year but taking its significance from the actual significance of his death, which was terminal to all the energy he had to give to argue sanity, rationality, morality, and excitement, all at the same time — if, indeed, that did end the greatest speaker for that condition, favorite word of his, then January 1970, in fact, did end something with his death which was, beyond his mere death, obviously — I mean, everybody dies.[1]

Dorn goes on to emphasize Olson's exhortation to write "poetry," not "your own poetry," an emphasis that itself echoes Dorn's own gesture of 1969, when "I," a character in Dorn's classic *Gunslinger* (a place we used to get the news from), left the stage, maybe forever.

In this country, even our ghosts seem to have ghosts, and each generation encounters its own, refracted back in others as if through a prism, part fun house, part unfathomable abyss. News travels, eventually. I, for one, feel like I've been waiting a long time to find out what happened. Ken Warren has been delivering the news for some time, primarily through *House*

---

1 Edward Dorn, *Charles Olson Memorial Lectures*, ed. Lindsey M. Freer (Center for the Humanities, 2012), 39.

Organ (the remarkable newsletter he edits and publishes and that I first encountered on Vincent Ferrini's desk at 126 East Main Street in Gloucester, then later, on a visit to Joanne Kyger in Bolinas), and the unique *Lakewood Observer* project, whose principles and plan appear as an enormously useful postscript to this collection. Beyond these venues, Warren has been an indefatigable and alert commentator on the times we live in, through essays and reviews, primarily of books and music but also of movies, all published disparately and exceedingly hard, until now, to track down. For anyone who wants to gain a truer understanding of the "psycho-geography" of North American culture, particularly from a present vantage point looking back into futures we might once inhabit, there is nothing quite like *Captain Poetry's Sucker Punch* available.

One of the many virtues of Warren's extraordinary collection is that he writes from positions that the prose itself both enacts and interrogates. These positions can be economic, intellectual, political, historical, emotional, cosmological, esoteric, or even pharmacological. But, because of the clarity of their deliverance, they are always felt to be earned and, as such, present a challenge to the reader to respond in kind, to find a place from which to read. In the very first essay, a review of Lewis Hyde's *The Gift*, a book that became popular among certain poets, we are given a taste of Warren's method, an approach that often allows potentially contradictory or divergent directions to be thrust upon the reader, forcing one to actually think about where one stands in relation to the ethical map Warren's prose and intellect delineates. When Warren writes, *"The Gift* is especially popular with poets who value state-supported fellowships," he takes the kind of personal risk that has faded from the world of criticism long ago. Once upon a time (outside of those doing hatchet-work), people who reviewed things — whether books or music or movies or artworks — thought that writing from a particular position, even if it might shift over time or cause a rift in the social network, was a necessary part of the endeavor. And the work under scrutiny, in addition to a desire to make it more known or express what one might think laudable or even dangerous about it, was also a vehicle for establishing values.

In this sense *Captain Poetry's Sucker Punch is,* to use another well-worn cliché, like a "bucket of ice water on a sweltering day." Disparate, opinionated, and sometimes unwieldy, it is also a huge sigh of relief in the monotonous, jargon-filled, mystifying, pretentious, back-scratching, ass-kissing terrain that purports to consider itself criticism these days. In his writing on music, for example, Warren achieves something exceedingly difficult: He manages to convey very clear arguments without the reader necessarily having to be familiar with the particular cultural figures he refers to. For instance, when he writes, "Long before the Ramones had cast Karen Quinlan as the decade's terminally sedated icon, the New York Dolls had already embodied in pill-box trash odes to battered psyche the sad truth that America's energy crisis had numbed the rock and roll ego," we don't really need to know who the Ramones, the Dolls, or Karen Quinlan are to grasp the strength of his statement. The presentation of this kind of argument is at complete odds with how pop culture gets written about now: If you are unfamiliar with the references, the writing is unintelligible because the references are not being used to create meaning or establish value, and so they gain no traction beyond the glitter of their own gaudy display.

All in all, there is much to recommend: Few critics I can think of are able to write seriously on the Christian context of heavy metal, and directly follow with an essay on the complexities of Simone Weil's relationship to the Ancient Near Eastern, Hebrew, and Greek legacies. There are essays on poets we should know more about, such as Daniel Thompson, and essays on writers we are familiar with (Jack Kerouac, Gregory Corso, Anne Waldman, Eileen Myles, John Wieners, and so many others), but are given a new angle on. The juxtaposition of an essay on L=A=N=G=U=A=G=E poetry with substantial essays on Robert Duncan's *Groundwork* and Ed Dorn's *Abhorrences* is truly illuminating, pitching the terms and trajectory of given thought far beyond the usual polemics attending the remains of what came to be called the "poetry wars." There is a superb essay on Gilbert

Sorerentino in which Warren — against all the facile readings of Sorrentino's inventive and apparently Oulipean forms — insists that Sorrentino remains largely preoccupied with social and economic class, not the gymnastics of "postmodern" invention.

Finally, in addition to the erudition and intelligence that courses throughout, two sections in particular set the rest in relief: the essays on John Clarke ("Between Language and *Ta'wil:* Robert Creeley, Jack Clarke and Poetics in Buffalo after Olson," and "John Clarke and the Constellation of Epic Intent"), and the longest section of the book "Charles Olson's Breath of Conspiracy." In an odd way, while the methodology is similar, the approaches to Clarke and Olson are almost at opposite poles. Since Clarke's work is so much less known and commented upon than Olson's, Warren provides an introduction to Clarke, certainly the best one I am aware of. And since Olson's work has assumed such presence, even if, in many ways, it remains to be further explored, Warren chooses to approach it with what might almost be called shock therapy. By concentrating on the amplified implications of a detailed reading of Olson's political and social formation, Warren provides a completely new framework for thinking about Olson's unique placement as a conduit through which some of the twentieth century's most vexed issues were channeled or found expression. Here, perhaps more openly and clearly than anywhere else in the book, we are given a substantial framework and structure of interpretation that, even if one were to violently reject or disagree with its premises, will still engender new and original thinking. This, it seems to me, is no small accomplishment, and provides a key to understanding the title of Warren's collection: Without poetry, and poetic thought, we are destined to remain bereft of sustenance, both hungry and deceived.

Vincent Ferrini: *Before Gloucester*

2012

I.

My first letter to Vincent was written in 1969, when I was 13. In 1975, a month after my nineteenth birthday, when I reported that I had gone through Ezra Pound's *ABCs of Reading,* Vincent declared that I was:

> summa cum laude! Right from this frameshop,
> so you'll know it's really authentic.

In retrospect, it was the degree that has mattered most. We continued exchanging letters, news, and books until his last year. Throughout, Vincent paid attention — he told me what he was reading, and embraced the political content of my work, enthusiastically recommending it to other friends. I have always been aware of the profound value of this exchange, how much I learned from it, and how important it was to me. Vincent's embrace was encompassing: when Jack Kerouac died in 1969 and I responded with all the piss and vinegar that a teenager could muster, complaining about the injustice of so much of his work being out of print, Vincent not only suggested I write to Allen Ginsberg but provided me with his address. I wrote and Ginsberg responded. When Vincent lent me some copies of

Diane di Prima's magazine *The Floating Bear* and I asked where I could get more, Vincent told me to write to her. I did, and she responded. Through these letters, I became part of a great continuum. Working on this project has made me realize even more profoundly just how much I was given and how much there is to return.

II.

Vincent Ferrini (1913–2007) grew up in Lynn and remained on the North Shore of Massachusetts, moving to Gloucester in 1948 to open a picture framing shop and "live from frame to frame." His life and work span crucial moments and movements in North American political and cultural history. The effects of immigration, industrialization, anarchism, Communism, the New Deal, the Cold War, deindustrialization, and the creation — through political and artistic involvement — of countercultures in face of the totalizing forces of repression, in whatever form they are manifested, are all things that pass firsthand through Ferrini's life. The range of his associations — found in political and civic action, publications, letters, and personal relationships — is staggering and mapping it will greatly enrich our literary, political, and cultural history. Despite various valiant efforts — Henry Ferrini's 1990 film *Poem in Action: A Portrait of Vincent Ferrini;* publication of *The Whole Song: Selected Poems,* edited by Kenneth Warren and Fred Whitehead, the first university press publication of his work; and the city-wide celebration of Ferrini's 100th in Gloucester, Massachusetts in the summer of 2013 — an introduction is still very much needed.

If Ferrini is known at all to readers, it is usually through his friendship with poet Charles Olson and, notoriously, as the object of attack in "Letter 5" of Olson's *The Maximus Poems.* More discerning readers will know that *The Maximus Poems* themselves began as a series of letters to Ferrini, then Olson's beachhead in Gloucester while he was away. Even more discerning readers will know, particularly through the scholarship of Olson scholar Ralph Maud and younger scholars like David

Rich, that, despite this incident, the relationship between the two poets was constant and life sustaining to both. Moreover, when Olson came to visit Ferrini in Gloucester in 1948 after having read some of his poems, he must have looked to Ferrini as a living example of the radical renunciation of any privilege society might then have offered, and as another way into the political economy of the poem. Ferrini had already published five books that put him in the mix with some of the most celebrated proletariat writers of the period; he had moved from anarchism to communism and then left the Party, only to see his work attacked in the mainstream communist press by no less a figure than poet Thomas McGrath; he worked as a union organizer in a key struggle that would define post-war labor relations, and taught at the radical Samuel Adams School for Social Studies in Boston, eventually shut down under pressure from the House of Un-American Activities. It is this aspect of things, the wealth of associations and experiences that Ferrini brought *to* Gloucester, that we are presenting here through a selection of poems from his early work and a key letter from long-time friend and interlocutor Myer "Mike" Hecht.

As he wrote in his autobiography *Hermit of the Clouds,* Ferrini's parents were "immigrants of the 1909 wave of the poor" and had come from Southern Italy to work in the shoe factories. Born in the New World as Venanzio Ferrini, under the sign of the patron saint of his father's Old World hometown of Raiano in Abruzzi, life's drama intruded upon his earliest memories:

> The tenement I am born in has a placard worn out, torn, weatherbeaten like the clapboards but the writing still legible: WHEN WILL THE LONG FEUD END?[1]

With the emergence of strong anarchist and labor movements in New England, Ferrini's parents, Rena DeCarlo and Giovanni

---

1 Vincent Ferrini, *Hermit of the Clouds: The Autobiography of Vincent Ferrini* (Ten Pound Island Book Company, 1988). The first quote is from p. 9, the second from p. 1.

Ferrini, found themselves in the midst of political and economic turmoil as so many key incidents of the period took place in their immediate environs. Bartolomeo Vanzetti, an omnivorous reader, just like Giovanni's son Vincent would become, met his first anarchist comrades in Worcester, Massachusetts, in 1912.[2] And Vanzetti sent in his first twenty-five-cent contribution to Luigi Galleani's essential anarchist journal, the Italian language *Cronaca Sovversiva* (which had recently relocated to Lynn from Barre, Vermont), that same year. Since Ferrini characterized his parents as "non-practicing Catholics, and my father as a Christian anarchist," it's certain that *Cronaca* would have made an appearance in the already politicized Ferrini household.

But this family was poor, and traumatized by poverty. In an oral history on his hometown of Lynn, Ferrini recalls:

> My father was unemployed. He'd been a shoe worker all his life and the whole family went on welfare. I would generally go with my mother to the welfare and oh you felt guilty for going. That's the way they made you feel. It was a hard time. Real bitter. At times during the winter it was really tough. I felt it the most then. I remember for instance that the house was always cold. My mother and father never had a warm house until their old age. I used to freeze all the time and she would get a hot water bottle and put it under our feet. We were always freezing. Sometimes my mother would take these hand irons and heat them up and wrap cloth around them and put them under our feet. We were always freezing. That's the one thing about poverty I'll never forget, is the cold. We lived on Bedford Street. The stove exploded. I was next to the high chair. My little brother was underneath the stove and the little girl, my sister on the highchair, got killed. I've got scars here and here [points to arms and legs]. It was

---

2 See Paul Avrich, *Sacco and Vanzetti: The Anarchist Background* (Princeton University Press, 1991), as well as the extraordinary *Letters of Sacco and Vanzetti* (Penguin, 2007).

a hard time. It was a real dose of poverty. That was the bitterest time.³

Already having witnessed death firsthand, Ferrini was a teenager when there is "a public murder" and the State "sizzles a harmless fish peddler and a humble cobbler,"⁴ Nicola Sacco and Bartolomeo Vanzetti, in 1927. He went to work in a shoe factory and tannery but his father's judgment (having himself been an aspiring opera singer) — that he was born in the wrong class to be a poet — led him to discover the Public Library. With shoulder length hair, arguing against "eating any kind of flesh," Ferrini describes himself then: "I am intense, a fanatic, I wear a long black coat down to my ankles, a black fedora hat, a black bag I fill up with Library books I cannot part with."⁵ In the library, he meets "the great dead, engaging them in long conversations."⁶ But he also meets Truman Nelson, a high-school dropout whose father, John Wilson Nelson, worked as a barber.

> …somebody taps me on the shoulder, I look up and stare, a square face with Hamlet's hair…
>
> I gaze up at this man in a Civil War uniform. I see a chameleon mind. Truman Nelson is a tenant of the Past. I, of the future present. We are two frontiers.⁷

The library remained a site of primal import:

> It was outside the library, on the Commons, where Ferrini and Nelson heard Ann Burlak Timpson, "The Red Flame" (so memorably described in a poem by Muriel Rukeyser),

---

3   Quoted by David Rich in the first Ferrini talk. Peter Anastas and David Rich, "Reading Ferrini: A Gallery Talk," CAM Video Lecture Series, VX09, Cape Ann Museum Library & Archives, Gloucester, MA. Transcript archived at: http://gloucesterwriters.org/mp3test/.
4   Ferrini, *Hermit of the Clouds*, 17.
5   Ibid., 22.
6   Ibid., 19.
7   Ibid., 23.

cry out against their oppressors. It was outside the library where Ferrini was handed a copy of the *Daily Worker,* the newspaper that persuaded him to place his faith in the Communist Party for several years.[8]

A lifelong friend, Nelson would emerge as one of the most respected radical historians and novelists of the mid to late twentieth century, lauded by W.E.B. DuBois, James Baldwin, and many others. He was also a factory worker and shop steward at General Electric, along with Ferrini, who eventually found Olson's former Harvard professor F.O. Matthiessen (also involved in the Samuel Adams School), as a mentor.

In Henry Ferrini's film *Poem in Action,* Nelson talks of Ferrini and how the hopelessness of those times bred such great ambitions:

The series of poems that he wrote about the depression are absolutely unique and...I always tell people if you want to recapture that feeling — because here he was, you know, an unemployed worker, no prospects, none of us, see that's the irony, none of us had any future as workers or as executives or as businessmen. So what do we do, we aspire to the highest, I wanted to be Tolstoy and he wanted to be a great poet, you see, and it allowed that, we had nothing but our fantasies, we had no prospects. So we didn't have to go to school to learn welding… there's no goddamn jobs welding — so what did we try to learn? We tried to learn to be great geniuses.[9]

In the process of learning to be "great geniuses," alliances in the world around them — part of "THIS LONG FEUD" Ferrini had sensed as a child — were shifting rapidly. Of this period Ferrini

---

[8] Vincent Ferrini, *The Whole Song: Selected Poems,* ed. Kenneth A. Warren and Fred Whitehead (University of Illinois Press, 2004), 27.

[9] Henry Ferrini, dir., *Poem in Action: A Portrait of Vincent Ferrini* (Ferrini Productions, 1990); a good introduction to the work of Truman Nelson can be found in *The Truman Nelson Reader,* ed. William J. Schafer (University of Massachusetts Press, 1989).

writes: "Money for me has one purpose: to buy books: with my usual fanaticism I go after the sublime dead." But:

> It's 1932, the bottom of the Great Depression. The mightiest empire on earth is useless, stumbling on three crutches.
> Not even the broken down shadow of a job.
> Russia is a lighthouse in a dark world. And the message in a thunderblast: MAYAKOVSKY.
> I cannot get the breadlines out of my sockets. Hunger is as permanent as City Hall, the administration of an alien morality. Society is as stratified by Money as persons are.[10]

While gripped by second-wave anarchism as represented by a journal like *MAN!*, something Ferrini mentions reading in 1932, the Communist Party was gaining followers. Having finished high school, Ferrini found work with the WPA in 1935, reading ships' logs at the Peabody Museum, and teaching civics, health, language, philosophy, and social studies in Lynn's Armenian, Greek, Irish, Italian, Jewish, Polish, and Russian fraternal organizations. His friend Truman Nelson, on the other hand, got dismissed from the Federal Theater for trying to organize its workers; with no high school diploma, he was relegated to manual labor. Peter Anastas has stressed that Ferrini's political activities were constant, mentioning that he was involved in organizing Lynn's first teacher's union, in the formation of WPA workers unions, in Party faction meetings and caucuses, and in the struggles between two factions in the Electrical Union at GE.

It was during this period that Ferrini began to send his poetry out and get published, appearing in a wide array of little magazines, from the anarchist *MAN!* to *Smoke, Bozart-Westminster,* and the *Young Communist Review.* This meant that his work appeared alongside key modernists such as William Carlos Williams and Marianne Moore, formally radical poets like Lorine Niedecker and Louis Zukofsky, highly politicized writers like Kenneth Patchen and Muriel Rukeyser, as well as those

---

10 Ferrini, *Hermit of the Clouds*, 28.

explicitly allied with communism or labor movements such as novelist Mike Gold. One of Ferrini's early champions, Gold was a key figure in the twentieth-century American Left, founding editor of *The New Masses* (in 1926), and author of the classic *Jews Without Money* (1930). This is the period of Ferrini's first full-length unpublished manuscript, *Onions & Bread,* completed in 1936 but only rediscovered in 1998, while cleaning out his frame shop to prepare for winter.

1936 marked deeper shifts — Italy's war against Ethiopa resulted in colonial occupation beginning in May of that year. While Mussolini consolidated power in Italy, it became common for black-shirt fascist gangs to circulate within Italian-American communities in New England or even present themselves officially. David Rich's intrepid scholarship has revealed an example of this, when, at the end of June, the traditional "St. Peter's Fiesta in Gloucester was co-opted into a celebration of Mussolini's invasion of Ethiopia," with the Italian consul from Boston lauding Mussolini's exploits as he was greeted by the crowd with the fascist salute and cries of "Viva Mussolini."[11] The outbreak of the Spanish Civil War followed immediately in July and, just as Ferrini got a hold of the *Daily Worker* and signed on with the Party, news of two deaths arrived: a friend and comrade from Lynn, killed in action in Spain, and the poet Federico García Lorca:

I hear of Federico García Lorca. Langston Hughes brings me his Cante Jondo, I am entranced, intoxicated. The supreme imagist! He is a blood brother. His poems come after me and I go after them.

---

11 Recounted by David Rich in the Ferrini talks: Anastas and Rich, "Reading Ferrini," along with an account in *The Gloucester Daily Times* from June 29, 1936, that Rich found. Interestingly, Ferrini himself notes: "Attilio Boverini patrols the ghettoes on his Mussolini motorcycle" (*Hermit of the Clouds,* 9).

Abe Cohen is killed in the dry lands of the bull and the guitar, and we feel amputated. Each of us has an organ missing.[12]

III.

When researching Ferrini's archive at the Cape Ann Museum in Gloucester, we were immediately struck by the range and volume of correspondents: one of the last letters filed, for example, was written to Ferrini at the age of ninety-three, just a year and a few months before his death. Ferrini had written a poem to Camille Paglia about her new book *Break, Blow, Burn,* which he had been emphatically recommending to friends. She wrote back to him: "<u>Wow</u> — I'm absolutely staggered. For you to have written a poem about my work is an honor that, for once, leaves me speechless."[13] Spanning generations, one finds letters from Meridel LeSeuer and Joy Harjo; substantial correspondences with George Butterick, Jack Clarke, Larry Eigner, Jack Hirschman, and Paul Metcalf; queries from young poets that extend into decade-long exchanges; years of letters between Ferrini and then-imprisoned Gloucester sculptor and decorated Vietnam veteran David Bianchini, serving a ten-year term for dealing marijuana.

But one thing stands out when examining these materials: the earliest letters found in the archive date from 1948. We know, for instance, that Ferrini corresponded with poet and translator Aaron Kramer beginning in 1945, but the first of Kramer's letters to be found in Ferrini's archive dates from 1949. In fact, except for a copy of the manuscript of *Onions & Bread,* no written documents or correspondence dating from earlier than 1948 can be found. This massive absence, for someone who meticulously kept all his letters, is, most decidedly, a missing organ in

---

12 Ferrini, *Hermit of the Clouds,* 37.
13 Letter from Camille Paglia, dated August 4, 2006; Vincent Ferrini Letters and Papers, Archive Collection A16; Box 39, Folder 1; The Cape Ann Museum, Gloucester, MA.

the life-body of Ferrini's work and a profound gap of our knowledge of the period.

The years between 1936 and Ferrini's move to Gloucester in 1948 (when he declares that he has "quit the Church of Politics,"[14] with an emphasis on "Church," since Ferrini always remained politically active, though unaffiliated), were years of intense struggle, with repercussions that continued to affect him and his family. Ferrini's then wife, Margaret "Peg" Duffy, a brilliant Radcliffe-educated teacher who eventually had an auditorium named after her at a North Shore regional high school, was blacklisted from her profession for many years.[15] Given Ferrini's membership in the Communist Party, and his involvement in UE (United Electrical, Radio, and Machine Workers of America) and the Samuel Adams School for Social Studies — both infiltrated and aggressively targeted by the House of Un-American Activities — Rich has surmised that Ferrini most likely destroyed all his correspondence and personal papers, for fear of implicating friends and co-workers. This could have been at any number of points: perhaps when Ferrini was first mentioned in a HUAC hearing, in Walter S. Steele's massive 1947 testimony,[16] when informant Herbert A. Philbrick began making public accusations in 1949–1950 (resulting in the indictment of eleven people involved in the Samuel Adams School), or when Senator Joseph McCarthy and Roy Cohn staged a televised tribunal in Lynn in which many members of Ferrini's former local were interrogated.

From 1941 to 1950, with the war machine finally providing employment, Ferrini was a bench hand at "the vast General Electric complex in Lynn" and worked "as a polisher and as a collector of scrap wire (which he sometimes took home and

---

14 Ferrini, *Hermit of the Clouds,* 86; both David Rich and Peter Anastas have emphasized this conclusion as well.
15 In the Ferrini talks, Peter Anastas discusses Peg Ferrini's life and character. Anastas and Rich, "Reading Ferrini."
16 Steele's full testimony is available here: http://www.archive.org/stream/testimonyofwalte1947unit/testimonyofwalte1947unit_djvu.txt.

made into sculptures)."[17] But the atmosphere of the war plant was radically different than the shoe factories of his youth:

> I know shoes, woodheelings, stitching, lasting, soles, channels, boxing, and shipping.
> This is indifferent, strange, and alien.
> A world of complex machinery, intricate windings, oil caked on floors, workers isolated at their machines, great spaces between persons, I feel as though I am inside some inhuman brain, and apart.
> The people are unlike the shoeworkers, who labored close together, breathed the same air, felt the same thoughts, talked as a family... and quarreled as a family, and the Union their own flesh.[18]

As more Communists entered the Union, Ferrini felt more familiar and immersed himself in a struggle that would determine the divisions and politics of unionized labor following the war. The UE, founded in 1936, grew to become the third largest Congress of Industrial Organizations (CIO) body, with over half a million members at the end of the Second World War. But fissures had begun in 1941 when Albert J. Fitzgerald, a leftist from GE in Lynn, defeated the anti-communist James Carey to become UE president. Thus the infiltration, repression, and witch-hunts began, as leftist and Communist-affiliated GE workers on defense contracts were accused of sabotage and espionage, ultimately culminating in purges and deals that would largely ally labor with government and big business.

Ferrini was enormously productive during this fervent time, producing *No Smoke* (1941), *Injunction* (1943), *Blood of the Tenement* (1945), *Tidal Wave: Poems of the Great Strikes* (1946), and *The Plow in the Ruins* (1946); all except *No Smoke* (reprinted in 1999), some poems reprinted in *The Whole Song*, and the selections published here, remain out of print and exceedingly hard

---

17   Ferrini, *The Whole Song*, 21.
18   Ferrini, *Hermit of the Clouds*, 62.

to find. Yet, this series of texts, written by a largely self-educated factory worker, provide a perspective on the cataclysmic arc illuminating life in the mid-twentieth century available almost nowhere else. Throughout this period, Ferrini never wavered from his position as a worker, remaining skeptical of any kind of dogma and recognizing bosses wherever they might appear, even in the Party. Although committed to the work he was doing, Ferrini sensed the fissures:

> The books do not jibe with the shifting Changes. The theory is object to the subject, and I instinctively rebel at the Practice...
>
> The roots of the Party are in Russia, and they have an alien smell, like clothes handed down to us that do not fit...
>
> The Party is not Indigenous. And we all know it.[19]

Eager to put his knowledge, experience, and creative energy in service of furthering working-class culture, Ferrini became involved in several other endeavors during this period, most notably the Samuel Adams School, founded in Boston in 1944, and the People's Culture Union of America, where he served as vice president and director of publications. According to Rich,

> the Culture Union tried to continue that mid-1930s Proletarian movement, encouraging working people to write their own stories, after the Communist Party switched its tactics, closed the John Reed Clubs, and initiated the Popular Front. During the Popular Front, the Proletarian writers earlier encouraged by the Party were essentially discarded, and Ferrini was actually attacked in the pages of the *New Masses* for lacking artistic polish; Popular Front methods involved trying to co-opt prestigious, bourgeois authors formerly condemned as decadent, while dismissing the very working-class authors, such as Ferrini, who were previously written about glowingly. In the pages of *Great-Concord Tide*, the

---

19 Ibid., 55, 77.

organ of the Culture Union (which Ferrini was involved in producing), the Union went on the attack, condemning the *New Masses* for having betrayed the Proletarian movement.[20]

In many ways, as Rich also points out, the result of Ferrini's independence of mind and worker's perspective was that "the Communist Party left him" and not the other way around.

The Adams School was part of a loose affinity of "people's schools" that included the Jefferson School in New York, the Abraham Lincoln School in Chicago, the Ohio School of Social Sciences in Cleveland, the People's Educational Center in Los Angeles, the Walt Whitman School in Newark, the Philadelphia School of Social Science and Art, the California Labor School in San Francisco, and the Seattle Labor School. The Adams School featured a mixed group of academics, artists, union members, and people of some means with leftist sympathies. Classes were given at night and tuition was $6 a term per class; classes were also given in union halls or in an extension program in homes, churches, or community centers. Ferrini taught the "Contemporary Writers Workshop" on Friday nights. People involved in the Adams School included Ann Burlak's husband Arthur E. Timpson, MIT mathematician Dirk Jan Struik, sculptor George Aarons, and F.O. Matthiessen, founder of the American Civilization program at Harvard, former teacher of Charles Olson and mentor to Ferrini's friend Truman Nelson. Matthiessen's involvement is significant since his dramatic suicide in 1950, both as a closeted gay man and following accusations by Herbert A. Philbrick of communist sympathies, gained such notoriety. And it was Philbrick who may have played a significant role in Ferrini's life as well.

A Boston area advertising executive, Philbrick was paid by the FBI to infiltrate the Communist Party starting in 1940; by 1949, he began to make public accusations, and his lengthy testimony to HUAC in 1951 resulted in the conviction of eleven people. In addition to Matthiessen, two of Philbrick's prominent

---

20 David Rich, email communication.

targets happened to be the GE plant in Lynn and the Adams School in Boston. Ferrini's previous mention as a teacher at the Adams School was embedded in a much longer testimony, but Philbrick's public accusations and concentration on the Lynn GE local was of a different order. Ferrini decided to leave GE one year before becoming eligible for his pension, while Philbrick went on to write a best-selling memoir, *I Led Three Lives: Citizen, Communist, Counterspy*, which was quickly turned into a movie and then a television serial that ran for 117 episodes between 1953 and 1956.

IV.

With Ferrini's move to Gloucester in 1948, and the absence of any correspondence pre-dating the move, extant archival documents become weighted by what's missing. Some of the earliest letters found in the archive, dating from 1948 and 1949, while still written in friendship and solidarity, reveal either ambivalence or direct critique of the new directions Ferrini's poetry took after leaving Lynn. The most substantial batch, also revealing various literary connections, are by Ensi Wirta. Raised in the coal-mining country of Pennsylvania, Wirta had participated in the epic 1935 Humboldt County lumber strike in Washington state and been arrested there. His Finnish background may have connected him, somehow, to Gloucester, since there had been a prominent Communist and Socialist group of Finnish immigrants in Lanesville, the "red Finns." He writes with familiarity of the struggles in Lynn so there may have been some connection to Ferrini through union activities. He did seem to know Muriel Rukeyser, and mentions her three times in connection to the loan of several of Ferrini's books.[21] Most significantly, though,

---

21 From Ensi Wirta's letters to Ferrini, November 30, 1949: "I've tentatively gone through all books except 'Blood of the Tenement' — that one being out (Muriel Rukeyser has it on loan, & I haven't been able to reach her — maybe she's out of town — she was up in Br. Columbia, or Alaska, or some damn place recently, among native Indians — doing research or something — the Jt. Anti-Fascist Refugee Committee had a hell of a time

in long, elaborate letters discussing poems in detail, replete with prosodic analysis, Wirta is disturbed by an ideological slippage that he reads into Ferrini's poetry, quoting from and critiquing *Sea Sprung,* the first Gloucester book, published in 1949:

> My God, Vinnie! This shocks me! "I shall melt his fist / with love" — a fascist to be met with love? Not with militancy, resistance, etc.? No, it is not one power arrayed against the other — but love is not the power we use exclusively with people in general — we use above all struggle, and we love those struggling with us — but police, and others — not love.[22]

Clearly, both Wirta and Ferrini struggled with these ideological issues, and their import for both the form and content of writing; the level of care and analysis displayed in these letters, written from one worker to another, is extraordinary. Materialist in his assumptions, Wirta critiques the image of a single bird in flight appearing in one of the poems and writes:

> I object to this on these grounds: first, the playing up of the solitary nature of the bird is an individualistic bourgeois-romantic poetic concept (Shelley was great on such stuff & it also characterizes the Auden-Levis-Spender bunch).[23]

---

finding her to send her as a delegate to the Mexico City Peace Conference, where she finally went by plane)." In another, undated: "On your letter, Muriel Rukeyser must be out of town yet — got no answer per telephone on several calls — so haven't been able to get her reaction to your Tenements and Ruins, copies of which I left her." And in yet one more, February 26, 1950: "Dammit, Rukeyser, I hear, has gone out of town, and with her, one of your volumes that I had been hanging onto dearly. I understand she's moved out. No, I haven't read her latest book, the critical one, but I hope to do so." Vincent Ferrini Letters and Papers, Archive Collection A16; Box 38; The Cape Ann Museum, Gloucester, MA.

22 Letter from Ensi Wirta, October 29, 1949; Vincent Ferrini Letters and Papers, Archive Collection A16; Box 38; The Cape Ann Museum, Gloucester, MA.

23 Ibid.

Later in the letter, Wirta asks Ferrini if he has read Pablo Neruda's recent speech given at the Continental Congress for World Peace, held in Mexico City:

> He said there <u>that his poetry of the past no longer served its purpose,</u> "that they (the poems), carried with them the furrows of bitterness of a dead speech." I think that you should reexamine the content of your past influences critically, like Neruda, & discard that which is harmful, & create out of your own total of the past that which is good & useful. And that includes Neruda himself as an influence. And surrealism, too —[24]

Ultimately, these ruminations lead Wirta to accept, at least provisionally, the new direction Ferrini's work has taken:

> After our conversation back there, when I read it the first time, I read it with a disturbed mind — for I felt at the time that you were involved in some kind of retreat before the ideological pressure of present hysteria. But a second reading made me feel better; I got a better perspective...
>
> As to content, on 2nd reading I suddenly realized a major point — namely, that you were immersing yourself in a new poetic milieu, utilizing Gloucester's imagery to the full — & that is & will be, greatly to your advantage. Your industrial imagery in "Blood of the Tenement" was really brilliant, & I hope that fishing, Gloucester, the sea, & related themes, will similarly afford a rich source. In this volume, you have made an excellent beginning. There are lots of concrete images. You get a feeling for the material essence of the area. In this sense, your poetry is a reflection — imaginative, of course — of reality — & that's my #1 criterion in judging art.[25]

---

24 Ibid.
25 Ibid.

Clearly, Ferrini's work continued to center on Gloucester, culminating in his multi-volume *Know Fish* (Books 1–7; 1979–1991), the evolution of which is traced brilliantly by Kenneth Warren: "Ferrini commandeered a lexicon through which the red memory of party dogma, shop-level torture, and shattered comradeship could be transformed into its opposite — *The Community of Self,* as he would eventually put it in the title to Book IV and V of *Know Fish*."[26] Among many other themes and preoccupations of *Know Fish,* it features long sections of poems written in Gloucester dialect, a kind of Southern Italian/Portuguese-American lingo almost reminiscent of the Jamaican Linton Kwesi Johnson's dub poetry; such texts are materialist to the very syllable, and reflect aspects of the city's historical reality and legacy even buildings cannot preserve. Although Ferrini left "the Church" the Party had become for him, the principles that brought him there — and created the kind of dialogue he had with Wirta — remained deeply embedded in his perspective on both life and art. Yet, for whatever reason, and despite the intensity of their exchange, no later correspondence with Wirta can be found in the archive and we have no basis on which to understand the further evolution of their friendship.

The only correspondent from this early period who continues to write to Ferrini regularly into old age is Myer "Mike" Hecht, excerpts of whose letters appear after the selection of poems. We don't know how they met, but they seem to already know each other well as the letters commence in 1949. There is an enticing reference in a letter to "the cultural conference in New York," as well as a connection to the legendary Jack Conroy, novelist and founder of the important journals *The Anvil* and, with Nelson Algren, *The New Anvil.* Always a champion of Ferrini's work, Hecht writes to his friend about delivering a copy of his new book while visiting Conroy in 1989, just before his

---

26 This was to have appeared in a book planned by Warren but which never came out due to his untimely death in 2015. Kenneth Warren, "Political Agency and 'Participation Mystique' in Ferrini's Life and Work," paper presented at Holy Local: Vincent Ferrini's Literary Legacy, The Cape Ann Museum, Gloucester, MA, June 22, 2013.

death, in Conroy's hometown of Moberly, Missouri, once also a center of shoe-manufacturing. This connection, given that Ferrini published in *The New Anvil*, squares the circle, bringing us back to the 1930s, the time the poems in the following selection began to be written.

V.

For writers who survived the 1930s, and those coming of age in the 1950s, personal correspondence was a lifeline, a way to make friends, exchange ideas, formulate plans, and establish political and aesthetic principles. As new findings by Rich, Peter Anastas, and others come to light, our sense of Vincent Ferrini's role at a pivotal time in American culture has found new articulation, shaping a new history. The range of correspondence Ferrini carried on with so many different kinds of people is extraordinary. Going through the boxes, we were intrigued by letters from people we had never heard of, with pointed political discussions and extended aesthetic critiques. One correspondence stood out, not only for its longevity, but also for the range of references and experiences depicted. This is the correspondence of Hecht (1919–2009), of which, at this point, unfortunately, Ferrini's side is mostly missing.

By all accounts, Hecht was an extraordinary man with whom Ferrini corresponded from at least the 1940s through the 2000s. We don't know how they actually met, but surmise that it took place through print, by Hecht contacting him after reading a poem of Ferrini's in one of the little magazines he first appeared in during the 1930s. In any case, by 1947, they were involved in the People's Culture Union of America, a group of writers still loyal to the Proleterian movement of the mid-1930s, despite various controversies and sharp ideological and aesthetic differences. Perhaps the connection between Hecht and Ferrini was through Conroy; the mid-western novelist and editor had published Langston Hughes and William Carlos Williams, collaborated with Arna Bontemps, and published Ferrini in *The New Anvil*. This important journal, co-founded with Nelson Algren in 1938, was a response to the New York takeover of the original *Anvil*, which became the *Partisan Review*, and typified the deep conflict between midwestern working-class populism and what Conroy called "the ideological tempests raging in the New York coffee pots."[27]

An inventor and polymer chemist who held many important patents, Hecht was also a member of the Steelworkers' Union who wrote plays, sang in the opera, and had a theater column for the radical *Chicago Star*, a newspaper founded by Frank Marshall Davis, a major figure who bridged the New Negro Renaissance of the 1930s with the Black Arts Movement of the 1960s. We later find Hecht corresponding with Studs Turkel; writing to poet and Vietnam veteran W.D. Ehrhart after discovering his groundbreaking anthologies of veteran writing; visiting Jack Conroy just before his death; connecting Ferrini to Earl Robinson (author of the lyrics to "I Dreamed I Saw Joe Hill"),[28] and always standing up for his friend's work, ordering new books from Ferrini and sending them to anyone he thinks will find them of interest.

The excerpts from Hecht's letters that follow seem pivotal, opening new vistas on unknown connections, and providing a window into the complexities faced by politically active writers during the first years of the Cold War. The following excerpt from a 1949 letter to Ferrini, written by a common friend who remains unidentified, gives some sense of the atmosphere at the time:

---

27 In Michael Denning, *The Cultural Front: The Laboring of American Culture in the Twentieth Century* (Verso, 1998), 215.
28 Embedded in the Hecht Folder is a fascinating exchange between Earl Robinson and Ferrini following an introduction by Hecht, involved in a tribute to the once-blacklisted songwriter on his eightieth birthday. Though his songs were revived by Joan Baez, Bob Dylan, and others, Robinson had largely been forgotten. Ironically, being blacklisted led him to seek other work and he eventually became chair of the Music Department at Little Red School House/Elizabeth Irwin in New York City where he was "rediscovered" during the folk revival.

> I expect to see Mike today. We meet quite rarely, chiefly because there is a complete absence of any literary activity in this enormous small town. Perhaps something will shape up this winter. Mike as you may know, copyrited [sic] a one act play, 'What's In The Name?' He has been trying to stage it in several small theaters. The other poets and play writers are mostly in isolation like myself. The situation and the outlook are rather dismal.[29]

Hecht's first letter, also from 1949, begins with some doubts as to the direction Ferrini's new work has taken in Gloucester, while commenting on other poets allied to working-class culture, including Alex Bergmann, Milton Blau, Kenneth Fearing, Sol Funaroff, Aaron Kramer, Lou Lande, Thomas McGrath, Michael Quin, and Henry George Weiss.[30] Throughout his letters Hecht always differentiates between "the big names" and the people, the rank and file. His cultural and political instincts are acute, and his curiosity boundless. By the time of this letter, Ferrini had already started to correspond with Robert Creeley and had met Olson. With HUAC proceedings moving into full-force, and Ferrini about to embark on a new poetic trajectory, the correspondence with Hecht must have allowed him to keep at least one foot in a world he was largely leaving behind.

The second letter, dated February 26, 1950, addresses Ferrini's idea to start a new magazine, what would soon become *Four Winds,* the object of Olson's attack in "Letter 5" of *The Maximus Poems.* After an extensive elucidation of how unpropitious the social, cultural, political, and economic conditions are for such a venture, we are given an extraordinary postscript in which Hecht describes a cultural evening that included poetry read-

---

29 Vincent Ferrini Letters and Papers, Archive Collection A16; Box 39, Folder 2; The Cape Ann Museum, Gloucester, MA.

30 An introduction to some of these neglected poets can be found in *Revolutionary Memory: Recovering the Poetry of the American Left* (Routledge, 2003), and *Repression and Recovery: Modern American Poetry and the Politics of Cultural Memory, 1910–1945* (University of Wisconsin Press, 1989), both by Cary Nelson.

ings, discussion, and the presence of various luminaries. In the space of a few paragraphs, we again encounter Jack Conroy, live this time. We encounter the great poet Gwendolyn Brooks, along with her husband, Henry Blakely, the "poet of 63rd st."; poet Margaret Danner Cunningham who later moved to Detroit to participate in the renaissance that took place there through independent Black publishing houses like Broadside Press and Lotus Press; and artist and writer Margaret Taylor Goss Burroughs, founder of the DuSable Museum of African American History and one of the initiators of the South Side Community Art Center, a key African American institution. Finally, we see Paul Robeson addressing "the negro community," though, at least in Hecht's eyes, he sees Robeson as a "big wheel," coming around late to battles that people like himself had already been waging for years "with only bruised heads and bleeding hearts to show for our efforts."

In this letter, and these brief ending paragraphs, invisible lines of transmission reappear and worlds never thought connected are conjoined. The huge political and cultural ambitions of people whose sensibility and aesthetic were formed in the cauldron of the 1930s can be seen more starkly in light of the Cold War and the postwar period. This juxtaposition dramatically demonstrates a crucial but very under-examined historical phenomenon that characterizes the transitional nature of the time. On the one hand, the kind of ambition described by Hecht, and characterizing the midwestern, populist bent — embracing popular culture and social justice — found itself drastically diminished and in retreat. On the other hand, those who set out in new directions on their own, cut off from known institutions, demonstrated a different courage and an almost visionary apprehension of the radical changes taking place in the newly configured human universe. In short, a letter like this causes one's head to turn around and around, like in a cartoon, and seek a new place from which to reconsider the historical narratives we have been given; in closing, Hecht writes:

"FOLLOW THE PERSON"

I left with my head in the clouds. Truth is, I'm still drunk. Don't blame
me if I sound giddy. History was made last night — and I was there shaking
hands with it.

17

Rimbaud via Rukeyser: An Editorial Note

2019

I.

That Arthur Rimbaud can continue to elicit shock from readers — certainly for different reasons at different times — serves as testament to the novelty of his vocabulary and the radical nature of his attack, including what we can call his "racial imaginary." Perhaps even more remarkably, what a reader might find startling or disturbing now ("Bad Blood" or "Night in Hell," sections two and three of *A Season in Hell*), must have been most suggestive and liberating for Black Francophone writers like Aimé Césaire, Leopold Senghor, and Léon Damas, founders of the Negritude movement, and others who followed in their wake.

Originally, *A Season in Hell* was called *The Pagan Book,* or *The Black Book,* meant as a caustic indictment of a system whose "civilization" offered only war and submission, as baptism, servitude, and work — it was a vision of life in which "hell" ought to last only a season, and not be the eternal foundation of behavior through fear.¹ As one of Rimbaud's contemporary translators, Paul Schmidt, writes, *Season* "was an attempt to relate bourgeois capitalism, bourgeois science, and the bourgeois Christianity of the nineteenth century to some fundamental innocence to be found in past history and past time, and in the non-Western world of the East, or Africa; to come to terms with personal salvation in historical terms." As he also notes, "The opening and closing metaphor of *A Season in Hell* is battle, and victory."²

A clear indication of this insight can be seen in one of Césaire's most important texts, "Poetry and Knowledge" (1944–1945):

> As for Rimbaud, literature is still registering the aftershocks of the incredible seismic tremor of his famous *lettre du voyant* (the seer's letter):
> "I say that one has to be clairvoyant, to make oneself clairvoyant."
> Memorable words, words of distress and of victory...
> Henceforth, the field is clear for humanity's most momentous dreams.³

These "momentous dreams" have to do with the next sentence of the letter, left out by Césaire, but certainly known to his readers: "A poet makes himself a visionary through a long, boundless, and systematized *disorganization of all the senses*."⁴ This included rejecting all the entitlements bestowed by Enlightenment, something Rimbaud systematically catalogs in "Bad Blood," moving from his own barbaric Gallic ancestors whose only advantage is a "declaration" that eventually might enable

---

1   These and many other insights are indebted to Suzanne Bernard and André Guyaux's brilliant notes in *Oeuvres de Rimbaud*, ed. Suzanne Bernard and André Guyaux (Classiques Garnier, 1991), 459–65 in particular.
2   Arthur Rimbaud, *The Complete Works*, trans. Paul Schmidt (Harper Perennial, 2008), 217.
3   Aimé Césaire, *Lyric and Dramatic Poetry, 1946–82*, trans. Clayton Eshleman and Annette Smith (University of Virginia Press, 1990), xlv.
4   Rimbaud, *The Complete Works*, 116. Schmidt uses the word "visionary" which, in the translation of Césaire's text, is rendered as "clairvoyant."

them to become part of the bourgeoisie: "I know every family in Europe. I love them like brothers, the bloods who date back to the Rights of Man." To go further, one must be of "an inferior race, eternally" and "leave Europe behind" where "my eyes are shut to your light" and baptism can only come through submission or capture, turning any form of "innocence" into pure irony. One must become an outcast, seeking life among "the true children of Ham," outside the system of original sin and eternal damnation. The resonance with Césaire's famous line, "as for me I have nothing to fear I am before Adam,"[5] is unmistakable.

Clearly, these are some of the core ideas that inspired Césaire, struggling to find a wedge between his French education, newly acquired knowledge about Africa, racial politics, decolonization, and Communism. These issues came to the fore during a seven-month stay in Haiti in 1944, where he was lecturing on Stéphane Mallarmé and Rimbaud but emerged with a book length essay on Toussaint L'Ouverture; a play on Henri Christophe, another major figure of the Haitian Revolution; and new found political energy that saw him elected Mayor of Fort-de-France upon his return to Martinique in 1945.

II.

As a provincial child of both war and colonialism, Arthur Rimbaud has become a symbol and myth of and for many things he had little or nothing to do with, a subject meticulously covered in René Étiemble's *Le mythe de Rimbaud* (1952), a book that Frantz Fanon, the indispensible theorist and practitioner of decolonization, is known to have had in his library, along with another lesser known 1945 study, *Rimbaud. Le précurseur,* by René Silvain.[6] Given that Fanon's personal library was not large,

---

5   Aimé Césaire, *The Collected Poetry,* ed. and trans. Clayton Eshleman and Annette Smith (University of California Press, 1983), 109. See Clayton Eshleman and Annette Smith's extraordinary introduction to their translation for further background.
6   See the list of Fanon's known library in Frantz Fanon, *Écrits sur l'aliénation et la liberté* (Éditions la découverte, 2015); interestingly, Fanon also had

everything in it is significant. Interest in Rimbaud would surely have been part of the legacy of Fanon's beloved teacher, Aimé Césaire, in their native Martinique, then a French colony. Fanon encountered Césaire as his secondary school teacher in the late 1930s, before leaving Martinique in 1943 at the age of 18 to join the French Free Forces, eventually receiving the *Croix de guerre* for serving in Alsace and the colonies of Morocco and Algeria.

Around the time Muriel Rukeyser took up her student translation of *A Season in Hell*, Césaire was in Paris, studying and writing about key African American figures of the Harlem Renaissance such as Langston Hughes and Claude McKay. He also paid close attention to the infamous Scottsboro trial, in which nine African American boys and young men, ages 13 to 20, were falsely accused of raping two white women on a train in 1931. Through local activism, demonstrations in Harlem, the Communist Party USA, the NAACP, and others, the trial received international attention. Rukeyser reported on it, worked for the defense of the accused, and was arrested in 1933 while in Alabama because of leaflets found on her person announcing a Black student conference. Eight of the defendants were initially sentenced to death by electric chair, followed by years of appeals in which each defendant met a different fate, with some eventually paroled.

Although direct contemporaries (both were born in 1913), their circumstances couldn't be more different: born a Black colonial subject of modest means, Césaire turned racism on its head, coining the term "negritude" in 1932, becoming one of the twentieth century's foremost poets of global decolonization and an active politician who held office for decades in Martinique; white and born to a family of some means, Rukeyser attended private school, then Vassar and Columbia, mainly working in film as a way to support her truly unique literary work and scholarly investigations, accumulating a sizeable FBI file while remaining politically outspoken throughout her life. Ironically, while Rukeyser's encounter with Rimbaud was fleeting, repre-

---

Ezra Pound's *Cantos* and Walt Whitman's *Leaves of Grass*, 587–655.

sented by this early, unpublished translation, Césaire's encounter with Rimbaud was profound and continuous, almost a dialogue of sorts, and one that he explicitly acknowledged.

As Robin D.G. Kelley writes in the introduction to Césaire's essential *Discourse on Colonialism* (1956), "it should be read as a surrealist text, perhaps even an unintended synthesis of Césaire's understanding of poetry (via Rimbaud) as revolt and his revision of historical materialism."[7] There are so many instances, of style and substance, in which *Discourse* feels like a rejoinder, an echo of *Season*, and a close reading of the two would make a useful study. For example, Rimbaud's "victory" at the end of the *Season*, despite identifying as "pagan" and "black," is "to possess reality in the compass of one soul and one body," an ultimate rejection of western dualism and metaphysics. Describing the racism of psychologists, sociologists, and other professionals in Discourse, Césaire calls upon René Descartes, a most unlikely ally to uphold human commonality, citing a universal creed, so unlike Rimbaud's bitingly ironic and self-lacerating application of "the Rights of Man" to his barbaric ancestors and other once baptized European pagans:

[E]ach of these gentlemen, in order to impugn on higher authority the weakness of primitive thought, claims that his own is based on the firmest rationalism — their barbaric repudiation, for the sake of the cause, of Descartes's statement, the charter of universalism, that "reason...is found whole and entire in each man," and that "where individuals of the same species are concerned there may be degrees in respect of their accidental qualities, but not in respect of their forms, or natures."[8]

One of Césaire's later works, *A Season in the Congo* (1966), depicting the 1960 rebellion and the fate of assassinated Prime

---

7   Aimé Césaire, *Discourse on Colonialism*, trans. Joan Pinkham (Monthly Review Press, 2000), 10.
8   Ibid., 56.

Minister Patrice Lumumba, has unmistakable parallels to Rimbaud's *Season*. This dialogue continued, even after Césaire's death in 2008. In 2011, a celebration took place to christen *rue Aimé Césaire* in Rimbaud's provincial hometown of Charleville, a focal point in the ongoing Rimbaud myth.

III.

Rimbaud's mother, Vitalie Cuif, was, in some sense, "brought to market" by her father at the less than marriageable age of twenty-seven, moving from the tiny hamlet of Roche to the more prosperous Charleville in 1852. Napoleon III had just established the Second Empire through a coup, and a soldier in his army, Frédéric Rimbaud, a Captain in the 47th Regiment, would quickly become her husband. His trips to Charleville were brief, almost each one bringing Vitalie a new child. After the birth of Arthur in 1854, the Captain would serve in the Crimean War for several years, a key campaign that greatly increased France's imperial reach. Captain Rimbaud, something of an Arabist, had already served in Algeria; having translated the Quran and compiled a collection of Arabic jokes, he left a large variety of other manuscripts behind. But by 1860, with the briefest of sojourns spent in Charleville, he would come through again and leave, never to return.

With the Franco-Prussian War in 1870, the school in Charleville shut down and Rimbaud, not yet sixteen, began the continuing series of journeys that would end only with his death in 1891. He had already written some extraordinary poetry, including the 1869 "Jugurtha," a prize-winning Latin composition sometimes construed as a paean of Arab resistance to French colonization, and quoted by the Algerian revolutionary poet Jean Sénac in *The Sun Under the Weapons,* his fierce rejoinder to Albert Camus over their irreconcilable choice of sides in the war for Algerian independence.

For the next several years Rimbaud lived what for many others would have been considered several intense lifetimes. An arrest for vagrancy in Paris after running away from home, scenes at the Paris Commune: the wild long-haired kid from the provinces with dirt under his fingernails and ill-fitting clothes scandalizing bourgeois society in every way imaginable. He befriended the poet Paul Verlaine, soon breaking up Verlaine's marriage to have an affair with the older poet, causing scenes that restlessly took them between France and England and Belgium until Verlaine shot Rimbaud, superficially wounding him in the wrist, for which Verlaine was sentenced to two years in prison.

Returning to Charleville, Rimbaud wrote *A Season in Hell* and had it published in 1873, salvaging only a few copies because he couldn't afford the printer's bill. After this, more movement: England again, and Germany. Then Vienna where he enlisted in the Dutch colonial army which he deserted for Java. Back in France, he crossed the Alps on foot, then Italy, Egypt, a construction crew in Cyprus, Aden, and, finally, what was once Abyssinia, now Ethiopia, where he would be based as a colonial trader until illness took him to Marseilles to die in a European hospital. And, of course, there were the languages: Rimbaud spoke and read Arabic, and had at least a working knowledge of Amharic, Adarinya, Oromo, and Somali. He may also have communicated in several other languages including Agroba, Tigrinya, and possibly Kotou, a language that became extinct by 1937. In the most recent English biography of Rimbaud, Graham Robb offers the following useful distinction about this part of Rimbaud's life: "Excuses made for Rimbaud are also excuses made for the colonial enterprise as a whole and, more recently, for the secular evangelism that underlies the academic enterprise. Rimbaud was by no means the worst of the Europeans. [...] In Rimbaud's eyes, Europeans and natives were all human beings and, therefore, equally deserving of scorn."[9]

IV.

Texts and translations have complicated histories but both are made of words whose histories are even more intricate and

---

9   Graham Robb, *Rimbaud* (Norton, 2000), 411.

complex. A new edition of *A Season in Hell* and *Illuminations* appeared in 1892, and then a *Collected Poems* in 1895, both with prefaces by Verlaine. The publication of *The Symbolist Movement in Literature* by British poet, critic, and translator Arthur Symons in 1899, with a revised and enlarged edition in 1919, did much to bring Rimbaud's work to the attention of Anglophone readers and writers. Henry Miller describes his first encounter with Rimbaud as having taken place in 1927. By the time Rukeyser finds him, in the early 1930s, the myth of Rimbaud continues to grow and, alongside, the sweeping rise of racial consciousness through political movements and the interest in and appropriation of African art and culture. Thus, even as African diasporic cultures of the Americas have a global impact, the French word "nègre" becomes a key transformative term and it is on the cusp of this word and its translation that an interpretation of Rimbaud's *Season* may rest for contemporary readers.[10] While Rukeyser misses certain things at the level of the language, she captures other things unflinchingly, as in this caustic line in "Bad Blood," as clear an indictment of European or even white privilege as had been penned until then: "Well, who made me lie, who protected my laziness?" She also clearly understands that it may be necessary to expand the semantic breadth of "nègre," to include Black, Negro and, in one instance — the dance of the houris in "Night in Hell" — the pejorative and racist usage, in order to capture Rimbaud's ideologically antagonistic attack on the feigned "whiteness" at the heart of a Europe cleansed of its pagan origins, a myth he wanted to shatter. This is, undoubtedly, a slippery slope, but we felt an attempt had to be made in order to provide some deeper context for these vexed terms whose histories — and the policies implemented behind those histories — continue to have such impact on the life and fate of people.

---

10 See Brent Hayes Edwards's brilliant discussion, "Translating the Word Nègre," in *The Practice of Diaspora: Literature, Translation and the Rise of Black Internationalism* (Harvard University Press, 2003), 25–38. Also see Eshleman and Smith's introduction to Césaire for an excellent discussion of their translation choices and historical context for uses of the word "nègre." Césaire, *The Collected Poetry*, 27.

18

You Don't Know Jack: On Jack Kerouac

2017

When Jack Kerouac died in Florida in October of 1969, it was a local event in New England. The *Boston Globe* clipping I still have, "Jack Kerouac's Days on the Road Are Ended," has a Lowell, Massachusetts dateline, noting that "last night this dreary old mill city, dominated by factories and tenements, sadly remembered its native son." Of course, Kerouac's "days on the road" had ended long before. By the time *On the Road* came out in 1957, many of the books Kerouac is most well known for were already written but unpublished (and once they did come out, many went out of print during and after his lifetime). Only now, at a remove of more than forty-five years, are we starting to get a fuller picture of the enormity of Kerouac's achievement, and the extent to which it has been misunderstood, denigrated, and distorted. Because of the vastness of Kerouac's archive, held in the New York Public Library's Berg Collection, the need for serious textual scholarship and intelligent editing has been paramount. While Kerouac himself was a meticulous archivist, organizing all his work carefully, the editing quality of the posthumous work has varied, sometimes wildly.

These two superbly presented and edited books, *The Unknown Kerouac* (Library of America, 2016), edited by Todd

Tietchen with translations by Jean-Christophe Cloutier, and *La vie est d'hommage* (Boréal, 2016) edited by Cloutier, boldly stand out and finally give us a more sustained and coherent reading of Kerouac's full oeuvre and his conceptualization of "the Duluoz legend," the interlinking of all his novels as a series of episodes in the larger tale. For Tietchen, this is his third edited volume of Kerouac and the quality of his work remains exceptional.

One of the great revelations here is that Kerouac wrote serious work in his mother tongue, the French he grew up with in Lowell, with its "Little Canada," as a member of a community that had landed in New England during the great nineteenth and early-twentieth century exodus from Quebec, when some 900,000 people emigrated in search of work and better wages, with a reputation for being ready to take on anything. In fact, Pierre Vallières, political activist and intellectual leader of the Quebec Liberation Front, wrote a book about these communities, translated into English in 1971 as *White Niggers of America,* something that might offer perspective on Kerouac's background and the social context in which he was seen and saw himself.

Indeed, Kerouac, the scholarship kid, didn't speak English until he went to school and had an accent into his twenties, only making it out of the "dreary" mill town of Lowell because of his talent as a football player. Tietchen's meticulous biographical timeline makes a point of mentioning the jobs Kerouac actually held: gas station attendant, construction worker, short order cook, worker in a ball-bearing factory, security guard, baggage handler, kitchen worker in the US Merchant Marine, parking lot attendant, and railroad brakeman. Tietchen also mentions that when Kerouac's sister Caroline (known as Ti Nin) died in 1964, she was buried in an unmarked grave because there wasn't enough money to pay for a headstone. He also marks the known incidents when this "Beat legend" was beaten up outside of bars: broken arm, broken nose, and possible concussion in Greenwich Village in 1958; two broken ribs in Florida in 1965; and cracked ribs, again in Florida, in 1969.

The Unknown Kerouac is full of treasures, early journals, and a breakthrough journal he wrote in 1951 while recuperating in a VA Hospital from an acute case of thrombophlebitis. In it, Kerouac finally finds the language and form we have come to consider most his own. But we also find out, through Cloutier's mind-bogglingly brilliant translations and notes, that Kerouac only finds this form and language through his movement in and out of French. Two of these longer texts, *The Night Is My Woman* and *Old Bull in the Bowery* are, in effect, almost co-productions, since there are English passages by Kerouac in the original French text which are now blended in with Cloutier's flawless translations.

In the introduction, Tietchen deftly notes the attention Kerouac pays to Geoffrey Chaucer's Prologue to *The Canterbury Tales* in a 1949–1950 journal called *Private Philologies, Riddles, and a Ten-Day Writing Log:* "Not only is this allusion perfectly at home among the searching experiments of Kerouac's road-worn journal, but it shows that his interests in migratory experience and road narrative have as much to do with long-standing archetypes of pilgrimage and quest as they do with the longings of the postwar period, or the history of the French-Canadian diaspora."

One gets the distinct feeling, in reading this and similar passages, that more than some literary and historical contextualization might have been forced to the cutting room floor. This institutional tendency to want to short-circuit broader interpretation and reception of our most vital cultural figures is, of course, endemic in the realm of US publishing, but Tietchen seems to have done the best he could under the circumstances.

In addition to an array of shorter pieces, *Memory Babe,* a sweet recollection of youth in Lowell, and *I Wish I Were You,* Kerouac's reworking of his collaboration with William S. Burroughs, eventually published as *And the Hippos Were Boiled in Their Tanks,* fill various holes in the Kerouac oeuvre, making us aware of the extent to which he continually reworked and reconceived his material. There's also a lengthy written exchange between Kerouac and trusted friend and novelist John Clellon

Holmes that provides the most unadulterated and direct self-assessment of Kerouac's work on record.

For those dedicated Kerouac readers able to read French, Jean-Christophe Cloutier's *La vie est d'hommage* is truly the pièce de résistance. We are given almost all the extant French texts Cloutier was able to retrieve and reconstruct from the archives, as well as an extended essay, expanding greatly on the shorter essay included in *The Unknown Kerouac*. We soon come to see the very different understanding that our French speaking neighbors to the North have of Kerouac's importance, where he is often considered Quebec's earliest "post-colonial" writer in that he was one of the first to commit the spoken language to writing, often spelling phonetically to capture the nuances of local speech and language patterns. Cloutier's attention to these details, as well as to the larger social and historical contexts, provides a new understanding of Kerouac's unique contribution to American English, to the point where Cloutier can write: "In a sense we've always been reading Kerouac in translation." But Cloutier also enables us to get at least some feeling for Kerouac's central place in the writing of *survivance,* that unique combination of survival and resistance that was the "rallying cry" of the Québec diaspora, and connect it seamlessly to the linguistic torment, so eloquently delineated by the late Édouard Glissant (as Cloutier points out), in the transition from oral to written language undertaken by colonized people; it is within this matrix, finally, that we can begin rereading the stunning lifetime work of Jean-Louis Ti Jean John Jack Kérouac.

19

Introduction for Amiri Baraka's Olson Lecture

2017

If performance, image, object, and sound-making are forms of knowledge, then what we now call art gives a unique view of how things in the world are or are not responded to.

In 1944, the great Martinican poet Aimé Césaire wrote: "Poetic knowledge is born in the great silence of scientific knowledge," AND, "what presides over the poem is not the most lucid intelligence, the sharpest sensibility or the subtlest feelings, but experience as a whole."[1]

That same year, Césaire's student, Frantz Fanon, perhaps aspiring to also become a writer, found himself in Algeria as a French soldier, and was horrified by what he experienced; it would lead him to become one of the twentieth century's most innovative psychiatrists, its most important theorist of race and colonization, and an Algerian revolutionary.

On this side of the Atlantic, in the only hemisphere so thoroughly dispossessed that, up until very recently, not one single state used a native language officially, Bebop had already come into being, a phenomenon that Jack Kerouac called "the lan-

---

1 Aimé Césaire, *Lyric and Dramatic Poetry 1946–82*, trans. Clayton Eshleman and Annette Smith (University of Virginia Press, 1990), xlii.

guage of America's inevitable Africa" expressing the "enormity of a new world philosophy."

In 1944 Kerouac met Allen Ginsberg and poet Robert Duncan published "The Homosexual in Society," announcing a new doctrine of human liberation that would also insure his continued UN-recognition as one of the century's greatest poets. In 1944, alerted to changes in US policy in which Nazis and war criminals got filtered through the OSS and State Department to become key policy makers and scientists, Charles Olson resigned from his post at the Office of War Information in the Roosevelt Administration to become, of all things, a poet.

Just some months before that, in a trial in Alabama over his status as a conscientious objector, Herman Poole Blount, known as Sonny, and later Sun Ra, did the unthinkable and unheard of: He told a white judge, in the deep south, that if he was forced to learn how to kill "he would use that skill without prejudice, and kill one of his own captains or generals first. The judge said: 'I've never seen a nigger like you before,' to which Sonny replied, 'No, and you never will again,' a response that immediately landed him in jail." His psychiatric report echoed those of Lester Young, Charlie Parker, Bud Powell, Charles Mingus, and so many others, in which he was described "as a psychopathic personality," but also as a "well-educated colored intellectual" who was subject to "neurotic depression and sexual perversion."[2]

These are the over and undercurrents of the world Amiri Baraka grew up in. Born Everett LeRoi Jones in Newark, New Jersey (the city his son Ras is now running for Mayor in), in 1934, Baraka's importance and multiple legacies are truly mammoth.

In a review of a book about Billy the Kid, Charles Olson wrote:

> [W]hat strikes one about the history of sd states, both as it has been converted into story and as there are those who are

---

2   John F. Szwed, *Space is the Place: The Lives and Times of Sun Ra* (DaCapo, 1998), 44 and 46.

always looking for it to reappear as art— what has hit me, is, that it does stay, unrelieved.[3]

This sense of the "unrelieved" and the pressure that brings to bear on what poet Ed Dorn called "this permissive asylum," is enormous, and we know that the past cannot simply disappear. Given the circumstances of destroyed languages and peoples, slavery, and layered diasporas, we have a human, political, and cultural amalgam on this continent that is as dense and complicated as any the world has ever known.

The explosion of expression following World War II—Bebop, Abstract Expressionism, the New American Poetries, the Black Arts Movement, Free Jazz, Afro-Futurism, and a host of other groupings and labels—is a massive response to this complexity, and represents an era of creativity that measures up to any known age of accomplishment we can think of. At the same time—facing the academic, ideological, and political straightjackets of the Cold War—these artists were first and foremost thinkers, and their work constitutes a vast realm of hardly explored concepts about the world we actually live in.

Amiri Baraka is one of a handful of the remaining key representatives of this era, and his personal, artistic, and political life cuts through almost every significant intersection of the age. There are no other living American writers able to traverse the traditional generic trio of poetry, prose, and drama, then move into the realms of essay, criticism, autobiography, and scholarship, while making an authoritative mark in each form. In fact, if we take the great British scholar Gordon Brotherston's definition "that the prime function of a classical text is to construct political space and anchor historical continuity,"[4] then Amiri Baraka is one of our truly CLASSICAL writers.

---

[3] Charles Olson, *Collected Prose*, ed. Donald Allen and Benjamin Friedlander (University of California Press, 1997), 311.

[4] For this important definition, see Gordon Brotherston, *Book of the Fourth World: Reading the Native Americas Through Their Literature* (Cambridge University Press, 1992), 4.

His disruptive and political practice refuses to conform to style or manner, allowing imagination to roam between the placard and the eulogy, between eyewitness reports stating facts and cosmic journeys reinstating the kinship of souls. He has both been "anchoring historical continuity" and redrawing the political boundaries of time and space, first in Newark, New Jersey, then in New Ark, out and gone, an otherworldly place through which he channels radio shows, movies, street banter, memories, diatribe, drama, scholarly study, fable, fiction, science fiction, investigative poetics, calculated public rhetoric, and on-the-spot reporting. He is a fantastic witness both to the astonishing unreality of the daily real and an example of what can be done to answer it.

He has constantly exposed himself and his ideas to public scrutiny, even attack, opening a window into participation in the amalgamation of selves and ideas that form the creative, political subject. Amiri's example has served as a constant reminder that such selves, ideas, forms, even communities, are won through struggle and confrontation with oneself and the world. They are not cheaply packaged and exchangeable things to pick up or drop for personal gain or according to dictates of fashion. Finally, though, this clarity of purpose rests in a stance, a position, a place one has to come to in consciousness and over which there can be no negotiation. The visibility of such a stance, bound to a real historical context, is itself a call to action, to activate those parts of one's own consciousness and meet such a challenge in like terms. In recent years, Amiri has been quite explicit about the need to emphasize and carry on his diverse legacies. He has been extraordinarily generous in working with the *Lost & Found* project; this began with a small collection of letters between him and Ed Dorn, finally resulting in the complete correspondence, due out from the University of New Mexico, edited by Claudia Moreno Pisano. Most recently, Amiri has lent his support to *Il Gruppo*, a gathering of writers initially convened to debunk a recent book claiming that Charles Olson was an exemplar of US imperialism, and that "Projective Verse" was based on a military paradigm. Amiri actually published

"Projective Verse," so if Olson is a big imperialist, perhaps, by association, Amiri is a small one. Without further ado, let's give it up for Amiri Baraka.
(APPLAUSE, which should continue…)

20

On Amiri Baraka: An Interview with Özge Özbek Akıman

ÖZGE ÖZBEK AKIMAN: How did you get to know Amiri Baraka and/or his work?

AMMIEL ALCALAY: I was a weird kid. I encountered *System of Dante's Hell, Tales,* and *Blues People* as a teenager, and I never stopped reading him. This would have been 1969, 1970, 1971, those years. I can't remember when I first actually saw him read or met him. I know I saw some plays in the 1970s and I believe I also heard him read somewhere in that period. But I was close to people who had been close to him: Gilbert Sorrentino, for example, who was a teacher of mine, and then a good friend. By hearing Gil talk about "Roi," I felt like I knew him before I got to know him, it felt legendary! I certainly got a feeling for his unparalleled sense of humor, which I got to know first hand later.

I was out of the country for about eight years in the late '70s and '80s but when I got back I was an adjunct teacher at Rutgers University, just at a time when Amiri was teaching there and, apparently, having some problems. I met him then and I also remember posting a little sign on the bulletin board that I can't imagine won me any popularity contests there — I wrote something like: "REMEMBER THIS: Amiri Baraka has forgotten more about poetry than most of the faculty here ever knew!" He used to play John Coltrane and Sun Ra in the hallways and I think that somehow upset the order of western civilization or something.

I then got to see him more, at readings, some visits to his house, and it was always a thrill and a pleasure. When he introduced me to his wife Amina, he said: "This is the brother that the Zionists are giving so much trouble to." Wow, that was really an honorable way to be introduced, I thought. I had the honor to introduce him on several public occasions, once at a huge festival celebrating the Black Arts Movement at Georgetown University, for his keynote lecture, and then again at the annual Olson Lecture in Gloucester, not that long before he died.

He was incredibly supportive of our work in *Lost & Found,* the publishing project that I am the founder and General Editor of. We did a lot of work on Ed Dorn and Amiri was very close to Ed and retained enormous respect for him and his work. One of our earliest projects was a selection of letters between him and Dorn, from the late 1950s to 1965, and that eventually became a book, an award-winning book edited by then Claudia Moreno Pisano, now Claudia Moreno Parsons. Amiri was very happy about that and made time for us. As always, in retrospect, one always wishes there had been more time, more occasions, but I feel very lucky to have gotten to know him at all.

ÖÖA: Can you cite him as one of the inspirations to write poetry?

AA: Absolutely, and I think that's still true. In Amiri's case, though, it wasn't just "writing poetry." It was more like Charles Olson in the sense that the intention of poetry was much wider, it had to do with finding things out, with activating knowledge, with being part of an ongoing nexus of activities. But as far as poetry goes, strictly speaking, I've been thinking about some of his poetry more and more recently. In the 1980s Ed Dorn wrote a series of poems called *Abhorrences* that a lot of people were horrified by: They were short, caustic commentaries on so-called public life. And they were a great influence on Amiri, who embarked on a series he called *Low Coup* (definitely not haiku) poems. Well, for the last few years, I've been writing such a series, in homage to Dorn, called *Imperial Abhorrences (& Other Abominations)*, so I've been thinking about and reading Amiri's poems.

He also had an extraordinary way of shifting registers, even within a sentence. There's a piece of his called "Something in the way of things" that I read at his memorial at the Poetry Project at St. Mark's Church, and it moves from the most condensed vernacular to an almost Elizabethan elegance in a flash. I think he got a lot of that from listening to music, from concentrating on how these great geniuses, players of so-called jazz, were able to transform the most banal tunes into great works of art. He talked about first doing a gig with Max Roach and a few other musicians and he showed up, you know, with a folder of poems, and notebooks, and they looked at him and said: "What's that?" And Amiri said, "My poems." They just laughed and said, "Nope, you have to play like us, no sheet music." So there was incredible agility and variation in his tone, I love that.

ÖÖA: What turning points or phases in his career strike you as the most important? Why?

AA: Ah, the proverbial $64,000 question. Of course, Amiri was like a whirling dervish in that sense, here one day and someplace very different the next. But there was a real logic to it, and he carried the load as he went from one station to another on the journey. In many ways, I think he exposed himself, maybe not all parts of himself, but many public parts of himself, in order that other people might feel permission to try something different. I think that's a big problem in how people think about him now: they have their favorite Baraka but not the whole person.

Certainly a big turn came on his trip to Cuba, something that made him fundamentally question a lot of the assumptions he had and a lot of what he was doing. There were many people, for instance in the Black Panther Party, who were deeply against his Black nationalist phase, and thought it very damaging, and ill-informed. At the same time, once he went back to Newark, he really dug his heels in, and became a real institution in and for the city. The result of that, for sure, is the fact that his son Ras is now Mayor of Newark, something that Amiri, unfortunately, didn't get to see before he passed on, even though I think he knew, in his heart of hearts, that Ras would win!

To me, all the phases are important: we have to remember that, early on, in editing *Yugen* with his then-wife Hettie Jones, they really consolidated all the disparate, non-academic poets across the country, something no one before them had been able to accomplish. The publication of Yugen really makes possible Donald Allen's landmark anthology, *The New American Poetry*. I've found some of his less read, less popular periods — some of the more ideologically driven political work — incredibly helpful as a way to imagine ourselves out of various assumptions. Anything he wrote on music is of enormous value. His eulogies are legendary. I saw him give the eulogy for Larry Neal, it was absolutely breathtaking.

ÖÖA: Do you have any personal favorites among Baraka's work? Could you talk about one? Or any that you felt has grown in significance in time for you?

AA: That's a tough one — there are so many. His earliest story, "Suppose Sorrow Was a Time Machine," is something I reread all the time. It's an absolute masterpiece, and still haunting. I teach *Blues People* whenever I have the opportunity, and I teach it as part of a group of texts that include things like Muriel Rukeyser's *Willard Gibbs,* Olson's *Call Me Ishmael,* Dorn's *The Shoshoneans, The Family* by Ed Sanders, David Henderson's biography of Jimi Hendrix, and a number of others — these are what I call books of poetic knowledge, areas in which poets ventured across so-called "disciplines," particularly during the Cold War and aftermath, in order to explore something and treat it very differently than a standard academic or mainstream approach might. Interestingly, Baraka writes at the beginning of *Blues People* that it is a "theoretical" work. There is a lot involved in teaching students weaned on structuralism, post-structuralism, and every other imaginable kind of theory, to make them understand that, yes, actually, *Blues People* is ALSO a theoretical text. I love *Tales of the Out and Gone,* later fiction, especially some of the 9/11 related pieces. The piece I mentioned earlier, "Something in the way of things," is a text I have very deeply imprinted and ingrained in my head and heart.

ÖÖA: Could you comment on the politics-poetics relationship in the context of Baraka's work, which partially forms the way Baraka's work is received? Do you find that discussion fruitful?

AA: This is one of those US red herrings — there are those who like Baraka more before he became so-called "political" and those who don't like him at all before he became so-called "political." The most political poems published in the US may be those *New Yorker* poems about clams on Long Island, because they appear next to very expensive ads for luxury items, and pay more than a dollar-a-word. I think they actually pay by the column inch. But I guess they probably don't publish as many of those now since they can claim to be more au courant. But the ads remain, that is the context of those poems, no matter what the poems "say."

So unfortunately, the discussion is generally NOT fruitful, though it should be. But in order for it to be fruitful, most "educated" United Statesians, and I stress educated, would need to de-educate themselves of many assumptions about what politics consists of. Under the ideological reign of terror prevalent in the US, politics means "those things I don't agree with." This is the liberal middle ground of consensus through which sanctions got imposed on Iraq, killing hundreds of thousands of people. What, I ask, is the real difference between Martin Heidegger maintaining a university post and being a member of the party during National Socialism, and liberal American academics voting for Bill Clinton and his sanctions on Iraq? That things took place further away? So I think a fruitful discussion would have to start out with some common terms as to what is meant by the "political."

To get back to Baraka, this is very unfortunate because some his most strident works are great instruments by which fruitful discussions might be had, but few people are willing to get past the surface of things, the assumptions behind those surfaces, and examine what intellectual work might look like from very different perspectives. The great example of this is the general reaction to his poem "Somebody Blew Up America." I find it absolutely astonishing that more people got angry about a poem, a poem, and not, let's say, a government order, a thing that actually has policy repercussions, that can bomb a country, impose sanctions, kill people, torture them, or put them in prison.

So there was more anger over the poem than over things that actually happened on 9/11 and how those things were reported: For example, was it possible for a single plane to topple a skyscraper like that? Many engineers say it wasn't. Why were all the remains of the buildings hauled off and not forensically examined? Why were claims made that fingerprints were found in areas where the temperature of the heat was high enough to vaporize aluminum and steel? Why were there gaps in the timeline of the air controllers, and a thousand other things that an informed public should have been outraged over, or at least questioned? Well, instead, people got angry about a poem.

ÖÖA: To what extent was Baraka internationally concerned with politics?

AA: I think Amiri got to a point where he was able to look to certain political situations, and writers and thinkers involved in or emerging from them, as a kind of litmus test on how to proceed from where he was. In other words, he was FROM HERE, but, of course, via Africa. So Newark, New Ark, a place that was home but never home and always home. A contradiction right off the bat. Pastoral poems out the window, not about flowers and clams like those silly old but very political *New Yorker* poems, but about what he saw out the window, in Newark: someone nodding out, a drug deal, a street walker, broken windows.

Toni Cade Bambara has this great thing where she writes: "And I understand that the world is big, that the actual and potential audience for Black writings is wide. People in Cuba, Iran, Vietnam, Brazil, the Caribbean, New Hebrides, the Continent, all over are interested in knowing how we in the belly of the beast are faring, what we are doing, how we see things." This is a very important concept, and I think one that Amiri was acutely aware of. In other words, he drew a lot from other parts of the world, from other struggles, but he also understood that he was able to speak from, report from, a very unique position, one that could help inform the world as to things also of importance to them.

ÖÖA: Could you name poets, writers, thinkers whom you would align Amiri Baraka with? It could be across time and geography.

AA: I once did a useful thought experiment in a class in which we looked at work by writers who were all born in 1934, taking into account an interesting developmental timeline that Robert Duncan had once set up (i.e., crucial ages, nursing, standing, walking, talking, etc.). So the 1934 generation would be generally walking and starting to talk by the time the Spanish Civil War starts. These include, just as the tip of the iceberg: Amiri, Ted Berrigan, Ray Bremser, Diane di Prima, Henry Dumas, George Economou, Anselm Hollo, Hettie Jones, Joanne Kyger, Audre Lorde, A.B. Spellman, and John Wieners. What was interesting about this was that, writers who at first glance might seem to have little or nothing to do with each other, might still, at some level, be addressing similar concerns.

In any case, although Amiri was a deep student of W.E.B. DuBois, and there is much to learn by looking at them in relation to each other, I think it's important to look at him in relation to Charles Olson and Ed Dorn, two people that remained very important for him. There is an extraordinary poem in *The Maximus Poems* about Amiri, whose father, like Olson's, also worked for the postal service, and it was Amiri who first published *Projective Verse* as a stand-alone pamphlet. The relationship to Dorn was more as a friend and contemporary but also someone whom Amiri trusted implicitly and through whom ideas were tested, even when they were out of touch.

And then I would say that Amiri's insight into the intellectual stance of musicians, into the positions that their music embodied, would provide an extraordinary source of cross-pollination. So that would mean looking deeply into the worlds and works of Thelonius Monk, Sun Ra, Ornette Coleman, Archie Shepp, Albert Ayler, Cecil Taylor, and so many others, and trying to figure out how to translate their poetics into textual form.

ÖÖA: What do you see is missing generally or understood properly in recent Baraka scholarship?

AA: In a piece that I wrote about Amiri, I quoted the great British scholar of the Indigenous Americas, Gordon Brotherston, someone whom Dorn worked with closely. Brotherston wrote that "the prime function of classical texts is to construct political space and anchor historical continuity." This is an incredibly useful statement, and it would be hard to find a more classical US writer than Amiri—to begin with, he wrote in all the traditional genres: poetry, drama, and prose. And then he wrote scholarship, polemics, autobiography. One can hardly think of anyone else who did that, and had such an impact in each area. I don't think, for instance, that even such a basic concept as this is taken into account when looking at his work.

For quite a number of years, and more so as he got older, Amiri kept bringing up the value of writers he had been associated with earlier, insisting that without keeping them alive in some way, they too would get "disappeared." I'm afraid that there is some such disappearance underway with Amiri now, under the aegis of "having gotten past all that," the incredible "presentist" tyranny that subjugates the past to some supposed notion of progress. Unless I've missed something, this publication in Turkey would be the first such gesture, a special issue of a journal, since Amiri's passing, and it doesn't surprise me. So I think, just to begin with, that it's very important to keep exploring his archives: There is a tremendous amount of work that still needs to be published, correspondence, plays, poems, essays. We've just offered, through *Lost & Found,* a modest research stipend for a student at the Graduate Center of the City University of New York, to do archival work on Amiri. I truly hope something comes of it.

21

For Jimmie Durham, Poet

2021

Although I wonder why Jimmie Durham isn't generally thought of as a poet or a writer in the US, actually, once I start thinking about it, I don't have to wonder that much, because he is, or should be thought of, in relation to a company I know well, but a company that continually seems to be losing ground. I remember encountering Jimmie's first book, *Columbus Day,* when it came out in 1983, and thinking, even then, even for me, steeped in the furthest out of poetry and poetics: "Ah, here is something, something different, something of great beauty and truth, but also filled with something like documentation, reports, dispatches from the front." Need one ask for anything more?

I remember when Amiri — Amiri Baraka — was interviewed on television, on CNN even, by Connie Chung, after so much was made of his poem "Somebody Blew Up America," following 9/11, and he said: "My responsibility is to truth and beauty. That's what Keats said and that's what DuBois said. That's my responsibility." But Jimmie also uses tools and digs, looking in back of the language, under it. He once wrote to me: "So many people speak English as a second language without having a first. I am waiting for that to free up our ways with English."

I wondered about contemporaries — poets — and whether there had even been cognizance of each other *as* poets or whether such meetings had taken place under some other circumstance. Since Jimmie was born in 1940, I thought of Simon Ortiz, born in 1941. So, of course, I wanted to know more about that and, sure enough, Ortiz, in welcoming Jimmie "back" to a US in 2017 that he actually hasn't yet returned to, mentions how he had met Jimmie in North Dakota in 1976, in the context of trying to put together the International Indian Treaty Council. And it reminded me so much of poets I knew in the Middle East, who had met at a demonstration or an activist meeting, but had little or no idea about each other's poetry.

I thought of Ortiz's most amicable forward to a reprint of *The Shoshoneans,* a brilliant road trip of sorts by poet Ed Dorn and photographer Leroy Lucas, the man who had burst into the 8th Street Bookshop in 1965 while LeRoi Jones (Amiri Baraka) was reading, to say that Malcolm had been shot, Malcolm had been shot. And so Ed Dorn went to the 1965 Berkeley Poetry Conference "as a substitute forced on the organizers by LeRoi Jones, who had begun to withdraw from such contact. And that's how I went along as the Indian."[1]

Close to the beginning of Dorn's presentation, he says: "I'm not talking about the 'Ugly Americans' or going to Europe and insisting on water when people don't have it or all the crudenesses that we know *do* exist. That's not it, that's another situation altogether. This is simply a matter of how trustworthy can you be if you come from this context. And I assure you, you can't be very trustworthy. Nobody trusts us. You *don't* have to talk about Vietnam. You don't have to talk about South America. You can talk about Nevada. That's much closer to home."[2]

And this business of "removing oneself," Simon also speaks of this in relation to Jimmie leaving the hardness of New York ("Jimmie was poor in New York city in the 1970s, no denying that"), in relation to a trip he, Simon, had once taken to the Southern states in search of people who never left, the Trail of Tears, "Indian Removal," and whether such things could at all be equivalent to Jimmie's voluntary "removal." Perhaps, Simon

---
1 Edward Dorn, *The Poet, the People, the Spirit* (Talonbooks, 1976), 6.
2 Ibid., 11.

ponders. I think of poet Ted Joans writing from Europe in 1995 to his friend Amiri in New Jersey: "So, brother Baraka, I remain, as usual, outside the outsiders... I marvel at your patience with the U.S.A. I no longer tolerate the blatant isms of the masses of this powerful unhip jive giant, I have graduated from it all. May you stay in the best of health."[3] As Jimmie once wrote to me: "No more business with the US. no reason to go there."

The point, I think, is that everything still needs to be pieced together, always. Poet as "maker," Jimmie as maker, of breath and sound, vowel shape and consonantal stop: from voice and harp, trail and leaves, roots and wood and scrap, tin and fabric, word and tear.

In the marvels of these vinyl grooves ridden by a fine needle there is electromagnetic magic, Tesla overriding Edison's wax cylinders, sound coming into our midst, vibrating our ear. And because the poems are their own length, the limitations that a three-minute version of Bird's "Cherokee," for example, imposed upon the ensemble, or the earlier lament of singers from Asia Minor on the Lower East Side of New York that "los fonógrafos nos siegaron los garones / phonographs have cut our throats (1922)," are not a factor.

No, instead, as Jimmie writes, "you need to get your bearings straight," with words to dance by, laugh with, mourn together: "I was far away / almost everyone who did not attend the wedding was far away / and as I write distance ourselves / become more far away." This, about a US bombing of a wedding in Afghanistan. From the everyday to deep time, there is a dexterity to these words because, like when using tools, they can come back to cut you: "the long tongue of the law / shorthand for offhandedness." And elsewhere: "Truly, humankind has fallen. / Any colt will tell you, horsekind has fallen too, / And all the kinds of moving life, / living to devour, living by devouring, / Watching always fearful of the bite. / We live by death of course." Even though he might be "held back by many stones," in these poems,

---

[3] Ted Joans, *Poet Painter/Former Villager Now/World Traveller*, ed. Wendy Tronrud and Ammiel Alcalay (Center for the Humanities, 2016), 51–52.

in all his art and being, Jimmie grabs onto any "piece of fallen star" he can find, with an enormous embrace that is of shadow and light, life and vision, humor and wisdom.

22

Getting Out of the Western Box: Dennis Tedlock's *The Olson Codex*

2018

Despite the remarkable fact that poet and thinker Charles Olson still remains quite outside the consensus of what passes for US literary culture, more and more of his work continues to become available. Recent books include *Contemporary Olson*, a collection of essays edited by David Herd; *Letters for Olson*, a unique gathering edited by the late Benjamin Hollander; *The Collected Letters of Charles Olson and J. H. Prynne*, edited by Ryan Dobran; *An Open Map: The Correspondence of Robert Duncan and Charles Olson*, edited by Robert J. Bertholf and Dale M. Smith; and *Imagining Persons: Robert Duncan's Lectures on Charles Olson*, also edited by Bertholf and Smith. A book by Olson on William Shakespeare completed in the early 1950s but never published, and a critical edition of one of his key but long-out-of-print texts, *The Special View of History*, are in the works. And yet, even among these riches, there is nothing quite akin to the late Dennis Tedlock's *The Olson Codex: Projective Verse and the Problem of Mayan Glyphs*.

In the present context of enforced identity boundaries and claims, it becomes that much harder to give credit where credit is due: Olson's curiosity expanded Tedlock's lifelong immersion into Indigenous languages and cultures. Tedlock's standing as the translator of both the *Popol Vuh* and *Rabinal Achí,* as well as his essential and innovative work on the transmission of oral texts in written form, place him in a very particular position of authority, as distasteful as that word has become to many. But Tedlock's authority, in this case, derives from his long experience of working with Mayan glyphs, and what he has made known by continually sifting materials through a poetics that was, in large part, inspired by Olson's innovations and audacity, as well as his reach. This reach went far: One of Olson's attempts to connect Ancient Mesopotamia with Ancient America was thwarted by a rejected grant proposal in 1951. (As he wrote to poet Robert Creeley after getting the news: "I imagine I did say to you that I doubted State wld take a risk on me at such outposts of the empire as Istanbul or Teheran, simply, that in such places, they can't afford more than pink-cheeked servants.")

But Olson did get to the Yucatán in 1951, spending about six months in Lerma, from where he wrote of his experiences with great excitement, primarily to a then twenty-three-year-old Creeley he would not even meet for several years. It proved to be a formative experience in which Olson discovered new methods and materials with which to forage his way out of the Western box. Creeley later edited Olson's side of the letters for a small book called *Mayan Letters,* and this is Tedlock's primary source, though he uses other letters and writings by both Olson and Creeley. After a lucid and illuminating foregrounding of the myriad issues Olson's poetics brought to both transcription and performance, Tedlock outlines the heart of his project: "In my reconsideration of Olson's letters, I have brought him deeper inside the Mayan world than he could have gone at the time. In addition to Mayan dates, I have reconstructed the corresponding stars, planetary positions, lunations, birds, beasts, deities, and divinatory readings." He goes on to note that this is part of the Mayan tradition of "daykeeping": "Daykeepers measure the rhythms of time, watch the skies, pay attention to dreams, and listen to the stories people tell about themselves, seeking clues to events that are hidden in the past or have yet to happen."

In a stunningly beautiful production, *The Olson Codex* utilizes all manner of visual material. Photographs, glyphs, astrological and astronomical figures, typography, and fastidious attention to detailing the movement between oral, written, and visual texts in composing the poetic line—all go into projecting a very particular time and place while opening our minds, eyes, and ears to myriad new possibilities. In addition to the profound erudition brought to bear on Mayan sources, the *Codex* proves to be an extraordinarily moving tribute, not just to Olson but to the particulars of a series of significant events in the life of a poet and thinker, the implications of which could hardly be fully explicated at the time.

Like almost everything else of the period, decoding the Mayan language was also part of the Cold War struggle, something Olson instinctively knew when he wrote to Creeley on March 22, 1951: "Racism has to be kept at the end of a stick." Most Western scholars simply could not accept the fact that the Mayans were capable of creating such a complex visual orthographic alphabetical system. As Tedlock notes, the "Soviet invasion of the world of bourgeois Western scholarship" was "taking shape" in the form of Yuri Knorosov's work. Less than a year from Olson's letter, the Russian scholar would "crack the Mayan code." At the Carnegie Institute of Washington, J. Eric S. Thompson, the foremost Mayanist of the time—and someone Olson critiqued—would be "quick to reject Knorosov's decipherment, branding it as one more example of false Soviet claims." Olson would be dead by the time Knorosov's work was fully accepted in the West, but, interestingly enough (a fact Tedlock does not mention), he was reading another important US-based Russian scholar, Tatiana Proskouriakoff, before he went to the Yucatán.

Despite great plans and the desire to continue studying Mayan culture, Olson had a job to go back to: teaching at Black Mountain College, complete with room and board for himself and his wife, and $100 raised by students to entice him there. Finances would improve at only a few points over the course of the rest of his life, but he remained fully aware, as he famously declared at the Berkeley Poetry Conference in 1965, that "I'm the White Man, the ultimate paleface, the non-corruptible, the Good, the thing that runs this country, or that is this country. And, thank god, the only advantage I have is that I didn't." While many obstacles remain to a clearer understanding of Olson's true stature, Tedlock's unique efforts to reanimate a singular and inspiring experience preserved only through letters from one poet to another opens new vistas that demand further consideration.

23

Digging Our Way through the Data Midden

2018

Over a span of close to sixty years—from his 1961 debut *Poem from Jail,* written after being arrested for attempting to board a nuclear submarine, to his 2018 *Broken Glory: The Final Years of Robert F. Kennedy,* a text over thirty years in the making— the very public work of Ed Sanders has both embodied and extended the work of his two great "bardic mentors," Allen Ginsberg and Charles Olson. Between these two points Sanders has inhabited the very mercurial fate of what it might mean to be public in this country. Inhabiting the roles of poet, political activist, rock star, publisher, bookstore owner, investigative journalist, memoirist, biographer, environmentalist, author of local zoning laws, and visual artist, he has also been the inventor of new poetic forms and technologies, from the glyphic poem to the "Talking Tie," an electronic instrument meant to take the place of the lyre in the electromagnetic age whose new muse Sanders has dubbed "Retentia," guardian of magnetic tapes, compact disks, hard drives, and all our new forms of memory management and storage.

The specifics of these roles include initiating the notorious *FUCK YOU: A Magazine of the Arts,* opening the Peace Eye Bookstore on the Lower East Side, being a founder of the renegade rock group the Fugs, finding himself on the cover of *Life Magazine,* deep involvement in key political events of the 1960s, and writing the definitive book on the Manson family after years of research. Unquestionably, his massive and singularly organized personal archive constitutes one of the essential resources for future histories of the counterculture and its aftermaths. All the while, too often under the radar, he has continued to write epic verse for our era, histories whose power and intent become more and more evident as time passes.

The coincident appearance of *Broken Glory: The Final Years of Robert F. Kennedy,* with its extraordinary illustrations by veteran cartoonist Rick Veitch, and a new edition of the long unavailable classic *Investigative Poetry* (brought back into print by Dispatches Editions, publishing wing of the lively and essential web journal *Dispatches from the Poetry Wars*), is yet another indication of just how far what ought to be considered one of our most vital cultural and political resources has drifted from the map of our collective attention.

In many ways, the modern history of the United States moves along parallel lines: One line emerges from the ideological propaganda, cognitive dissonance, and psychological warfare pioneered by Walter Lippmann and Edward Bernays starting in the 1920s, becoming fully weaponized by the 1950s to expand US imperial interests exponentially and subjugate domestic dissent. Another line emerges from archival documentation, eyewitness accounts, common sense, and willingness to relentlessly question the basic assumptions of the constructions of reality that have become both surround sound and something almost like a second skin, enclosing and suffocating the parameters of our rational and imaginative faculties.

There is no better source to explore the need for these rational and imaginative faculties, along with some very practical considerations and advice, than *Investigative Poetry*. Originally presented as a lecture at the Naropa Institute, *Investigative Poetry* takes its rightful place among some of the most important manifestos and documents in poetics of the twentieth century. As Sanders notes in his introduction: "This is the Age of Investigation / and every citizen must investigate." In the body of the lecture, he goes on to say: "My statement is this: that poetry, to go forward, in my view, has to begin a voyage into the description of *historical reality*." And further: "There is no end / to Gnosis: / The hunger / for DATA." Thus, in the "RELENTLESS / PURSUIT OF DATA!," history is open to the citizenry, no case is fully closed, and it is the right and duty of any one of us to "NEVER HESITATE TO OPEN / A CASE FILE / EVEN UPON THE BLOODIEST OF BEASTS OR PLOTS."

While Sanders has written many single and multi-volume histories in verse, (including *Chekhov; 1968: A History in Verse; America, A History in Verse;* and *The Poetry and Life of Allen Ginsberg), Broken Glory: The Final Years of Robert F. Kennedy,* feels like a summa of some kind, a further honing of the methods that *Investigative Poetry* lays out and that his other histories have created the foundation for. Though so many books dealing with the details of political assassinations, particularly of the 1960s, get put in the "conspiracy theory" bin, the fact is that the legion of dedicated researchers and archivists working on such topics often present the most solid and lucid philosophical and epistemological response to the unreality and cognitive dissonance created by propaganda and the actual conspiracies perpetrated by the US government.

Although the seeds of Sanders's work on the assassination of Robert F. Kennedy were sown during the research he undertook in the early 1970s on the Manson Family, a law enforcement source led him to believe that there may have been a connection between one of the Manson murders and someone who knew something about Sirhan Sirhan, the alleged assassin. Sanders worked through material from 1974 to 1980, gathering some 4,000 pages of FBI files and related documents and then kept the project on the back burner, collecting and filing clippings until more abundant archival material began appearing in the later 1980s and 1990s. The big break came with the opening of the large Robert F. Kennedy Assassination Archive at the University of Massachusetts, Dartmouth, "assembled by author and professor of political science Philip Melanson and the RFK Assassination Archive Committee of the University Library." As Sanders goes on to note in his introduction: "Original materials, including research files, audiotape interviews, videotapes and news clippings were donated in several installments by a number of private individuals investigating the case." This brings into play the citizen investigator, called upon to act by Sanders in *Investigative Poetry,* without whom the record of "historical reality" would be much impoverished.

Thus, the data midden, along with Sanders's own experience as an active intelligence involved in political life—observing, sleuthing, organizing, contemplating—are elements that go into the dramatic narrative presented here with such mastery. And it is the flow of the narrative itself that must be paid attention to. While the poem begins right after John F. Kennedy's assassination in 1963, and touches on Robert F. Kennedy's 1965 run for the Senate, his 1966 speech in South Africa, and early background on Sirhan Sirhan, it moves quickly to events of 1967 and 1968. There is a significant section on Martin Luther King Jr., starting with the Memphis Garbage Workers Strike and ending with King's assassination and the ensuing uprising that swept the US, a sequence in which Rick Veitch's drawings are particularly powerful. This sequence ends with Sanders's own stunning rendition of the Ancient Greek text of Aeschylus that Kennedy cited in his tribute to King.

But given the rapidity and accrual of major events in this period, once we get to the Ambassador Hotel in Los Angeles for Kennedy's victory speech in the California primary on June 4, 1968, the day he was shot, the poem almost seems to stand still, taking up over 150 pages of this 350 page text. And we remain in the moments following the speech and the various possible routes out of the hotel and through the kitchen for a good part of these 150 pages. While the stop-action and repetition is quite reminiscent of Bruce Conner's dazzling film *Report,* a dizzying collage of found footage on the JFK assassination, Sanders is able to achieve a density of the moment through his shifting verse patterns and data clusters that cannot be easily approached in a non-textual medium.

This counter-intuitive narrative flow seems to lie at the heart of Sanders's method: While we know all too well the tragic fate of Kennedy, it is as if only by freezing the action and turning the prism over and over again can we be given any hope of staving off the inevitable. By presenting it like this, we come to understand that, though Kennedy has been assassinated, the case is still open. And the only way to know more about it is to relentlessly comb through the testimony of all the people that were in the kitchen when he was shot, to consider every perspective, detail, and inference, while grasping the powers at work that have cut those sources off to us.

We find out, for instance, that Coroner Thomas Noguchi definitively determined that the shots killing Kennedy could not have been fired at a distance of more than three inches away from his head, eliminating any possibility of making Sirhan Sirhan the assassin. Even more damningly, we learn that after an independent analysis had determined that the bullet entering Kennedy's neck could not have been fired from Sirhan's gun, the LAPD itself revealed, years later, that they had already been sitting on their own independent analysis, corroborating these findings.

Throughout the text, Sanders displays an uncanny fluency, moving in and out of prosaic passages that nevertheless are deeply embedded in full prosodic value. His own appearance as narrator or commentator is highly limited but quite significant. Just before the Chicago Convention in 1968, Sanders begins seeing something in Kennedy ("I liked Robert Kennedy / I was hungering for his Presidency") that differentiates him from some of his compatriot demonstrators and activists. In the midst of a particularly vexing set of versions of an event, even he must admit that: "The past is like quicksand." By the end of the poem, he is ready to declare what he by now knows must have happened:

Is there no Justice
Is there no Ancient Feather of Justice
to judge against

"FOLLOW THE PERSON"

> Evil?
>
> Here's what I believe
> occurred by the Ice Machine

As he goes on to name names, by referring to the "Ancient Feather of Justice," Sanders also returns to an early discipline of his, the study of ancient Egyptian hieroglyphs. In many ways, Sanders has hewn a new form of narrative glyph in his historical poems, an indelible data cluster delivered in the form of a story, the kind of story we need to tell ourselves over and over again if we are to survive with any shred of self-respect.

Getting to the roots of history, of finding out for yourself, has always been at the center of his work. As Sanders writes in *Investigative Poetry*:

> Lawyers have a term: "to make law." You "make law" when you're involved in a case or an appeal which, as in Supreme Court decisions which have expanded the scope of personal freedom, opens up new human avenues.
>
> You make law.
>
> Bards, in a similar way, "make reality," or, really, they "make freedom" or they create new modes of what we might term Eleutherarchy, or the dance of freedom.

Sanders' effort to "make reality" and "make freedom" are made manifest in his historical and biographical poems, his reports from the field, and his steadfast refusal to knuckle under to nonsense and received versions of history. But it has also been made manifest in his tireless search for new form and new means with which those forms can be enacted. This collaboration with Rick Veitch, dubbed a "graphic history" adds a powerful new vector to the catalog. One cannot help but think that the sheer magnitude of Sanders's work over the years, his commitment to diving deep into the data midden of information overload to fend off what fellow Fug Steven Taylor has called "memoricide," to make "fact fable again," as Olson put it, and tell us stories that we need to know, presents an urgent example of historical revisionism that demands both closer and wider attention.

24

An Interview with Marwa Helal

2018

MARWA HELAL: Did you always want to be a poet?

AMMIEL ALCALAY: I'm not even sure how to answer that since I think the terms of "being a poet" have changed pretty dramatically over the course of my lifetime. We tend to think of these titles or categories as some kind of timeless essence but "being a poet" has and can mean a lot of different things in different situations. There are times when it has meant being the propaganda mouthpiece of a ruling fiefdom or glorifying an imperial empire. "Poets" have instigated genocidal wars and they've also been witness to those same situations. For me, I think it was "writing" rather than the category of poet particularly, and I came to understand that poetry — under certain very specific historical conditions — can be a unique and very useful form of knowledge, a take on the world that might be unavailable elsewhere, but that seems more and more rare. I was an avid reader and happened to grow up in an environment in and around Boston where I had access to all kinds of people who happened to be poets. My high school years were 1969 to 1973 and so I didn't really go to school much. There were local deaths of people who seemed heroic to me: Jack Kerouac in 1969, Charles Olson and then Steve Jonas in early 1970. I understood that the way they lived — and died — was intimately connected to what they wrote and how the society we were living in considered them, or didn't. I think my relation to poets had more to do with a specific form of attention that might have been more generally prevalent then but was expressed very directly in conversation, in being together. It's recognizable to me immediately, when it still happens. I got to know John Wieners, for instance, as a teenager, and I'd walk around town with him, sometimes talking, sometimes not saying much. That was the case with many others, sometimes with a group of adults going through various very significant things but who never saw me as a bother or an intruder. In retrospect, that's quite remarkable. My first writing "mentor" was the poet Vincent Ferrini, to whom *The Maximus Poems* began as letters. Vincent was exuberant and generous: he operated a frame shop in Gloucester, a very small place that he also lived in, and which has now, happily, become the Gloucester Writers Center, a far cry from the usual "artist retreats." I've written extensively about Vincent and his experience in radical politics in the 1930s and '40s. To have that kind of historical transmission and sense of attention, that to me, I think, is what "being a poet" can mean.

MH: What has surprised you most about your dedication to this path?

AA: I guess I would say that what I have found surprising in the past few years is how little actually writing or producing poetry has to do with "being a poet." There is no "coin of the realm" in this country anymore. Of course, this is something Ezra Pound put at the center of his work: "Usura slayeth the child in the womb," which puts it as strongly and as succinctly as possible. We've lived in a kind of banking hell joined at the hip with the British Empire since the creation of the Federal Reserve in 1913. With manufacturing and production now almost fully outsourced, we have also, in so many ways, internally outsourced our own culture, begun thinking of it and relating to it in terms that actually have little or no relationship to the historical conditions in which it was produced. There has been a tradition of poets in the twentieth century with a historical awareness of these conditions but I think the nature of systemic "incorporation," in which the publicity and propaganda machines have usurped almost all available space, has made it that much harder for poets to operate on that critical plane. I'm not sure if this, in itself, is surprising, but I think what I said earlier is. In other words, a deeper understanding that doing the work of poetry might not necessarily mean writing it.

MH: What has been inspiring you lately?

AA: I'm inspired by a young poet in Gaza, Mosab Abu Toha, who opened an English language reading library called the Edward Said Public Library, under conditions that I would hope we are all aware of. He would very much like to come to the US and study but, of course, he can't leave Gaza, nor has he ever been able to leave Gaza. I'm inspired by Dareen Tatour, a young Palestinian poet who has been under house arrest for several years for a poem she posted on the internet and for which she has just been sentenced to an Israeli prison. I'm inspired by Ahed Tamimi, a 17-year-old Palestinian who was just released from prison, along with her mother Nariman, after serving eight months for slapping an Israeli soldier trespassing on her family's land.

MH: What is the best thing about being a poet right now? What is the most difficult?

AA: On the difficult side, I guess I try to wear blinders because if I paid attention to certain things it would be damaging to both my mental and physical health. And I'm not talking about the circus that refers to itself as "Washington" but the careerist triumphalism that seems to permeate too much of the so-called "poetry world" these days. And I don't mean to paint with such a broad brush because I also feel very rooted in parts of this world, and close to many people participating in it, including myself! There is a tremendous pressure towards conformity, a fear of being critical, of actually expressing difference of thought and opinion, and of engaging in real debate. Of course this characterizes US society as a whole but the trickle down into the poetry scene is, to say the least, disconcerting and very stultifying, sometimes suffocating.

On the better side, again, taking all my previous qualifiers about "being a poet" into account, I would say that, having reached a certain age, I realize that I've accrued quite varied experiences and the knowledge of those experiences and I've been able to become more focused and selective in how I choose to transmit or make use of them. I've been having some fun over the past several years with my co-conspirators at *Dispatches from the Poetry Wars,* one of the few collective efforts out there trying to shake things up a little. My sense is that a lot of people actually follow it, using the equivalent of a brown paper screensaver so the neighbors don't find out, as we're probably considered very impolite, irascible, and politically incorrect. Satire is needed now more than ever and the poems that have been given me over the past several years, a sequence I'm calling *Imperial Abhorrences (& Other Abominations),* are mainly written while driving (I have a long commute), and are kind of bumper sticker like historical and political treatises, in homage to Ed Dorn.

MH: *Lost & Found: The CUNY Poetics Documents Initiative* is such a wonderful title because the publications carry that energetic charge of discovering a treasure — if you could tell us how it came to be and why?

AA: Thank you! Needless to say, I'm very proud of what we've been able to achieve, and the fact that we've lasted this long and really built a multi-pronged institution within an institution that has also gone out and resonated variously in ways I'm sure I'm not fully aware of. Most of the great mentors I've been lucky enough to have always grumbled about this or that great work that, of course, is "out-of-print." Having that as a kind of baseline, I also came to feel very strongly that the real work of the poets of the 1950s, '60s, and '70s that I am closest to has only begrudgingly begun to be recognized for what it is, and that is a concerted and deep intervention at the heart of how US cultural politics and the state organized itself in the Cold War. This might be more obvious in the case of some figures but less so in the case of others. I saw that students were accustomed to understanding geographical and formal distribution of poets through reading anthologies, thinking that poets divided into schools were like some kind of fish that wouldn't dare traverse "enemy" waters, and I wanted to find ways of making the culture and politics of the period cohere more to its reality. Finally, my academic training is more as a Medievalist and in Middle East Studies so that when I began teaching graduate students who were primarily involved in contemporary US culture, I realized that they needed more tools to understand the nature of historical contexts and I thought encountering an archive could provide a much more unmediated experience, in which a student would have to confront materials not surrounded by jargon or accepted vocabularies, and be forced to consider the object in itself and in relation to other actual things and events.

In addition, written in right at the very beginning, was the idea of using this great still-public university, CUNY, as a means of bringing this archival work—often so secretive and unknown—into public light. At the heart of this was the idea of the Living Archive, and of hosting older, non-academically affiliated figures who could come into the academy but also bring students out of the academy and into their communities. This is part of a broader approach to providing tools for the preservation of various legacies that are sometimes well-protected but sometimes just a moment's throw from a dumpster. We tend to think of our institutions as stable but, inherently, they're not. No one in Baghdad or Sarajevo expected some of the first hits to be against their archives, and it is essential that we understand how important the transmission of historical memory is. This is the heart of the project: putting students in situations in which they take it upon themselves to become the bearers of this transmission.

MH: A passage from something you've read recently that has resonated?

AA: I'm just now rereading David Ray Griffin's masterpiece, *The New Pearl Harbor: Disturbing Questions about the Bush Administration and 9/11*. I find myself drawn to the kinds of work that gets labeled as "conspiracy theory" but which I find to actually be the most solid and lucid philosophical and epistemological response to the unreality and cognitive dissonance created by propaganda. Such books actually propagate reality: in discussing Flight 77, the Boeing 757 that allegedly hit the Pentagon, Griffin writes:

> According to at least one version of the official story, authorities were able to identify victims of the crash by their fingerprints. To provide support for the official account, therefore, the fire would have to be hot enough to vaporize aluminum and steel and cool enough to leave human flesh intact.

This does the work of poetry: I've written a short "Imperial Abhorrence" in reference to this called "NEW HORIZONS IN PHYSICS." By exposing ourselves to the surround sound of propaganda that is everywhere with us, we are actually being forced to "take leave of our senses."

MH: What do you think of the term "decolonization" and how we all seem to be throwing it around casually these days?

AA: Useful but very problematic. We've barely begun to scratch the surface on this one and need to deeply educate and immerse ourselves in histories and peoples that have undergone the twin processes of colonization and decolonization, the second part, of course, being a hell of a lot harder to find true examples of. I've been a long-time student of Indigenous peoples of the Americas, of Palestine, and of Algeria, three very key areas. On the ground, the work of decolonization, as Frantz Fanon so eloquently puts it, is, by definition, violent. But that violence is often misunderstood — it can be through armed revolt but it also must be through a Rimbaud-like "deregulation of the senses." The old order must be completely overturned, internally and externally. This is not a simple process, by any means and, being in the US, the impulse is to simplify things to the point of incoherence or consumer convenience. Thus, on an academic level, for instance, we have the category of the postcolonial, which tends to skip over the difficult work of decolonization. While I mention this as an academic category, given that the academy is often pimping more arcane ideas that soon get repackaged to find popular outlets in the stunningly narrow bandwidth of mass media, this idea suffuses all kinds of discourse. So there are lots of theories bandied about but very few examples that demonstrate the actual work of decolonization. Just to give a recent and very particular example: A former student of mine, Kai Krienke, just translated an extraordinary work by the late Algerian poet and scholar Hamid Nacer-Khodja,[1] which is an almost book-length essay prefacing a translation, also done by Kai, of the correspondence between Algerian revolutionary poet Jean Sénac and Nobel Prize–winning author Albert Camus, also Algerian, and of similar poor, working-class background. This is a text through which one can learn a hell of a lot more about the actual mechanics of decolonization than shelves of theory. Moreover, we are ourselves colonized to vastly differing degrees by economic structures, racial categories, ideologies, and all manner of propaganda. The splintering of all this into identity politics only is also the work of a kind of colonization and makes deeper resistance incoherent and ineffective. I could go on...

MH: What is the key to a superb translation?

AA: Not mystifying the process. My friend Elias Khoury always says: "if a masterpiece can't lose twenty-five percent in translation, it probably isn't a masterpiece." I remain hooked, for

---

[1] Hamid Nacer-Khodja, *Albert Camus, Jean Sénac, or The Rebel Son,* trans. Kai Krienke (Michigan State University Press, 2019).

example, on the old Constance Garnett translations of Fyodor Dostoevsky, because those are the ones I read when I swallowed Dostoevsky whole. Now I know that there are supposedly "better" translations out there, but I remain indifferent to them because they feel unfamiliar. I would also say that knowing both the language one is translating from and the language one is translating into, though that might just seem like common sense, is essential! We've come to the point where people are doing all kinds of translations with little or no knowledge of the language translated from. There are, of course, some people with a certain genius for "language" who can perform miracles, but those are very "informed" miracles. We've also come to a point where the "translation" is set off like some sort of crown jewel, as if anything can actually be conveyed without deeper context. So many of the translation projects that get done in the US just reinscribe a kind of generic totalitarianism, upholding the values of "the poem" or "the novel." We need translations with deep context, with historical overviews, with interviews, with excerpts from letters, biographies, polemics, and literary, cultural, and political background. Too few of these get done though I think, hopefully, that is changing.

MH: What has been your favorite reading or moment at the Poetry Project?

AA: There are so many so I'll have to mention a few. In the mid-1970s, my very dear and old friend Kate Tarlow Morgan and I managed a bookstore in the West Village, a few doors down from a laundromat that I also managed part-time. One day we arrived to open the bookshop and there was a man in a blue suit sitting on a chair outside the shop. It was Robert Duncan. He spent some hours in the shop and, of course, we talked at length. He advised that we try and buy a Gestetner so we could start a small press. We had been planning to go hear him read at the Project that evening, which we did, and it was thrilling. Kate who, among other things, is a dancer and choreographer, created a performance piece called "Blue Suit" that we performed in Gloucester in 2010 at the Charles Olson Centenary celebration, so that encounter had much further resonance, thirty-five years later.

The Project has always been a welcoming place to me, an alternative to the "church" I don't go to. As the machinery ratcheted up towards "Shock and Awe," the war in Iraq, Anne Waldman and I organized a number of day long events at the project called "Poetry Is News." There were many great moments, in the spirit of teach-ins of the '60s. Our first speakers included a friend, Rebecca Murray, who had been involved with the International Solidarity Movement (of which Rachel Corrie had been a part), and she described riding with ambulances through the Occupied Territories in Palestine. She was followed by the great Lebanese novelist Elias Khoury who gave a rousing talk that was seized upon when I was later attacked by neo-cons for "bringing Arabs" to places like the Poetry Project! Then, picking the perfect dramatic moment, as usual, Tariq Ali showed up in the middle of the day, to a packed hall, and we just gave him the stage. Finally, a wonderful Naropa student whose name now escapes me brought a group of high school students from Bushwick to talk about the cognitive dissonance they were facing by Army recruiters, and their strategies to organize and resist it. That was a brilliant and great moment.

In 2005, along with Fred Dewey and Michael Kelleher, we organized an event called "OlsonNow." I bring it up because I feel like it was a watershed moment and an opportunity not further "exploited." The key to that event was to disturb the standard structures of stage and speakers or panels on subjects. We did UN-style three-quarter circular seating and put microphones all over the place so people could speak from where they were and encounter each other rather than face a stage and look at a speaker. There was no one really leading the discussion and it was run more like a town meeting, interrupted by performances. Some of the ensuing encounters were amazing, like a dialogue between Jack Hirschman and Susan Howe that I don't think could have occurred in a more conventional setting.

"FOLLOW THE PERSON"

Finally, on the downside, I will say that I was somewhat dismayed and almost shocked at the small audience that turned up for Amiri Baraka's memorial, and how so many of the readers qualified their feelings or thoughts about Amiri before their readings. This, to me, was an indication of a certain kind of malaise that I feel has permeated the so-called "poetry world," in which each person is almost conditioned to feel that they have to stand apart, declare a kind of position of superiority to some purported "bad politics" attributed to the person or subject at hand. I find this colossally smug, historically unconscious, often quite offensive, and usually just a real bore.

III

IN FRIENDSHIP

25

"a dance of freedom" /
In the Worlds of Etel Adnan

2013

In 1944, at the age of nineteen, Etel Adnan, born in Beirut to a Christian Greek mother and a Syrian Muslim father serving as an officer in the Ottoman military, declared that — since there was no school of architecture, her first preference — she wanted to become an engineer. Adnan had grown up between languages and cultures: Greek, Turkish, and Arabic; Damascus of the Orient and Beirut of a striven-after Paris, with French as the language of colonization and education, the language of everything in the world outside the world she actually grew up and lived in, outside the actual flora and fauna, sights, sounds, and smells of material reality and its imaginable horizons. As a newly created state under the 1916 Sykes-Picot agreement, in which the name of an English gentleman and the name of a French gentleman and the 'agreement' they came to would prepare the region for colonial domination and Zionism, "educated" Lebanon spoke French, creating a school system conforming precisely to the schools in France : "So I grew up thinking that the world was French. And that everything that mattered, that was 'in books', or had authority (the nuns), did not concern our environment. That is what is called alienation."[1]

Frantz Fanon, one of the twentieth century's most innovative psychiatrists and cogent revolutionary thinkers, would come to define "alienation" under the terms of colonialism. In *Wretched of the Earth,* he wrote: "Yes, the first duty of the native poet is to see clearly the people he has chosen as the subject of his work of art. He cannot go forward resolutely unless he first realizes the extent of his estrangement from them."[2] In 1944, Fanon was an aspiring young writer, a student of the great Martinican poet Aimé Césaire. Fanon's idealism had led him to enlist in the French army in order to spread the universal ideals of France and the spread of those ideals took him to Algeria, where what he encountered horrified him. Césaire, his teacher, put his finger on much of what would come to characterize the radical shift in the sources of artistic creation in the era following the death camps and the atom bomb, an era also characterized by fierce struggles against colonialism the world over, on the ground and in the mind.

In his 1944 text "Poetry and Knowledge," written while on a long visit to Haiti, the very site where the ideals of the French Revolution were put into almost immediate effect through the successful revolt led by Toussaint Louverture in 1791, Césaire wrote: "Poetic knowledge is born in the great silence of scientific knowledge."[3] And how could it not be, if the results of science had led to Zyklon B and nuclear fission, or what Chief Rabbi Moise Ventura of Alexandria called, in a 1945 sermon, "the historic moment of the spectacular explosion of materialism"?[4]

---

1 Etel Adnan, "Growing Up to Be a Woman Writer in Lebanon," in *Opening the Gates: A Century of Arab Feminist Writing,* ed. Margot Badran and Miriam Cooke (Indiana University Press, 1990), 7.

2 Frantz Fanon, *The Wretched of the Earth,* trans. Constance Farrington (Grove Press, 1963), 226.

3 Aimé Césaire, "Poetry and Knowledge," in *Lyric and Dramatic Poetry, 1946–82,* trans. Clayton Eshleman and Annette Smith (University of Virginia Press, 1990), xlii.

4 In Ammiel Alcalay, "Intellectual Life," in *The Jews of the Middle East and North Africa in Modern Times,* ed. Reeve S. Simon, Michael M. Laskier,

For Césaire, experience itself became the most valuable form of knowledge: "What presides over the poem is not the most lucid intelligence, the sharpest sensibility or the subtlest feelings, but experience as a whole."[5]

This impulse towards defining artistic work as a form of knowledge rooted in experience would reverberate throughout the world. Also in 1944, understanding that shifts in US policy would enable Nazis and war criminals to become the architects of a new war, defined as the Cold War, Charles Olson resigned from his post at the Office of War Information in the Roosevelt Administration in order to become, of all things, a poet, the one vocation he felt might encompass enough force to face the brutality past and to come. Poet Robert Duncan's 1944 "The Homosexual in Society," a landmark declaration for human liberation, would uncannily and with great prescience pick up on the terms of the age as he condemned the apportionment of freedom or humanity to any particular group. In a discussion of poet Hart Crane's lionization by a "cult" of homosexuality, Duncan wrote: "Where the Zionists of homosexuality have laid claim to a Palestine of their own — asserting in their miseries their nationality; Crane's suffering, his rebellion and his love are sources of poetry for him, not because they are what makes him different from his fellow-men, but because he saw in them his link to mankind; he saw in them his share in universal human experience."[6] This potential universality of human experience, something Césaire would so vehemently emphasize had been denied to colonized people, was brought to prominence by Duncan, in a very different context. It is in 1944, as well, that the Algerian Jean Sénac published his first poems. A pied-noir who grew up poor and remained poor, Sénac committed himself to the revolution (resulting in the end of his friendship with Albert Camus, another Algerian pied-noir), declaring his homosexual-

---

and Sara Reguer (Columbia University Press, 2003), 97–98.
5 Césaire, *Lyric and Dramatic Poetry,* xlvii.
6 Robert Duncan, "The Homosexual in Society," *Politics* 1, no. 7 (1944): 210.

ity openly by the late 1960s, with an understanding that "this poor body also / wants its war of liberation."[7]

For Adnan, the journey to understanding alienation and locating the body's revolution would be long and intricate, leading from the Middle East and Europe to the far west of the United States, and back and forth between these poles, in place, language, and form. Instead of becoming an engineer, the opening of a new school in Beirut in 1944 provided Adnan with a unique entry point, a way to project herself out of the world imposed on her by entering the French imaginary even more fully:

> The École des Lettres was founded by an exceptional Frenchman who was for years the chief administrator of all the French schools in Lebanon and Syria... Gabriel Bounoure was his name. He was an essayist and a major critic of French literature, sending papers on literature and poetry to the prestigious literary magazine called the NRF. He became, in addition to his official government functions, the director of the École des Lettres and gathered in Beirut a small but exceptional staff of professors.... I was one of the first ten or twelve students of the École. Gabriel Bounoure's classes were the equivalent of those mystic encounters one reads about either in the great sufis' writings of the Islamic past, or in the works of German Romantic writers such as Novalis or Herman Hesse. These were not ordinary academic teachings, but rather initiations into the life of the spirit as exemplified by the works of Pascal and Descartes or the poems of Baudelaire, Gérard de Nerval and Rimbaud. I entered literature through the grand door, I discovered the golden rule of the mind. I participated for three or four years in an experiment that Plato himself would have envied.[8]

---

[7] Jean Sénac, "Le Prince d'Aquitain," in *Oeuvres Poétiques* (Actes Sud, 1999), 602. Translation by Kai Krienke.

[8] Adnan, "Growing Up to Be a Woman Writer in Lebanon," 17.

The Egyptian writer Edmond Jabès, as well, was touched by Gabriel Bounoure:

> I was living in such an intellectual turmoil that Gabriel Bounoure became my life-raft. Today Bounoure is forgotten — an unforgivable injustice, I think.... He was considered a critic mainly focused on the past. This is wrong: his last essays, on René Char, on Henri Michaux, as well as the letters he wrote young philosophers such as Jacques Derrida, prove to the contrary his extraordinary openness to modernity... I should add that Bounoure himself was split between Western culture and his passion for the culture of the Orient which he discovered through living there for more than thirty years, first in Lebanon, then in Cairo and finally in Morocco, as a teacher and cultural advisor. His influence in those countries was enormous, especially in Lebanon. In Beirut he founded 'L'École des Lettres,' which made its mark on several generations of intellectuals. An avenue of the city is named after him.[9]

Bounoure's presence was felt far and wide, not only by those already mentioned but across generations and cultures, from the great Orientalist Louis Massignon (teacher of the extraordinary anthropologist Germaine Tillion, French resistance fighter, survivor of Ravensbrück, and courier between Saadi Yacef of the FLN and President de Gaulle during the war in Algeria); to poet and playwright Georges Shehadé, born in Alexandria, he spent much of his life in Lebanon and was a longtime friend of Adnan; Lebanese poet Salah Stétié; Algerian novelist Assia Djebar; and, quite significantly, Moroccan poet and former political prisoner Abdellatif Laâbi, founder, in 1966, of the essential magazine *Souffles*. It was under Bounoure's tutelage that Adnan found her true calling:

---

9   Edmond Jabès, with Marcel Cohen, *From the Desert to the Book* (Station Hill, 1990), 52.

> This is where and when I convinced myself that poetry
> was the purpose of life, poetry as counter-profession, as an
> expression of personal and mental freedom, as perpetual
> rebellion. Poetry became a revolution, and a permanent
> voyage. With a few friends I felt I was living a parallel life,
> a life which cut all ties with home and country. I can say
> that I experienced the feeling of knowing what angels could
> be. The city itself changed in my imagination. It became an
> enchanted small town, orange trees perfuming some of its
> streets, movies and music becoming one with my thoughts.
> I was living at home but not seeing my parents any more, or
> seeing them as through a fog. I think this is what is meant by
> being enraptured.
>
> Gabriel Bounoure treated us as privileged children of
> enlightenment. There was an equality in fervor, a fullness.
> Body and soul were one. Rimbaud and Baudelaire became
> more familiar to us than anybody we knew or could know.
> They took residence in Beirut. Along with Rilke. And Gérard
> de Nerval, who had written in the late nineteenth century
> a 'Voyage to the Orient', came back resuscitated among us.
> Gabriel Bounoure called him Gérard, and Gérard was one
> of us. The ten or twelve students of the École des Lettres
> became thirty or forty, in a few years, but they did not dilute
> the intensity of the first years, rather they caught the fever,
> joined the paradise.[10]

I have chosen to dwell on some of these details because the poles of Adnan's worlds do not always extend into each other, or into the familiar zones of each other's audiences, causing deceptions and illusions to abound. The dictates of the North American academy, for instance, have embraced a quite decontextualized version of what comes through French, concentrating on theory but leaving out its roots in debates around colonialism and the war in Algeria, as well as the aftermaths of those phenomena. This creates a sense of familiarity with the subject, even though

---

10 Adnan, "Growing Up to Be a Woman Writer in Lebanon," 17–18.

that seeming familiarity is almost completely removed from the import of actual events, debates, and allegiances. The vocabulary and structure of this thought has seeped into almost all the poetic terrain Adnan's American readers might find themselves inhabiting. At the same time, the academy has also created the field of post-colonialism, based almost entirely on Anglophone histories, sources, and assumptions, leaving the world of French empire that oversaw Adnan's cultural and political formation largely unknown. And these are just a few of the many blocs of thought, knowledge, and experience that buttress and contextualize her work.

Having been brought up, in Adnan's words, "to consider France the center of the world," she knew that it was "only a matter of time" before she would find her way to Paris. In 1949, with Bounoure's intervention, she finally accepted a scholarship to study philosophy at the Sorbonne. Like the teenage Diane di Prima, devouring Arthur Schopenhauer that same year in the Brooklyn Public Library until she encountered John Keats, Adnan sensed that philosophy "after Hölderlin and Heidegger," found its "greatest expression in poetry."[11] In 1955, Adnan moved to the United States to pursue postgraduate studies. With the American language would come completely new blocs of thought, knowledge, and experience that further layered Adnan's approach to expression and form, opening her to the possibility of a political awakening and confrontation with her own alienation as a colonial subject. In 1958, Adnan began teaching at Dominican College in San Rafael, a position she held until 1972, and it was then she began writing poetry again, but language had become a zone of great conflict.

> It was during the Algerian war of independence. The morning paper was regularly bringing news of Algerians being killed in the war, or news of the atrocities that always seem

---

[11] "Introduction: Biographical and Career Highlights," in Lisa Suhair Majaj and Amal Amireh, eds., *Etel Adnan: Critical Essays on the Arab-American Writer and Artist* (McFarland & Company, 2001), 14.

> to accompany large scale violence. I became suddenly, and rather violently, conscious that I had naturally and spontaneously taken sides, that I was emotionally a participant in the war, and I resented having to express myself in French...I realized that I couldn't write freely in a language that faced me with deep conflict. I was disturbed in one fundamental realm of my life: the domain of meaningful self-expression.[12]

It was at that point that Adnan began to paint, leading her, eventually, to claim that she "painted in Arabic," the language that colonial circumstances had dispossessed her of. Her experience, if not already abundantly evident, defies simple categorization: Though she had once written in French and now writes exclusively in English, she is most decidedly an Arab writer. So how is one to define her, and who will lay claim to her?

In a recent interview, Abdellatif Laâbi, who continues to write in French, responded to the inevitable question about language, a response that could just as easily apply, in different ways, to Adnan:

> What is important is not the language in which they write, but what they do with that language.... Does their mother tongue disappear the moment they write? It's a good question and it must be raised. What must be done with these writers is to see how different linguistic registers are molded into their writing. That's perhaps what makes the particular soul, the breath, and the musicality of those writings.[13]

In fact, the example of Adnan's work should force us back into the historical dimensions of multilingualism and the poly-vocal, and away from the consumer driven need to define and categorize.

To fully explore the layers of memory needed to turn these experiences inside out would take many years and it is, perhaps,

---

12 Adnan, "Growing Up to Be a Woman Writer in Lebanon," 15.
13 "The Abdellatif Laâbi Interview," interview by Christopher Schaefer, *The Quarterly Conversation*, June 11, 2013, 4–5.

only in *Paris, When It's Naked,* published in 1993, that Adnan is able to fully face the earlier consequences. The book is the testimony of a lover whose conscience is stricken, whose awareness has been pierced by the fruit of other knowledge and experience. The lover is Adnan herself, the object of her desire is Paris, and the forbidden fruits are her past and present allegiances. The relentless honesty, openness, and accumulated memory implicit in Adnan's writing probe the idea of Europe as margin and center in ways that are increasingly important for us to grasp. Describing an encounter with a Parisian friend, Adnan writes:

> Paris is beautiful. It aches to say so, one's arms are never big enough to hug such an immensity. Claude can say it innocently. It's harder for me to say so, it's also more poignant. It tears me apart. Paris is the heart of a lingering colonial power, and that knowledge goes to bed with me every night. When I walk in this city I plunge into an abyss, I lose myself in contemplation, I experience ecstasy, an ecstasy which I know to be also a defeat. Look, look how ugly are the Arab Quarter's pimps, how dehumanized the Algerians who squat in it, how destroyed their women, how degrading their prostitution to the very ones who vote for their expulsion. And I consider this monstrous being called Paris to be beautiful.[14]

At the same time, Adnan never assumes the role of victim. Her gaze penetrates the cityscape, the objects and people inhabiting it, but never at the cost of sparing herself, of abdicating responsibility. She roams the sites that had been projected onto the now distant but ever-present soil of Lebanon, implanted within her through language, in order to interrogate herself through those very signs, cultural icons and ways of life that once stood for both total liberation and defeat. But the relations are never simple, for this amalgam of the "implanted" has formed, as well, the deepest recesses of her being. As she writes:

---

14 Etel Adnan, *Paris, When It's Naked* (Post-Apollo Press, 1993), 7–8.

> Dear Parents, why did you lie to me? You told me the sky was blue while we watched it together, in Beirut, by the sea, and the sunset was a flame. You fooled a whole generation, then you destroyed it, the city is destroyed. The sky is not high either, as you taught me, it is so low, low, below my ceiling. I wonder if the rain will come in and spoil my books as it does my bones. I feel them, tonight, these bones you gave me. Neither one of you ever saw Paris, or intended to. Your trains never ended at Gare de Lyon. You thought France as an intruder into the order of things as you knew them. Paris was a place of perdition, you said. Be reassured: I did not lose my soul in it. I only lost my illusions. And you.[15]

Adnan does not simply refer to aspects of a place, a culture, or a people; rather, she partakes in and of them. And her range is exhilarating: from retracing the steps of Djuna Barnes, saying "hello to her at least once a day" and "dreaming of her," to recording the very same colonialized pain, aspirations, and defeats of the cogs that make the great machine of Paris operate so smoothly:

> A lot of immigrants work in factories and create a major problem: how to make them work without having them breathe our air, live in our cities, or look at our wives and husbands? This equation has not been solved. They go on with their menial jobs, genuinely happy to make a living. They love rain, asphalt, warm bread, goat cheese, industrial oils, long grocery hours. They see work as energy and life. People think it's incongruous that they smile in traffic jams. Paris is the machine that eats them and could reject them. What would you say if you became spit? You wouldn't know it. Spit doesn't think; it evaporates pretty fast. I'm not going to spit carelessly anymore. Out of respect for the street.[16]

---
15 Ibid., 101.
16 Ibid., 59.

Adnan's next major phase of encounter, through her embrace of the counterculture and activities against the war in Vietnam, added yet another layer to an increasingly intricate and complex amalgam of experiences and perspectives:

> The cultural revolution that was taking place in America had Vietnam as one of its sources, and one of its consequences was that the war issue became also a literary rallying point, a concern for the poets, and a dynamic subject matter. Poets wrote against the war, or rather, fought against the war through poetry [...]. I was entering the English language like an explorer: each word came to life, expressions were creations, adverbs were immensely immense, verbs were shooting arrows, a simple preposition like 'in' or 'out' an adventure![17]

It was in this context — as a teenager in the late 1960s, drawn into a life of continuous encounter, outside, on the streets — that I first found Adnan's poetry, through the Walter Lowenfels anthology *Where Is Vietnam? American Poets Respond,* one of many collections featuring poets who fought on formal grounds but were able to meet in political solidarity. Adnan's poem, "The Enemy's Testament," one of her first written in English, is narrated from the point of view of a Vietnamese soldier; in the second stanza, she writes:

> They got me out of my lair
> for I was infesting my own land,
> and they, the foreigners, came to
> liberate me,
>   liberate me of my share.[18]

---

17 Adnan, "Growing Up to Be a Woman Writer in Lebanon," 16.
18 Etel Adnan, "The Enemy's Testament," in *Where Is Vietnam? American Poets Respond,* ed. Walter Lowenfels (Anchor Doubleday, 1967), 3.

In the voice of another, in a new language, Adnan was able to begin writing her way through and out of the terms she had been given, testing the sound and play, the give and take of words like "land," "foreign," and "liberate." This period also signals a further immersion in American poetry and poetics and an awareness of the singular import of the period; as Adnan recollects in *Journey to Mount Tamalpais*:

> The early workshops participated in the newness of the world. Yes, they were at the very beginning of the Sixties, yes, they participated in the prophetic spirit of a decade which has its equals in History in the Pre-Socratics, or, closer to us, in the decade which preceded the Russian Revolution and was made by Malevich, Tatlin, Kandinsky... This time a whole nation was again being involved in a Great Experiment, unabashedly, through street marches, songs, underground movies and millions of silent events which tried to uproot a culture and plant a new one, a new forest.[19]

While involvement in this "Great Experiment" forms a significant layer of her language, there is a breadth of permission and emotional directness in Adnan's work that allows phenomena into the field of the poem that are increasingly rare on the American scene, a cross between the mysticism of medieval figures like Rabia and Hildegard of Bingen, the mysterious lucidity of Emily Dickinson or Lorine Niedecker, and the passion of H.D. Yet she is also more than capable of embracing the litanic line of Walt Whitman or Allen Ginsberg, refusing to succumb to the dictates of political or poetic correctness, constantly crossing the boundaries that would posit one world there and a completely other world here. Much more than bearing witness, her work enacts what Ed Sanders has called "eleutherarchy," that "dance of freedom" that "makes reality."[20]

---

19 Etel Adnan, *Journey to Mount Tamalpais* (Post-Apollo Press, 1985), 37.
20 Ed Sanders, *Investigative Poetry* (Spuyten Duyvil, 2018), 9.

Before the prominence of the sun in Adnan's 1980 masterpiece, *Arab Apocalypse,* there was the moon of Adnan's first book, *Moonshots,* dedicated to "the virginity of the moon" and published in Beirut in 1966. This was a book that somehow found its way to me around 1970 or '71, a period in which yet another key phase of Adnan's work would begin to unfold. Sandwiched between the assassination of Malcolm X in 1965 and the assassinations of Martin Luther King Jr. and Robert F. Kennedy in 1968, the Arab defeat in the June War of 1967 signaled a sea-change in American cultural politics and foreign policy priorities. Heroic images of Israeli commandos came to take the place of dead American GIs, fighting an increasingly unpopular war. The ensuing years would see the rise of evangelical fundamentalism, the idealization of Israel as a military giant that knew how to "get the job done," and the exacerbation of one-sided policies that would continue to lead the US into one disaster after another right up to the present.

From that point on, almost everything coming into the US from the Middle East was filtered through a mainstream Zionist narrative, from political history and cinematic representation to the availability and boundaries of novels and poetry. The key component in this propaganda war was the utter obliteration of any Palestinian reality, including even the idea of its very existence as a historical actuality or entity. Resistance to the ongoing trauma of colonialism and the fall of Palestine — the Naqba or "disaster" — became an active force shaping the imaginative horizons of US artistic and political culture, a process akin to what Native American artist Jimmie Durham describes as a fundamental component of American reality:

> Nothing could be more central to American reality than the relationships between Americans and American Indians, yet those relationships are of course the most invisible and the most lied about. The lies are not simply a denial; they con-

stitute a new world, the world in which American culture is located.[21]

Thus, the suppression and obliteration of a particular history becomes a motive force, the engine not only driving but enabling and enhancing various political and cultural fictions. In this context, it isn't surprising that Adnan was one of the first poets to specifically link the colonization of the New World and the destruction of Native America with the destruction and displacement of Palestine, something that became a central trope of Palestinian poetry and, later, Arab poetry as a whole.

On the cultural front, the movement to establish such a Palestinian and Arab existence and reality was taken up by a handful of people, and forward progress was very slow. One of the first books to appear, a bilingual selection of poetry called *A Lover from Palestine and Other Poems: An Anthology of Palestinian Poetry,* edited by Egyptian scholar Abdelwahab Elmessiri, with illustrations by the Palestinian artist and translator Kamal Boullata, came out in 1970. Boullata, also a close friend of Adnan, was a pioneering voice in championing Palestinian and Arabic culture. His still-unexcelled anthology of Arab women poets, *Women of the Fertile Crescent,* in which Adnan is included, appeared in 1978, followed by *The World of Rashid Hussein,* a selection of work by the exiled Palestinian poet, done in collaboration with Mirène Ghossein. But these were very lonely voices, with little or no institutional backing or support. It is in the context of these kinds of projects, and the surrounding political world centered on Palestine and the wars in Lebanon, as well as her own journalistic work in Beirut in the 1970s, that Adnan's Arab and Arab American identity takes its particular shape. Her landmark 1978 novel, *Sitt Marie Rose,* based on the story of a Syrian woman living in Lebanon who betrays her affiliations by siding with Palestinian refugees, only to find herself kidnapped and murdered, placed Adnan at the forefront of

---

21 Cited in Rebecca Solnit's *Storming the Gates of Paradise: Landscapes for Politics* (University of California Press, 2007), 32.

chroniclers of the effects of war in the chaos of states formed in the wake of colonialism. The novel took on a life of its own, finding very different fates and trajectories in each of its translations, while presaging a whole generation of women writers exploring the region and its conflicts with a new range of directness and intimacy.

In Adnan's work there are angels and astronauts, Algerians, Indians and Canaanites, women who walk veiled or naked, prisoners and freedom-fighters, white men on the moon and red men in Alcatraz, Charlie Mingus next to Gamal Abdel Nasser and Charlie Mingus at Baalbek, George Jackson and San Quentin alongside the fedayeen and refugee camps of Jordan and Lebanon: It is a world where "the dead are coming back in order to fight again / because the living are cowards!" Adnan's texts present a continual challenge — whether in the dramatic visual field of *Arab Apocalypse,* strewn with a hieroglyphic idiolect that ventures where words cannot go; the cinematic jump cuts in character and perspective of *Sitt Marie Rose;* the juggernaut of the *Beirut-Hell Express;* the relentlessly deceptive depth of epistemological inquiry of *There;* or the almost unbearable scrutiny of *Paris, When It's Naked.* Where many are blinded by the effects of a mythology, Adnan remains focused, unflinching, a teller of sequences and events:

    o Palestine

o shipwreck
one hears at night the
moaning of your valleys
where even the dead have some tears

And later in *Jebu,* a poem of ancient gods and present catastrophes, these extraordinary lines resound:

Palestine is a land planted by eyes
Refusing to be closed

I focus on these figures because Adnan's establishment of the poetic fact of Palestine creates a ground of the real she can then fully inhabit, not in the simplistic and much exploited figure of the exiled writer but in the paradox of Heraclitus: by being estranged from that with which she is most familiar, Adnan is equally at home anywhere in the world, and that is a deep a source of her unique powers. As poet Benjamin Hollander wrote in an homage to Adnan:

> The first time we met, we talked at length among a throng of people, as we inadvertently isolated ourselves in an alcove on the first floor of a friend's house, talking poetry, politics, the Middle East, baseball, film, while the so-called party was going on upstairs. It was then I realized what I was to discover over and over about Etel's presence: the reality of it, the directness of it, the warmness of it, as we sat down close and bent over listening to each other, her manner, her bearing, her being — right there, the real thing. "Poets," Etel once wrote me, "are great realists (even when they see angels, if they do, like Rilke does)." Etel is a realist of ideal integrity whose love for others radiates outward... She gives herself vulnerable permission to simultaneously inhabit and confront a spectrum of emotions in a moment, joy and sadness at the same time, an inner life which shows itself about her person, which is inclusive, without question.[22]

Simply put, Adnan's presence, and the presence of her experience in many places at once, has opened up cultural, political, and imaginative space that did not previously exist in this country, or that had been occupied by various kinds of interference. The occasion of this collection is momentous since, though she has been living in the US for more than fifty years, the pleasures and generative force of her work remain the privilege of far too

---

22 Benjamin Hollander, "Etel's Presence," in *Homage to Etel Adnan*, ed. Lindsey Boldt, Steve Dickison, and Samantha Giles (Post-Apollo Press, 2012), 51.

few readers in this country. To be in the presence of Etel Adnan's work is to finally grasp that poetry's only ideology is attention and, in her case, that attention is turned to the great human themes: love, death, war, the meaning of meaning, the extinction and creation of words and worlds, of being and beings. But that attention is always activated: a call to look more closely, a call to think more deeply, a call to put yourself in someone else's proverbial shoes, a call to find your voice and raise it, a call to remain steadfast, no matter what. I have always felt her there, ready to respond. She has recognized things in me I could barely articulate, and she has never withdrawn her attention, no matter where my journey has taken me. One could hardly ask for anything more.

26

In Friendship, for John Wieners

2015

> Why is it a major poet seems impossible
> to write about, while the ingratiating success yields
> odes of dazzling elegy & national award.
> — John Wieners, in "The Cut"[1]

I learned about the death of John Wieners in 2002 through a phone call from poet and old friend Duncan McNaughton. He had died on my birthday and I was attending an academic conference, very rare for me, on the partition of India, Ireland, and Palestine. I had gone mainly to be with old friends who seldom had a chance to gather. But after speaking to Duncan, I realized there was no one there I could share the news with, or at least no one who would immediately grasp the significance of the loss. The details came later, from John's stalwart friend Jim Dunn, about how John had left a party and collapsed on his way home, found by a parking lot attendant and taken to the hospital. Not having any ID on him, it was only through the persistence of a social worker and some nurses that he was identified at all. This

---

[1] John Wieners, "The Cut // *After Reading Gerard Malanga's Interview with Charles Olson in The Paris Review, Summer 1970,*" in *Cultural Affairs in Boston: Poetry & Prose 1956–1985*, ed. Raymond Foye (Black Sparrow Press, 1988), 155.

scenario almost played out John's answer to scholar Robert van Hallberg's 1974 question, posed in a rare interview: "For whom do you write?" he asked. "For the poetical, the people," Wieners responded, "Not for myself, merely. Or ever. Only for the better, warm, human loving, kind person. The guy on the street who might hold open a door for you...stops to give you instructions, spares some change, lets you in his bookshop. Friends I take for granted, like the future."

My encounter with John Wieners was early, and personal. That is, I met him as a teenager while hanging out either at what was then Gordon Cairnie's Grolier Books or the Temple Bar Bookshop, run by Jim and Gene, the O'Neil brothers, both in Cambridge. Cambridge MASS, with an emphasis on the long broad "A" that the rest of the country once might have been familiar with through President John F. Kennedy. Since then it's only been an occasional movie or, among poets, the singular voice of Eileen Myles. That's part of a bigger story, in which the Boston John Wieners came from and mainly lived in was/is an actual place, peopled by a particular accent that, in John's case, was immediately recognizable, almost archaic.

This first encounter would have most likely taken place sometime in 1969. I had just become a teenager and was drawn to everything *outside* of school: playing hockey at the Commons; taking in triple features at the Stuart in the combat zone while ducking the truant officer; shooting pool from one end of town to the other; going up the fire escapes to sneak into the Boston Garden with friends from the North End; sitting in the right field grandstands at Fenway for less than two bucks; listening to young men, not that much older than me, seeking asylum from the draft at the Arlington Street Church; talking to kids from Roxbury selling the Black Panther Party paper which I bought religiously every week and read from cover to cover; gravitating from bookstores to demonstrations and back again, depending on what might be happening in the streets of our world.

I often found myself in what might have seemed strange circumstances, but I never questioned them. All the while I raided my parents' bookshelves, loaded with little magazines of the

1950s and '60s: *Black Mountain Review, Big Table, Evergreen, Yugen,* and so many others, never thinking it unusual. When Jack Kerouac died in November 1969, I was irate, knowing he'd been forgotten, and viscerally feeling that he'd somehow been assassinated by society. I knew that most of his books were out of print because you couldn't find the ones we had at home in bookstores. I asked family friend Vincent Ferrini, the Gloucester poet to whom Charles Olson's *The Maximus Poems* were first addressed as a series of letters, what to do. He suggested I write to Allen Ginsberg, which I did. I then suddenly found a use for school and proceeded to write a militant twenty-five-page typed single-spaced paper in which I went on the offensive, reviewing Kerouac's work for a teacher I was sure would be uninterested or taken aback by my attitude, and I poured it on, making damn sure that would be the case.

Not long after Kerouac's death came the news of Charles Olson, going into hospital in New York. Through a conversation at one of the bookstores, I was given to understand that a book dealer had appeared with a stack of books for Olson to sign. Outraged, I wrote a near-libelous letter to the dealer who was ready to sue me until he heard how old I was. Throughout, John was a presence. I would see him at the Grolier and we'd walk to the Temple Bar, or the other way around. Sometimes I'd sit with him at the Hayes-Bickford's in Harvard Square. Other times I found myself at gatherings with a group of older people, not knowing exactly what they might be going through, but never feeling unwanted or uncomfortable. Along the way he'd give me books or broadsides, always signed to me: *Ace of Pentacles, Asylum Poems, The Hotel Wentley Poems, Nerves, Pressed Wafer, A Letter to Charles Olson.* Once he gave me an old copy of *Amiel's Journal,* by the Swiss philosopher-poet Henri Amiel, published in the 1880s. When my mother and I went to Olson's funeral in Gloucester, John was there, among the pallbearers, who included Ferrini, Peter Anastas (another old Gloucester friend), legendary patron of the arts and Frontier Press publisher Harvey Brown, scholar and translator Charles Boer, and poets Ed Dorn, Allen Ginsberg, and Ed Sanders.

"FOLLOW THE PERSON"

Back in Boston, there was a visit to poet Steve Jonas's apartment, somewhere near the Charles Street Jail, on the other side of Beacon Hill, in the palpably absent shadow of John's beloved Scollay Square, victim of the juggernaut wrecking ball of "urban renewal." There was a reading at the Charles Street Meeting House where I took pictures, as I often did then, with black and white film that I developed and printed, some of them gracing the walls of the Grolier or given to the poets when I had the chance. From that night there were pictures of John along with Denise Levertov, Anne Sexton, and Ron Loewinsohn. I always thought the reading must have been for some political cause but everyone I asked in Boston over the years couldn't remember or said no such event took place. It was only in 2012, while working on a *Lost & Found* project with poet Joanne Kyger, that she sent me the copy of a letter from John to her, dated February 22, 1970, in which he wrote: "Monday evening I gave a benefit for the Chicago 7 at the Charles Street Meeting House with Denise Levertov, Anne Sexton, Ron Loewinsohn, James Tate, etc." Jonas had died just twelve days before John's letter was written. I remember the shock wave that both Olson and Jonas's deaths had sent through this familial group of older poets that I found myself in the company of. I'm not sure what exactly I understood, but I knew that these events, like so many of the things we were demonstrating about, were momentous.

The intricacies of this particular history, what the late poet Gerrit Lansing has called "the occult school of Boston," is one of the many chapters of North American cultural and political life from the second half of the twentieth century yet to be fully documented or even remotely understood by those who weren't, in at least some way, part of them. While celebrated throughout his lifetime as a unique and masterful lyric poet by the most important poets of the period, the availability of Wieners's work has varied wildly. Receiving no critical acknowledgment or recognition during and even after his lifetime, gathering the work has mainly been the task of dedicated friends.

When most of his early small press books had become increasingly hard to find, Raymond Foye edited two superb volumes for Black Sparrow Press, *Selected Poems 1958–1984* (1986), and *Cultural Affairs in Boston: Poetry & Prose 1956–1985* (1988), gathering previous collections and uncollected works, as well as the few extant interviews that Wieners had given (with Foye, Charlie Shively, and Robert van Hallberg). The introductions to those books, by Ginsberg and Robert Creeley, provided, for the time, the clearest responses and assessments of his work. William Corbett, at some point, published a facsimile edition of *The Hotel Wentley Poems,* feeling the need for people to read something akin to the original version of that landmark book, published by the late Dave Haselwood as the first title of Auerhahn Press in 1958. Over the years, many people have sheltered, gathered, pirated, written about, and published the work of John Wieners, and a complete list would become a who's who of the poetry world of the past six decades. Happily, even after his death, new friends have emerged to continue building on this legacy. Robert Dewhurst has combed archives, letters, and leads of all kinds, to find poems that were either unknown or unpublished as he prepares a long-overdue *Collected Poems,* while Seth Stewart has edited journals and gathered, transcribed, and annotated the correspondence, covering important exchanges between Wieners and Olson, Robert Duncan, Robert Creeley, Denise Levertov, Michael Rumaker, Edward Dorn, Diane di Prima, Amiri Baraka, Philip Whalen, Joanne Kyger, and many others. As Stewart has so eloquently put it, "I consider these projects together as a *habeas corpus* mission, an effort to 'produce the body' of Wieners' thought, works, and life, liberating him from the institutions that subsumed him, that 'official verse culture' that could not accommodate a poor, homosexual, visionary poet who refused to be simply one of those things."

II.

In a 1972 text, Wieners wrote: "Since 1955, poetry or verse as some would prefer it be called has, despite all forebodings that it was dying, taken through a handful of writers in the United States, a stranglehold on established modes of thought, analysis, and attention." Marking this at 1955 meant, for Wieners, recognition of a now very obscure but enormously influential poem, Ed Marshall's "Leave the Word Alone," included in Donald M. Allen's landmark 1960 anthology *The New American Poetry*. He goes on to mention, among others, Charlie Parker, a figure that looms large for the poets of the period. Jack Kerouac delineated Parker's significance very particularly when he talked of bop as "the language of America's inevitable Africa," but an idiom "no one understands because the language isn't alive in the land yet." Making such a language live — a language arrived at in relation to the world, as a statement about the kind of world that had come into being — is certainly a strand running throughout the artistic stance of the period, in every medium, and part of the "stranglehold on established modes of thought, analysis, and attention" that Wieners refers to.

This troubling of generic representation is also, in this case, the multiply complex individual — John Wieners — that, as Seth Stewart emphasizes, could not be accommodated by either "official verse culture" or "the universe of discourse." With the greater availability of Wieners's work — particularly the journals and letters that express his stance towards the world, his thought — his crucial absence in the overly generalized historical record can start to be addressed.

While the universe that John dwelt in was filled with harsh reality — forced electroshock and insulin therapy, poverty, addiction, despair — he forged a world of truth and beauty out of it. His absolute mastery of form should, by all critical criteria, have put to shame all of his conventional prize-winning and celebrated contemporaries purportedly working in traditional forms. But such a thing could not be for it would signal an admittance of reality and historical consciousness into a world of propaganda, disinformation, and absolute counterfactual fabrication. In the face of a systemic violence that attempts to destroy any lasting record of the contradictory real, relegating the very material of our most intimate history to oblivion, I have no doubt that John's work will remain as an act of singular courage and testimony to the lives we actually lived.

27

Still Standing, for Gil Sorrentino

I grew up in an environment with a very realistic and somewhat jaundiced view of the public art world. My late father, Albert Alcalay, was a painter, and I remember him sitting around with other painter friends imagining all the awful things they might do to their dealers once the revolution came. I had a very clear understanding, as well, that artists, almost no matter what their stature, actually worked to a very small audience. This was certainly true of many of our family friends, like Charles Olson or Vincent Ferrini, for instance. As I began to write, it *wasn't* hard to think of myself as a "writer," however unformed that idea might have been — the trick was making a living. In 1975, in the midst of a dizzying variety of jobs and kinds of work (described at length in my book *Scrapmetal*), I decided to take a class at the New School with the poet and novelist Toby Olson. After Toby left, the class, to my great excitement, was to be taken over by Gilbert Sorrentino whose work I was familiar with through the cherished set of *KULCHUR* that I had liberated, along with *Black Mountain Review*, *Big Table*, *Evergreen*, *Yugen*, and so many other important little magazines, from my parents' library. I also had a number of Gil's books by then, both poetry and prose: *The Darkness Surrounds Us*, *The Perfect Fiction*, *Black and White*, *Steelwork*, *The Sky Changes*, and *Imaginative Qualities of Actual Things*. I found these books astonishing on many levels. Having been surrounded by the books, music, and art of the 1950s and '60s growing up, my relationship to the artists of that period was more like a kid with baseball cards: I knew the rosters frontwards and backwards, the stars, the utility players, the veterans, and the rookies.

In Gil's work I saw elements that were both highly indebted to that universe so familiar to me and yet completely unique. In fact, as I begin to understand the current reception of Gil's work, I am more and more aware that my own experience of both him and his work is markedly different from readers coming to him later, when his more well-known novels had become available. Just as there was, for better or worse, a "New American Poetry," so also was there a "New American Prose." And certainly Gil's work incubated in the now much neglected prose of that period, the work of Hubert Selby Jr., LeRoi Jones/Amiri Baraka, Robert Creeley, Douglas Woolf, Edward Dorn, Philip Whalen, Michael Rumaker, and a number of others as well. This was an exceptional time in all senses and more recently I have come to characterize the twenty-five-year postwar period of American creativity, 1950 to 1975, as comparable to already sanctioned and "great" historical periods of creative production, from western textbook examples like the Elizabethans or the Romantics, to other notable times and places, like the height of the Abbasid period in Iraq, the western caliphate in al-Andalus, or the Tang dynasty in China.

Gil's class soon became a focal point for me and there was a revolving and evolving group of us who attended with an almost religious adherence. Listening to him talk in class we felt exhilarated at being privy to what were undoubtedly hard-won truths and primary experiences of what now seemed legendary times. When I discovered Gil's walking route to class I would time myself perfectly to casually bump into him around 12th Street and Seventh Avenue. Likewise, when I figured his routine of getting the morning paper, since we lived just a few blocks away from each other, I made sure to coincide for the five or ten minutes of precious banter before he headed back home to work. Soon I found myself a frequent guest at the Sorrentino's, sometimes for lunch, sometimes for dinner. Before I knew it, I found my skills being put to use, "building boards," as Gil used to say, constructing shelves, storage units, and so forth, including the big carpentry project during the unforgettable summer of the Son of Sam.

Throughout, I felt a very familiar sense of the relationship between the "outside" and the "inside," almost seeing myself in Christopher Sorrentino, as he and his parents faced the obvious stupidity of much of the world out there. I felt I was being RE-EDUCATED, consciously now, in so much of what I thought I already to some extent knew. Most importantly, I felt that I was getting firsthand transmission of that bleak and magical time that had words like BOP, BEAT, and ABSTRACT ART attached to it, even though quite a bit of it was already familiar to me, but from a child's perspective. At some point Gil suggested I stop taking his classes and, as he put it, "study something real." I promptly enrolled at City College and began Ancient Greek and Latin, but, incorrigible, I still went to his class. In 1978, I took off on a journey to the old world, seeing the places and people of my immigrant-refugee parents' previous life. And during those two years I conducted a correspondence with Gil that still astonishes me. I have no idea what I might have been writing to him then but I am still amazed how his words on the page caused me, right out in public, to have convulsive fits of laughter. Laced in with his never-ending array of comic detail steeped in the minutiae of all forms of popular culture and great art, there was embedded a fierce and uncompromising assault on mediocrity and the grim trappings of American culture and life. There was, as well, an uncanny ability to incorporate everything at hand, to move deftly from one thing to another and have it appear completely seamless, as in this letter from the 28th of December, 1978:

LISTS OF GREATS AS RECENTLY GIVEN US BY THE TIMES BOOK REVIEW: John Cheever, John Updike, Irwin Shaw, Harry Crews. Denis Donoghue did end-of-year piece on "moddun poetree" in which he said that Charles Olson must be considered, along with Lowell, as a major poet. No other

> poets maudits were mentioned, and I assume that Chas. was thrown in to show us all that DD is no fucking stick in the mud. Blast and damn them all. Crazed Hasidim in Crown Heights literally wrecked their precinct house, injured 68 cops. Why? They're sick of the breakdown of law and order in their neighborhood. It just strikes me, by the way, that that phrase was invented by the Divine Marquis, although he had it "lore and ordure."

Throughout, Gil would refer to his own critical reception, at a time when *Mulligan Stew* was about to be published (after a string of by now famous rejections), while other novels, some to be renamed, were still in the drawer or circulating:

> My other two novels still swim out there in limbo, maybe if STEW gets some good reviews some courageous publisher will take them on, but I doubt it. Latest rejection of GHOST TALK is one of the classics: All dialogue, but no narrative to hold it together. This delivered as if I had somehow <u>wanted</u> to use narrative but, gosh, just didn't know how to do it. The letter was signed by someone with a monicker like Renfrew Dalton Cunningham—an admirer of Updike and you can bet your onion bagel on it.

Like so many of the painters of the 1950s that Gil admired, to whom success came late, his attitude towards the reception of *Mulligan Stew* was one of delight and bewildered amusement. As someone used to his books being remaindered or being published by small presses with print runs of 1000 copies or less, this was a new world:

> But as far as my fiendish STEW goes (a copy of which is "winging" its way to the sultry confines of olde Ierusalemme and that little street that Time Forgot upon which you "live") your industrious correspondent stands in starke amayze. To wit: rave reviews in Pub Weekly, Kirkus, Library Journal, Chicago Sun-Times, Sat. Review, a four-page mini-essay by

Kenner in Harper's, and a love letter by that doyen of N.Y. lit-hip in the Times, John Leonard (!). Barney has gone back to press for a second printing of 10,000 and the first printing (cloth) is all gone, the paper going fast. BOOKS & CO and 8TH STREET can't keep the little darling in stock, Is this your old nail-holder and hammer-getter talkin' on ya? Oc! as Arnaut Daniel would say. So you see, Willie, if you live to be 50, never engage in immoral acts, eschew the demon rum, and change your mind about politics constantly, you too may become a Famous Author. I am also going to get a review in next Sunday's TBR, but I don't know by whom. Grove may even take an ad out for my gamy goulash. When next you look for me, I will be the guy with the silk ascot, third from the left at the Plaza Bar, fly open, elbow couchant, geules vert, head on wrist, falcon moribund, lion toothless in left quadrant, motto: Sic Transit Gloria Swanson.

And with this success even came a British edition of the "gamy goulash," the cover of which allowed Gil to let fly at full force:

Got copies of the English MULLIGAN STEW last week. It looks good, but the jacket! Two legs in black nylons and high heels. Now I ask you! But it may sell to the fetish market, NEW BOOK BY YANK AUTHOR SHOCKS QUEEN! HOSIERY SHOPS SELL OUT OVERNIGHT! MASTURBATION ON RISE IN YORKSHIRE! WIFE COMPLAINS "I 'AVE TO DRESS UP ALL THE BLOODY TIME." PARLIAMENT TO PROBE WHAT ONE M.P. CALLS "UNDILUTED SMUT." AUTHOR ONCE WORKED FOR GROVE PRESS. CRITICS SILENT ON ISSUE. "NO FORM AT ALL" SAYS F.R. LEAVIS. GIRL READS BOOK, JOINS WHOREHOUSE. PUBLISHER SAID TO BE IN ARGENTINA. AUTHOR SAID TO COLLECT GARTER BELTS IN SPARE TIME. INTERNATIONAL INCIDENT LOOMS. "MUCK" SAYS BILLY GRAHAM IN LONDON. MINKOFF DENIES BEING EX-STUDENT. FRIEND CALLED "WILLIE" IN HIDING IN SEX KIBBUTZ. FEESER CHARGES AUTHOR WITH "HATING POETRY." LIMITED EDITION OF SEX TOME IN SHAPE OF PLASTIC LOAFER. POPE BLAMES CONTRACEPTION. CARTER THREATENS TO DROP

"FOLLOW THE PERSON"

"THOUSANDS" OF COPIES ON QUM UNLESS HOSTAGES ARE FREED. NEW JACKET DEPICTING ABE LINCOLN AT LOURDES PROPOSED. RABBI KAHANE CHARGES JEW-BAITING. MAILER TO PEN NEW REAL-LIFE NOVEL ABOUT SORRENTINO. POET CORMAN SAYS: it/is/not a/good/nov-/el. REAGAN DENIES CALIFORNIA PLAYED ROLE IN PERVERTING AUTHOR. FRANCO RISES FROM GRAVE. WILLIAM F. BUCKLEY CALLS FOR PUBLIC CRUCIFIXION. HOBOS COMPLAIN TITLE MALIGNS THEM. GLORIA STEINEM URGES WOMEN TO WEAR ANKLETS. BEGIN DENIES WEARING HEELS ON VACATION. ARAFAT ATTACKS ISRAELI HOSIERY MILL. DOW-JONES DOWN FIVE THOUSAND. HUGH HEFNER CALLS NOVEL "SICK." AUTHOR DROPPED FROM NEW SCHOOL POST. NIXON PROPOSES LEGISLATION AGAINST "DIRTY SEX." ARTS AND LETTERS GROUP STRIPS SORRENTINO OF HONORS. BRZEZINSKI REVEALS SECRET PLAN TO BOMB LONDON. TITO, CATCHING GLIMPSE OF BOOK, FINALLY DIES.

As I was contemplating "further" studies, Gil both helped me out and offered, of course, an opinion:

About CCNY: I paid them the $4.00 and they sent your transcript on, so don't worry about that. I'm glad that you are settling into some idea of how and what to study so that you won't be, as you implied in an earlier letter, a student to be a student. Your problem Willie is, if I may presume, clear to me, because it has always been my own: there is, like they say, the touch, the merest smidgen, a whisp, a soupcon, of the pedant about both of us. I basically loathe academics because they <u>pretend</u> to be pedants — the few academics I've loved ARE pedants. I put the pedant down because the worm is in <u>me</u>. I can see myself studying the Elizabethan-Jacobean masque for 20 years, easy, and writing monographs on "Anti-Nature in the Late Masques of Jonson." But, like, for real, not "academic" bullshit. Most academics, like most real people, don't know enough.

At the same time, before the idea of going to a place like Stanford could even form itself into a bare figment of Gil's imagination, there were classes at The New School (run, essentially, like sub-contracting work), and the remarkable visiting stay in Scranton, as described in June, 1979:

> My semester at Scranton, the Athens of the Poconos, is over. I delivered my "Edwin S. Quain, S.J., Memorial Lecture" in April, titled: "The Act of Creation and Its Artifact." You would have been proud. But for the fact that I was slightly drunk, sans jacket and tie, and with hands in pockets, I was the veriest model, the paradigm, nay, the cynosure, of Mr. Academo. The attendant Professors, so to speak, as it were, goggled and boggled. They still labor under the delusion that poets rush madly through the bush, leaves in their hair, fucking beavers and baying at the moon. Gibbous or otherwise. Gibbous?

Laced throughout this hilarity were some of Gil's clearest aesthetic insights and, on occasion, genuine perplexity at the meaning of his own work; in retrospect, these two facets meet and illuminate each other, as in the following excursus on "form" and the commentary on the meaning of the structure of *Mulligan Stew* which comes after, mentioning Jack O'Brien's essay that had appeared in *Parnassus*:

> I've been thinking for years now (did I ever tell you this?) about Creeley's "form is never more..." etc. O.k., I agree, but <u>what</u> is this "form?" Structure, yes? Now: what the hell is "content?" Can content be style? Can we say that "form is never more than an extension of style"? For instance, what is the "content" of a dance by Fred Astaire? Isn't a dance by Fred Astaire a formal pattern that reveals HIS style? I mean, you can get Joe Bush to do a dance that Fred Astaire has danced, via choreography etc., but it don't look like Fred A. Like a saxophonist who has mucho virtuosity and schooling and can play a chorus off a Bird record if you note it down

but that ain't Parker either. Now, taking this, ladies and gents, down the road a little into letters — what is Yeats's "content" or that of Baudelaire? The sum of the <u>whole</u> way these men, as any artist, look at the world and react to it makes for a <u>style:</u> and the way we apprehend that style is through form or, read: structure. What I'm saying is that there is no such thing as "content" at all. It has no meaning unless it has been refined into style and the style has (artistically speaking) no permanence unless it is evoked by formal patterning. The problem with the wild-man (sic) artist is that he is leaning on LITERALLY "content" — that is, THE MESSAGE. The solid citizens, like they say, always know this. The "folks" are enraged always always always by innovations in the form of art. They pretend to be shocked by the "message" but the message in a piece of slop may be as morally subversive as in a genuine work of art; the slop soothes, the other irritates, the "content" looks to be the same, but the style of the artist finds a new form; the style of the bum is nonexistent and therefore he cannot ever find or invent a form. So: we may distill this into the Sorrentino Dictum: CONTENT IS STYLE. Have I lost my marbles?

* * *

It's a marvelous essay, full of wit and terrific insights. Jack, of course, thinks it stinks, but he's wrong. The one thing he says that is really good and really on, how you say, le target, is that everything in the book is everything else or might as well be — alas, this is so. I myself am afraid to think my way back into the book, as against thinking my way OUT of it when I was writing it, because when I start to do that I get a terrible headache and, dollink, such anxiety! I mean to say, I don't understand the damn book. Oh, I understand it, but I don't see how it works the way it works. I feel a little like MacCruiskeen, the second policeman, with his amazing inventions, especially that spear with the invisible point, of which he says, on a bad day, if you try to think about it, you hurt your box! I'm working on a new novel, tentatively called BLUE PASTORAL, all about one Serge Gavotte, known as, among other things, Blue Serge: it is based on English pastoral modes: eclogue, elegy, georgics, idyll, and these modes are laid atop the "quest." In this case, the quest for "the perfect musical phrase." Oi, what fun I'm havink!

This becomes even more fun as I remember that a year or so prior to the letter above, Gil had written that "Lurch still plays his extraordinary piano, and figures to be the major character in a new book, just started, in which he figures as Serge Gavotte, known to all as Blue Serge." Lurch, of course, was a neighbor whose "extraordinary" piano could be heard through the walls. I am struck again and again, in reading these letters and thinking about my times with Gil and his family, that no matter to what fanciful or fantastic places his work could take you, it started at home, in plumbing the width and breadth of all permutations and senses of his beloved figure, the imagination. This included, of course, the inimitable recipes, like this one from August, 1978:

> I've saved my best news for last. It is a KRAFT recipe, which, if you are lucky, you should be able to whip up in Jugoslavia. If you can't get all the ingredients, you can surely improvise, or have them sent over. It's called, modestly, TOMATO MADNESS. Into a large bowl, chop rough chunks of baloney, celery, okra, and KRAFT American Cheese. Mix thoroughly with equal parts KRAFT Tomato Paste and KRAFT Bar-B-Q Sauce, until smooth and slightly sticky. Quickly shape into patties and line bottom and sides of large casserole with the patties. Dot each pattie with KRAFT Margarine, KRAFT Midget Marshmallows, and KRAFT Mandarin Oranges. Sprinkle liberally with garlic powder, oregano, KRAFT Pineapple slices, and cracked ice. Pour KRAFT Tomato Ketchup over all until the patties are completely hidden. Bake in 350 degree oven for 1 hour. Remove from oven, mix in one pint KRAFT Sour Cream, one large can beets, and three tbs. KRAFT Peanut Butter. Garnish with KRAFT Gherkins and carrot sticks, and

serve with plenty of KRAFT Vanilla Cookies, with pitchers of BROCCOLI-CHOCOLATE FIZZ. (See Recipe.)

Now, if this doesn't endear you to Tito, just write Mr. KRAFT.

As I historicize myself and those times, I am struck more and more deeply at just how sharp a turn this country had taken right around the time I got to know Gil, just after the end of the war in Vietnam and the restructuring of our aspirations and horizons, possibly an even more relentless and deadening assault against common sense and value than had taken place during the Cold War, and one that continues apace. His championing and irreplaceable criticism of seminal figures like Charles Olson, Jack Spicer, Louis Zukofsky, and Lorine Niedecker, just to mention some, stand out now like beacons of clarity in the self-congratulatory muddle of jargon and cant (one of Gil's favorite words), that we inhabit. In this light, Gil's brilliant and uncompromising stance and work, his insistence on the beauty of form, is a deep resistance to all that he was witness to. It seems fitting to close with the end of the last letter in this particular run, just before I was planning to return to New York in 1980:

> Can't tell you how happy I am that you are returning to "these States." There are very few people left to talk to or with anymore; the other night Vicki and I were saying that there's nobody hardly at all who can, how can I say this? — nobody at all who has anything to <u>tell</u> me that I want to know. Not even a fucking joke. I seem to be falling into some strange place, in which I am surrounded by, as they say, "interests" that nobody else has. Like I say: Jonson's masques!   Paul Valéry! Russian formalism! Etc. The reply is: E.L. Doctorow! Norman Mailer! Saul Bellow! This is indeed the provinces. And the smugness of it all!
>
> Vicki is well and sends her love. Chris is 17 and in the throes of that truly insane age. He's playing with a rock band that's just being formed, headed by some guy named Cohen. He, Chris, by the way, played in August at a rock club uptown

called THE EIGHTIES, his professional debut, as they say; he was sitting in for the bassist in a band called Hi-Fi. He is not a bass player. He rehearsed with "Cohen's Band" yesterday. I asked him how it went, would he be playing anymore with them, he said, "I'm in the band, Pop." One of the many gifts that parents must have is clairvoyance. In any event, these kids all seem to be "nize-a boys," albeit insane. One guy called Chris the other day, a kid that I didn't know. I asked Chris about him later and he said that he was a nice guy that he'd got to know this summer — he's the bassist for a band called THE OFFALS. Now what do you think of that? I look at him; I say: "Nu? He couldn't be a nice pre-dent? A nice B.Admin major? Maybe a CPA?"

We all await you. I passed the house on Hudson the other day. (That's a movie starring Bruce Cabot and Gail Russell: THE HOUSE ON HUDSON. WHAT TERRIBLE SECRET LAY BEHIND THE CURTAINED WINDOWS OF…THE HOUSE ON HUDSON?) It still seems to be standing.

28

In & Out of Place: Memories of Nissim Rejwan, Shimon Ballas, and Samir Naqqash

2021

I.

While the circumstances are so very different, I almost feel like Haroun Soussan, the narrator of *Outcast*, Shimon Ballas's masterpiece that I co-translated with Oz Shelach, still the only novel by Ballas in English. Like Haroun fumbling around for his glasses in the opening scene, I am fumbling around, looking for documentation, letters, and even tapes from my dear old and now departed friends Shimon, Samir, and Nissim. But those things, along with books they gave me, and various clippings I saved, are mostly in my office, now inaccessible because of the corona regime. So the only option is to speak, as Kazem, another character in *Outcast* remarks, "straight from the heart."

II.

I happened to be in London in 1987 just after the great Palestinian cartoonist and champion of freedom Naji al-Ali died, some five weeks after he had been shot in the street on his way to work, victim of an assassination. I went to the memorial at the Kufa

"FOLLOW THE PERSON"

Gallery and there, among the speakers, I saw the renowned Iraqi poet Bulund al-Haidari. I knew that Bulund and Nissim had been friends in Baghdad in the late 1940s, when Nissim managed the al-Rabitha Bookshop, a gathering place for local poets and writers, so I approached him. When I mentioned Nissim's name I saw Bulund's eyes light up: He told me to wait until the memorial was over and not to leave, under any circumstances, until we had a chance to talk. As I approached him after the event, he asked after Nissim with great curiosity and told me to wait until he got a piece of paper so he could write a short letter that he wanted me to deliver to his old friend directly, by hand. I knew from Nissim that they had attempted to communicate with each other at various times but to no avail, so I had a sense of the momentous nature of the occasion. Nissim and I always met in Jerusalem, sometimes at a café in town, sometimes at the Jerusalem Post where he'd gotten me on the list of reviewers, sometimes at the university to hear a speaker or attend part of a conference, sometimes at a press conference or political meeting on the East side of the divided and occupied city but, most often, we met at his place. Once I got back from London, I called and told him I had a surprise for him and, as usual, he said I should just come over, if that would be convenient. Once there, I handed him the letter, saying it was from an old friend. As he quizzically took the letter and opened it, I could see an expression on his face I'd only seen once before, some months earlier, when the Iraqi writer Khalid Kishtainy had managed to come to Jerusalem and we'd all gone out together to see a performance by the al-Hakawati Theater. Khalid had recently published his book *Arab Political Humor* and the whole time they were together, neither could stop laughing. Already having known Nissim for a number of years, I found this highly unusual. Of course, he had a wry sense of humor and one could, every now and then, glean a sparkle in his eye and see the edge of a grin develop, but almost as if he were grinning to himself, nothing like these full outward displays of joy. Seeing him like that, I knew that he hadn't always been the way I thought he was, that there were other parts of him left behind in another world. Like so many of his contemporaries, whether they admitted it to themselves or not, all they had been through because of the "Zionist entity," had surely taken its toll, and it was no different with Nissim.

III.

I met and did not meet Shimon in many places: We never, for example, met in Paris, even though it was his second home and the setting for one of his most important novels, *Last Winter*. In 1998, along with some other friends, we were absent together in Beirut. After having been invited by Elias Khoury for events centered on Arab Jews as part of the fiftieth commemoration of the Nakba, we were advised not to go as our safety couldn't be insured. But in our absence, others spoke for us, and the attempt to shut our appearances down had the opposite effect: People came from all over, as we heard later, particularly Palestinians from the camps ringing Beirut, to listen, to find out what all the commotion was about. They came to hear firsthand (or, in this case, because of the circumstances, secondhand), about the uprooting of Jewish communities from Arab countries, to hear about Zionism, paraphrasing Ella Shohat, a scholar with roots in Iraq, "from the standpoint of some of its other victims." In 2002 we met in New York, when I invited Shimon to participate in a momentous meeting with Elias and Juan Goytisolo, in that strange interlude between 9/11 and the war against Iraq, with the idea of making a statement of some kind, at least for the record. We once bumped into each other in the middle of Cairo, unaware that we would be there at the same time. He was with David Semah, a colleague and poet, one of the first to write in response to the 1956 massacre of Palestinians in Kufur Kassem, with his Arabic poem "He Shall Return." We walked for a while, as Shimon and I often did in Tel Aviv but here, again, like when I gave Nissim the letter from Bulund al-Haidari or when I saw him with Khaled Kishtainy in Jerusalem, I could see that in Cairo Shimon and David were attentive to and immersed in every sound and sensation, their ears bending and their mouths moving to different wavelengths. We were together in Toledo and Geneva, or maybe only one or the other, in meetings with the PLO at a time when such meetings were illegal. We often ended up together at political events, sometimes as speakers. We drove from Tel Aviv to Haifa on occasion, when Shimon had something to do at the university and he asked me to tag along. But, as with Nissim, we also often just met at his place, on Tchernikovski Street in Tel Aviv, the walls lined with books — in Arabic, Hebrew, French, and English — along with his wife Gila's oversized art books, rows and rows and rows of them, enclosing a living world of beauty and imagination within.

IV.

I only saw Samir at his home in Petah Tikva. I vividly remember the light coming through from the balcony, the warm welcome I would always get from his wife Vicki and their kids. But once inside, sitting on the sofa with Samir, it was like stepping into a parallel universe, and I would be transported to all the places he'd gone to in order to finally get away from where he was: over the border in the north to Lebanon while still a teenager, then to Teheran and Bombay, with the hope of returning to Baghdad, at the behest of his father's former business partner. After I'd left Jerusalem for good, he'd write me with an address in Manchester, or the possibility of moving to Cairo. But nothing ended up working, and he'd always return to the spot so close to where he arrived as a child, as a refugee from Baghdad. This emotional and political status — that of a refugee — is something that Samir fought fiercely for throughout his life, as an emotional category for his characters and as an existential condition for himself and those who had undergone a similar experience. While all the outward trappings seemed of the time and place, there was something that always made me feel privy to some secret, that there could be no better place to be than where I was at that moment, sitting and listening to Samir's voice coming from other realms he had traversed in both body and mind. While I can recollect everything as if I were right there now, it is hard to fully recapture the emotional texture of those visits, the oscillation of intensity, expectation, and human connection. Because of this, I am so grateful, as we should all be, to another Samir — the Swiss-Iraqi filmmaker, director of the masterpiece *Forget Baghdad* — for the loving portrayal of Samir Naqqash captured on film, in his own home, from that very sofa that we so often sat on, talking for hours.

V.

Although their experience was bitter, they were grounded, these friends, each in their own way. From his column in the *Iraq Times* in the late 1940s to the *Jerusalem Post* and an array of books that he wrote on Middle East politics, Israeli society, or the Jews of Iraq, Nissim remained a cosmopolitan among provincials. Absolutely steadfast in his allegiance to the language of his childhood, Samir went against all odds, writing incredibly layered and complex stories and novels in Arabic rooted in place, memory, and uncanny flights of imagination. His books depict not only lost worlds but also lost languages, dialects forged by ways of being that reach far back in time and custom. Yet the record of these utterances and interactions between characters are never frozen in an idealized past but always reanimated through present consciousness, through that reverie of almost unparalleled concentration I could always feel in his singular speaking voice. Reordering his own geography, Shimon worked through layers of illusion to create seemingly realistic worlds that were anything but realistic. His particular and unique gift, one that he honed to greater and greater effect, was the ability to depict lives no one else even imagined could exist, living in worlds no one would think possible. I cannot overemphasize this last point because it has so much to do with the breadth of Shimon's humanity. When I say that the lives and characters depicted in his novels are unimaginable, this is literally true — due to racist attitudes, narrowness of vision, and lack of imagination or experience — the society in which his books were received had a difficult if not impossible time accepting the existence of the people he wrote about. And all of this could as well be said about Samir, with a different slant. Of course, to actually create worlds that posit the existence of the people in them, has always been the most difficult job for a novelist and it is, unquestionably, a world-changing form of creation that is becoming that much more difficult, as our lives become more standardized and generic. I feel humbled and incredibly lucky to have had the opportunity to get to know these people, to spend time with them, and to count them as friends. But I want to emphasize — especially for younger people embarking on artistic or academic pursuits — that I took the time to be with them, to read their work, to come to an understanding of their worlds. I did this not just because we felt an affinity for each other as people but because I understood how important they were, how much particular history they carried, and how much of that history has been decimated and relegated to oblivion. And yet, it is precisely these tenuous threads that hold our world together, and they unravel unless we each act to find ways to reconnect them, and it is in that spirit that I think of them now.

From the Citadel: "I must have been an Arab once…"

To the memory of Kamal Boullata (1942–2019)

Why have you chosen this self-interview format through which to represent yourself?

I was happily surprised to be recognized as a contributor on Arab American literature by a French journal, particularly regarding the theme "home" and "homeland." Recognition of my immersion in these themes hasn't come readily in the US. I was once contacted by what one could only call a lazy journalist for "the paper of record," euphemistically known by the tabloids as "the gray lady,"[1] who queried me on this very subject, Arab American literature. Given the importance of issues of representation, I proceeded to ask her some questions. Once I understood that her familiarity with the subject was almost nonexistent, I simply gave her a list of writers she should interview and called it a day.

What do you mean by "representation"?

I am a child of refugees, but not from an Arab country. I heard, for instance, the Arabic phrase *mashallah* from the earliest

---

1 Reference here is to *The New York Times*.

age—there was no need to "translate" it, or even know the meaning, I knew *what* was meant, *how* it meant. In my family's case, that phrase took a long detour, lasting around a thousand years. In other words, my family origins of that more "recent" period in human history must have been in Iraq, and then, like many others, we probably moved west to al-Andalus after the establishment of the Western Caliphate, only to be scattered around the Ottoman Empire following the expulsions of Jews and Muslims from Spain. So in the case of the journalist, I thought people whose experience was more immediate ought to be consulted first, as being more "representative."

On the other hand, by the time I encountered this journalist, several years after 9/11, I had already been involved in a wide network of Arab writers, filmmakers, and artists for a few decades, writing about books, films, art, and political issues, and incorporating documentary materials into my own writing from the years I had spent in the region. Very few people, as far as I was aware, were using this kind of material: Of course, Etel Adnan had written *Sitt Marie Rose* in 1977, in French, based on an actual incident in Lebanon, and through the tireless labors of other dear friends like Kamal Boullata and Mirène Ghossein, the work of Rashid Hussein[2] made its way to English readers. There were things from the Arab world one had to keep an eye out for lest they vanish: small press publications from Arab student organizations, the series from Three Continents Press where one could discover Sonallah Ibrahim, Ghassan Kanafani, or Kamal's landmark anthology, *Women of the Fertile Crescent.* A masterpiece like Abdellatif Laâbi's post-prison memoir came out with a relatively obscure press and just disappeared: It was strangely titled *Rue de Retour,* even though it was in English, and the original title was *Le chemin des ordalies.*

There were older American writers, the novelist Vance Bourjaily, poets like Sam Hazo and Jack Marshall, for instance, and

---

2 See *The World Of Rashid Hussein: A Palestinian Poet in Exile,* ed. Kamal Boullata and Mirène Ghossein (Association of Arab-American University Graduates, 1979).

then a bit later, Naomi Shihab Nye, who kept probing at the visible and invisible lines binding her to America and Palestine. We shouldn't forget D.H. Melhem — her 1972 *Notes on 94th Street* is considered the first book of poetry published by an Arab American woman. D.H. finished her MA thesis, *On the Poetics of Charles Olson,* at City College in 1971. I dropped out of City College in 1978 but anyone who knows my work knows that Olson had been a family friend, that my memories of him are vivid, and his work remains a central presence that I continually think and write about.[3] In D.H.'s archive, one can see a copy of *A Primer for Blacks* lovingly inscribed by Gwendolyn Brooks: "For D.H., who has disclosed myself to me and to the World." Brooks was a close friend to D.H., and the subject of D.H.'s PhD thesis, still the most extensive study of Brooks's work. In Dudley Randall's *After the Killing,* D.H. analyzed the rhyme scheme for "I Loved You Once," translated from Alexander Pushkin's Russian, and wrote, at the bottom, one word: "exquisite."[4] I know we met numerous times over the years and her *Heroism in the New Black Poetry* is a book I often go back to and teach whenever I can. But this is a living history still being excavated, imagined, and created. There were memories of the literary activity that took place after the great migrations of the late nineteenth century, in Boston and New York. *Grape Leaves,* an anthology edited by Gregory Orfalea, was an early effort to tie some of this together. There was the largely Syrian "milk and butter district," centered around the grand old cast-iron buildings that were mostly torn down to make room for the World Trade Center.[5] There was Atlantic Avenue. There was 9/11.

---

3 See Ammiel Alcalay, *a little history,* ed. Fred Dewey (Re:public/UpSet Press, 2013).
4 For the source of both of these quotes, see Taylor Henning, "D.H. Melhem: Biographer and Friend of Gwendolyn Brooks," *Rare Book and Manuscript Library,* https://www.library.illinois.edu/rbx/2019/11/11/d-h-melhem-biographer-and-friend-of-gwendolyn-brooks/. On D.H. Melhem, see: https://dhmelhem.com/.
5 See Danny Lyon's documentary project, *The Destruction of Lower Manhattan,* originally published in 1969 and reprinted by Aperture in 2020.

And "FROM THE CITADEL"?

My name. In Arabic, *qala* is a citadel, so *al-qalá-ee,* would be "from the citadel." I remember when I was first introduced to Edward Said in the early 1980s, he immediately perked up on hearing my name and said: "I knew many Alcalays in Jerusalem." That was extraordinary to me because I'd grown up with all the attendant snickering about my name, that it had to do with battery acid, or a chemical, and so on, and Edward was, in fact, the first person I'd met outside my extended family who had immediate name recognition. The only other instance I can think of is recent, from a very different part of my life: Just a few months before he died last year, the poet Michael McClure (who, among so many other notable things, was the youngest person to participate in the Six Gallery reading where Allen Ginsberg first read *Howl* in public), left me a long and rambling phone message. After saying goodbye, he lingered a second and then added: "I've always meant to ask, Alcalay, that would be Arabic, Sephardic, right?" It was like him to know that but, still, a very rare occurrence indeed.

The theme is "HOME" and "HOMELAND": do you plan on addressing this?

I had thought of writing something different, somber, oriented towards catastrophe. I was very moved by a film given me to watch by an old friend, Ayreen Anastas, made with René Gabri,[6] on the question of Armenia, presently, filled with haunting and highly poetic phrases. My first attempts at the text were two blocks, like this, using some quotations from the film:

---

6   The film, *Black Bach Artsakh,* is not currently in circulation but was shown in March, 2021 at the Berlin International Film Festival.

I.

Through no fault of one's one, purely by circumstance, finding yourself born in a particular place, especially after or because of a war or the assassination and murder of family members, of a whole community, the need to flee, escape, leave, and so land, somewhere. Land. In the voice over, the narrator asks: "do you know people who return?" And the man responds: "there are people who return." He pauses, then says: "there are people who stay."

II.

More words, suspended over images, roads from a moving car: "is it less to ask, shall it be at our cost, crossing through our histories, who are we? How many homes, fields, worlds, were we forced to abandon? And when can the appeal to this ancestral past be understood as a longing for other futures, rather than a return?"

This reminded me of the title of one of my books, *Memories of Our Future,* that Juan Goytisolo wrote the introduction for, but it also felt a lot like the way I composed a piece based on the work of visual artist Jayce Salloum, for an exhibition catalog called *History of the Present.* When I began the piece you are now reading, I had in mind a form that I've written in for a long time, using numbered blocks of text, with many different kinds of material juxtaposed, often drawing on various other sources, including my own writing.

"Understanding Revolution," from 1990, is kind of the template, much of it using documentary material, including torture testimony and military tribunal accounts that I myself was involved in gathering in the 1980s, before and during the first Palestinian Intifada, a period that continues to inform how I think on an almost daily basis. The siege of Beirut in 1982, Sabra and Shatila, the assassination of Naji el-Ali in London, the kidnapping of nuclear technician Mordechai Vanunu in

Rome, the torture of fourteen-year-old Riad Faraj, the Maria R, seized on its way to provide food and medicine to people starving in the camps war in Lebanon. Naila Ayesh and her husband Jamal,[7] Faisal Husseini, trials, demonstrations: the bookstalls in Ezbekkiya Gardens. Much of this worked its way into *the cairo notebooks* as I moved towards making a world, expanding the parameters of what parts of myself might appear. "Home" and "homeland"? The D train: "empire of dreams, dreaming of empire, and a night at the opera, burning,"[8] a phrase that still haunts me, in which I am seized by layers of sound: the squeal of street cars in Cairo, like on the sharp curve between Boylston and Park in the Boston I was born to, the D train itself, heading down off the bridge, steel grinding against steel.

In 2019, I wrote a piece called "Reverse Migration," in the midst of a process in which, by listening ONLY to Cecil Taylor for about a month after he passed away, I learned how to HEAR again, after many years of having my ears stopped up to the sounds I had been most attuned to and moved by for so long, from Bud Powell to Mal Waldron and Don Cherry. The process of writing that piece led to an understanding of how long it had taken me to see that the primal conflicts within my own immediate family, things that had irrevocably shaped the course of my life, also stemmed from the fact that I was the only one who actually felt "at home."

But then, who is to say, why did I leave and spend so much time elsewhere, immersed not in some past but a continually accruing and increasingly textured present I am constantly in the process of recreating? Faraj, Faraj Bayrakdar, the Syrian poet and former political prisoner, describes the moment in prison when he heard, on the most rudimentary radio imaginable, the sound of Nizar Qabanni's "Kalimat / Words," sung by a woman, at a time when he had long been deprived of the voice of *any*

---

7   For more on Naila Ayesh, see Julia Bacha's 2017 documentary *Naila and the Uprising:* https://justvision.org/nailaandtheuprising.
8   From my piece "Understanding Revolution," in Ammiel Alcalay, *Memories of Our Future* (City Lights Books, 1999), 220.

woman.⁹ Just a few weeks ago, as I was proofreading the final version of his poems, *A Dove in Free Flight,* a project that a group of us have been involved with for more than sixteen years, I stopped at his description and sought out the song, sung by Majda al-Roumy. And I could now again *hear* this *other* music my ears had also grown so distant from. Home? Homeland? There have been a number of others in-between, including "No Return," starting from the Balfour Declaration and working its way through a dense catalog of political memories, embedded in my high school years, 1969 to 1973. In the build-up to the war in Iraq, students often asked me what we did "back then." And one thing I remember clearly saying is that we wore Army jackets, and wearing an Army jacket meant that you were identifying with the soldiers who were against the war. On my various haunts as a truant from school — between bookstores, pool halls, and movie theaters — I remember going to talk to young men just a few years older than me, harbored in churches, on their way to Canada to avoid the draft. These pieces can be pretty heavy, and I felt like I was hitting a dead end, as if it were enough. I wanted to be more direct, less dense and somber, so I dropped it and am trying this.

You mentioned Edward Said. That seems like a significant moment. Can you recount other significant moments related to the second part of your title, "I must have been an Arab once…"

Chronologically?

Not necessarily, however you see fit.

Often when I'm working on a project, events in the world encroach on it, and this has sure been the case here. Just today,

---

9 From an interview with Faraj Bayrakdar conducted by Muhammad 'Ali al-Atassi, in *A Dove in Flight,* ed. Ammiel Alcalay and Shareah Taleghani (UpSet Press, 2021), 101–2.

in fact, May 23rd, I was watching an interview with the filmmaker Elia Suleiman, whom I've known, shockingly, for about thirty-five years. He was talking about the long process of making a film:

> All of this takes quite a bit of time and you cannot exactly contain or arrest a moment, you just have to...accept the fact that you cannot just force imagination.... There is an intuition of the moment that you feel the weight of what you have written in all of these numerous notebooks, and this weight starts to invite you to see what it is that has been culminating.... Generally speaking, there is a sensation that comes to you, and this sensation comes also from two places: it comes from your interiority, but it also comes from an exterior because also my films are somehow — not that they are engaged with the immediate but they are engaged with an ambience, a social/political ambience, or shall I reverse it, a political/social ambience, so there comes a moment of the necessity to make a film because of what's happening around me...so, basically, the metaphysical relationship between the interior, meditative moments and what is happening is what drives one to go and feel the urgency to actually make that film.[10]

I've been thinking and making notes and waiting, close to a year, since I agreed to write this and, of course, I've been glued to the news from Gaza, and the rest of occupied Jerusalem and Palestine, in the weeks leading to the deadline. Over a week into the assault on Gaza, my friend Mosab Abu Toha, a person of rare spirit and resolve, sent me a short poem of his that I heard him read during an interview from there:

We are not stones in Gaza.

---

10 My transcription from an interview with Elia Suleiman conducted by Yasmina Tawil for the Arab Film Series, May 23, 2021.

> Even stones cry when they see our blood seep down our heads, arms, legs, and backs, when they smell the burns in our skins and hair.
> Stones wish they could stop the bleeding. They wish they had hands, soft ones, to dress our wounds.

After the catastrophic and criminal Israeli attack on Gaza in 2014, in which the university Mosab went to was destroyed and two of his close friends were killed, Mosab began gathering books from the rubble and collecting new ones, from donations, as a form of refusal, of resistance. As he describes the scene:

> By the end of the day, what had once been the English department lay beneath a heap of rubble. When I finally arrived at the site where I had spent hundreds of hours poring over the works of Wordsworth, Blake, Dickens, T.S. Eliot, Orwell, and Arthur Miller, the sight of thousands of books buried under rubble, especially the English-language books for which I felt such an affinity (I'd been teaching English to 6th and 7th graders in Gaza's UNRWA schools) struck me the hardest. [...] Hemingway, Faulkner, Twain, Steinbeck, Fitzgerald, Walker, Mailer, and James (to name just a few) lay smothered in dust and forced to sleep in the dark. Drones buzzing in the sky must have assaulted their ears. I wish I'd been able to brush the dust off their clothes; I was sorry I hadn't been able to hug them during the bombings.[11]

This initial gesture eventually turned into the Edward Said Public Libraries in 2017, beautiful and open spaces for children and adults to read, study and explore various imaginative activities, to resist the constant fear and enclosure imposed by US-funded Israeli terror by air, land, and sea.

---

11 This quote appears here: Mosab Abu Toha, "How the Edward Said Library of Gaza Was Born," *Arrow Smith Press*, https://www.arrowsmithpress.com/journal/said-library.

"FOLLOW THE PERSON"

During these most recent attacks, I watched the eleven-storey al-Jalaa Building, housing al-Jazeera, the Associated Press, and residential apartments, come down in real time. Everyone in the building was given one hour to leave. The images, while not surprising, are still shocking. I listened to an account by Youmna al-Sayed, an incredibly courageous journalist from Gaza, like so many other *actual* journalists there and in other parts of the world, describing how people in the building let elders and children use the single elevator to evacuate, as others, like Youmna herself, carried children down the stairs. She has four children at home, and described how her family fears for her safety while she goes to work, how she so often inhales tear gas and other chemicals, rubble from pulverized buildings, and has to seek cover from missile, drone, and other Israeli implements of terror, destruction, and death. After reporting directly from the site of the crumbled building, she removed herself to al-Shifa Hospital, where it was safer, and reported from there. But within half an hour, she returned to the site of her former office, to report from the ground. Just a few days later, on her way to work, the car in front of her slowed down before getting incinerated by an Israeli missile. Had the car not slowed a bit, she would have found herself incinerated as well. Yusef Abu Hussein, from al-Aqsa radio, wasn't so lucky: he was killed in a targeted missile attack on his house. And then there are the more recent escapades of contemptuous lapdog journalists — which is actually an insult to dogs, since they would never do such things — of the US, chattering on about "safe space" and "harm" from digital "violence," delivered not by missile but by tweets.

You seem to be getting somewhat off-topic — let's go back to that moment with Edward Said, can you continue in that vein? With other important moments?

I remember sitting on the porch in Beit Hanina with my friend Jamila, her mother inside making us lemonade. We'd met outside the family pharmacy, the Mina Pharmacy in the Old City, and we took a long walk before heading to her house. She told me stories about her father, how he was killed in the 1967 war.

I remember listening to Sari Nusseibeh discuss Ibn Sina, all the while twirling a lit cigarette between his fingers, right by his knuckles, as if it were a string of prayer beads. Everyone in the seminar just stared at the lit end of the cigarette, trying to follow both trails of Sari's thought.

I remember covering military tribunals with my friend Hagar before and after the first Intifada. We often had to go from one court to another as "hearings" would be scheduled and then cancelled, the prisoners moved between courts or back to prison. Even though we didn't know each other that well, we enjoyed being together and reacted to things similarly. Sometime after I went back to New York, she drowned in a wadi. I think of her often, and regret that her time was cut so short, that I didn't get to know her better.

I remember covering the trials of Faisal Husseini, transcribing the surreal and absurd circumstances when he was held in administrative detention, once because of an exhibition of Palestinian prisoner art at the Arab Studies Society in which there was a wooden letter-opener carved in the shape of Palestine and painted in the national colors.[12] A group of us always waited for him as he was led into a hallway, in wrist and leg chains, so his wife and daughter and son could greet him and then give us a few minutes to see if there was any unusual news circulating among the prisoners. Once he told us about some prisoners in the system that no one knew about, kidnapped at sea on their way to bring food and medicine to family members caught in the Camps War in Lebanon. This led to our research on the Maria R., and Israeli sea piracy in general.

I remember being in London in 1987, just after Naji al-Ali died, five weeks after he had been shot in the street on his way

---

12 See my text, "The Trial: A Real Farce," in Ammiel Alcalay, *Memories of Our Future* (City Lights Books, 1999), 163–72. An abbreviated version appeared in Ru Freeman, ed., *Extraordinary Rendition: (American) Writers on Palestine* (OR Books, 2015).

to work, victim of an assassination. I went to the memorial at the Kufa Gallery and there, among the speakers, I saw Bulund al-Haidari, the great Iraqi poet. I knew that Bulund and my dear friend Nissim Rejwan had been friends in Baghdad in the late 1940s, when Nissim managed the al-Rabitha Bookshop,[13] a gathering place for local poets and writers, so I approached him. But I've told this story elsewhere...

I remember, during the Camps War, sitting on the ground in a circle in front of the al-Nuzha theater in East Jerusalem with friends who had relatives up there. I'm not sure if we had candles or were surrounding a small fire we had set — mainly, though, we were trying to find a form for such a vigil, what it might look like, who might find themselves wanting to come into the circle or even ask what it was about.

I remember getting a letter from Abraham Serfaty postmarked "Central Prison: Kuneitra, Morocco," dated June 24th, 1991. I had met Christine Daure-Serfaty some months before, when she had come to New York to accept a human rights award in her still-imprisoned husband's name. Happy for the recognition but appalled at the institutional merchandising of pain and suffering she sensed in the proceedings, we immediately hit it off. She told me that the only visitors her husband might eventually receive had to be related. Because of our common background, she suggested I pose as a long lost relative, an American searching for "roots." I proceeded to write, not quite knowing what to expect. His reply began: "Your letter of May 2nd gave me great pleasure. I have read many of your texts in MERIP [Middle East Report] and I have long wanted to be in touch...."

I remember *not* being in Beirut in 1998, along with Shimon Ballas, Anton Shammas, Ella Shohat, and many others, after Elias Khoury had invited us to participate in the commemoration of the Nakba by exploring the history of Arab Jews in their present absence. As the date got closer, we were advised not to go as our safety couldn't be assured due to rumblings from Syria.

---

13 See Nissim Rejwan's "Bookshop Days," in *Keys to the Garden: New Israeli Writing,* ed. Ammiel Alcalay (City Lights Books, 1996), 46–55.

With empty chairs adorned with our names, others spoke for us, reading our work, and the attempt to shut our appearance down had the opposite effect: people came from all over, as we heard later, particularly Palestinians from the camps ringing Beirut, to listen, to find out for themselves what all the commotion was about.

I remember bumping into Shimon in the middle of Cairo, unaware that we would be there at the same time. He was with David Semah, a colleague and poet, one of the first to write in response to the 1956 massacre in Kufur Kassem, with his Arabic poem "He Shall Return." We walked for a while, as Shimon and I often did in Tel Aviv but here I could see that, in Cairo, Shimon and David were attentive to and immersed in every sound and sensation, their ears bending and their mouths moving to different wavelengths.

I remember being with Juliano[14] at various demonstrations, how much we enjoyed making up imaginative chants that turned standard slogans upside down. And then the big memorial in New York, after his assassination.

I remember rushing from the airport once, in San Francisco, and heading directly to the Book Fair. I immediately went to seek out Jalal Toufic. I think he was manning a table with some of his books and he told me to put my things down, that he would take a break and we could have a coffee somewhere. I'm pretty sure I had written about one of his books, we corresponded for a while and were eager to meet. But I turned inward for some reason, like so many other times in my life when I simply couldn't accept what was so generously offered, and said that I just needed to circulate among the books for a while. I know he felt like I had brushed him off and it bothered me for years. We met again, at an installation of his work in New York, and when

---

14 Juliano Mer-Khamis, 1958–2011, Palestinian actor, director, filmmaker, and activist assassinated in front of the Freedom Theater that he had established in Jenin. He co-directed the film *Arna's Children* (2004), about his mother's work in children's theater. A commemoration celebrating his work and life was held in New York on May 4, 2011, at The Church of St. Paul the Apostle.

it was over I insisted on driving him wherever he needed to go, and I was able to at least explain my state of mind at the time.

I remember walking around Brooklyn years ago with Sonallah Ibrahim and Elliott Colla. I think Ted Swedenburg was with us, but I'm not sure. Elliott went to Cairo right around the beginning of the pandemic and I asked if he could take some of my newer books to Sonallah. Then we began writing to each other and I was amazed by what he remembered and his response to my work.

I remember going to dinner after an event in New York with a bunch of people, including Goytisolo and Elias. When Susan Sontag came in late, Elias got up, and as loudly as he could, mockingly greeted her: "And how was Jerusalem, Ms. Sontag?" Despite the urging of many, including myself — having written an article pointing out precisely why she shouldn't have accepted it — Sontag had actually just returned from accepting the Jerusalem Prize.

Is there a way to even end this chain of associations?

Not really. I had wanted to use a poem by al-Ma'ari, about the dove turning its neck to see its nest destroyed, but I can't find it. I doubt that I'll travel any real distance in the foreseeable future, so I think more about places I've been and friends who are far away or no longer with us. Since I dedicated this piece to Kamal Boullata, it makes sense to end with him. I remember being in Amsterdam with Kamal and Lily, it was a good place to be, neither "here" nor "there" in any significant way, for us at least. For some reason, we spoke an invented Dutch half the time, and in between serious things, we laughed a lot.

I also remember wanting to take Kamal to Mansoura's, the once renowned Jewish sweet-maker of King Farouk, then in Brooklyn. I must have thought it would be some slice of "authentic" life, mummified, preserved over time and space. We went, and as Kamal began speaking to the proprietor in Arabic, the man leaned towards the back of the shop, calling out a helper whom he began to curse — for being an Arab — in the most vile manner imaginable. Kamal stared at the scene in disbelief. We bought just a few things and left quickly. I could see how affected he was, almost sickened. He and Lily soon left the US. After many years of living in Washington, DC, they felt it was no longer possible, with the Gulf War, Palestine, and the general sentiment in the air.

Just before they left, Kamal and I were working on a special issue of *Lusitania*, a journal published by another dearly departed friend, Martim Avillez. The idea was to present work for 1992, to mark the 500 years since the expulsions of Jews and Arabs from Spain, but with Palestine as a central reference point. When the siege of Sarajevo began, we realized that the focus needed to shift, and I took over. Before that happened, though, we had gotten a poem from Adonis, "The Other Body / The Other Home," that Kamal and I translated, which ended like this:

> This migration of mine is long in place, enduring even longer within me, as if I do not know myself…
>
> Once in flight I was intent to build a humble abode for the days of my past…
>
> I sat myself down among them, I mean my days, that are scattered, gathered by force. And instead of staring at them and inquiring and scrutinizing them, they began looking at me and probing and searching and asking. As if they were waiting for something else, another person. Beginning then I started to understand my flight, and those roads no one takes lest they be tempted to track some shadow, some harvest. Roads that always retain ashes as if they were a fire just now dying out, as if the road were a body shattered in the scent of jasmine left over from childhood. There is a tangled binding between me and my flight.
>
> I cannot presume that "return" itself would ever fully appreciate the damages.

"FOLLOW THE PERSON"

> I shall declare my life a home for my flight, and migration a home for my life.
> I shall tell migration: You are my expanse — you are vast.

Kamal had grown up in the Old City of Jerusalem, apprenticing himself at a young age to Khalil Halaby, a Palestinian icon painter who taught him how to paint from photographs, using the grid method. As he remembered sitting in front of the Dome of the Rock — where much of the provocation ending in the recent assault on Gaza took place — endlessly drawing the intricacies of its geometries, Kamal remarked: "I keep reminding myself that Jerusalem is not behind me, it is constantly ahead of me."[15] When he died suddenly in Berlin in August of 2019, the fulfillment of a last wish — to be buried at home, in Jerusalem — became a fraught war of nerves between Israeli occupation forces on one side, and Palestinian and international legal, ecclesiastic, political, cultural, and artistic forces on the other. Permission was finally granted and Kamal, after so much journeying, was laid to rest, according to his wish, in the very place he had grown up. Is that a "happy" ending? I really can't say.

---

15 See "Kamal Boullata," *The Khalid Shoman Foundation Darat al Funun*, https://daratalfunun.org/?artist=kamal-boullata.

30

CODA:
Following the Person

Some months into the coronavirus "era" I was asked by a magazine with a Jewish cultural emphasis to briefly comment on a poem I had been "holding close." I actually had been thinking a lot about Ezra Pound's famous canto on usury, "Canto XLV." In fact, I'd been reading a lot of him and about him, feeling that someone so unfashionable was just the right companion for the grim times we were in. Though I knew that presenting Pound, and that poem in particular, might cause some problems, I went ahead because it — and he — were much on my mind. After going back and forth with editorial suggestions, I was explicitly asked to at least make some reference to Pound's statements on Jews from a particular period. In what turned out to be a very interesting exchange, here is one of my responses:

> Thanks for your comments! I'll take a look at the stylistic stuff later but I just wanted to address the issue you bring up. In a weird way, the reaction that you & other readers had might be indicative of what I was trying to do: by not explicitly mentioning anything in that light, I hoped to give pause, or startle readers into not so easily accepting the terms as given; "anti-semitism," for instance, is an enormously fraught

term & one I don't use. To even begin any kind of explication, in a 500 word piece that's already complicated enough, seems to me a lost cause. Again, had I intended to open those connections, I would have. I explicitly don't for a lot of reasons. To me, it kind of closes the discussion: by leaving that out, I hope to jog a reader into perhaps looking into things on their own. By dramatically juxtaposing Pound with the war criminals who were filtered into significant positions of power, & not referring back to the immediate identification of Pound=anti-semite=usury/banking obsession etc., I want readers to explore the issues & think about the juxtaposition I'm making explicitly. The fact that everyone who read it had similar reactions indicates that the connection you want me to state isn't unknown. I don't see that I have to make evident that I also know it. Does that make any sense? I stick my neck out here more than a bit, writing about Pound in this context, & I've got a purpose behind it. As in other things I've written that go out on somewhat of a limb, my aim is to demonstrate that we really need to go out on a limb sometimes in order to activate thinking outside given terms ... I hope this makes some kind of sense to you — eager to hear your thoughts.

At one point, I suggested that we include some of our exchange, as a way of opening the editorial process up to readers, so they could understand how conflicting perspectives are negotiated. In the end, though, it still felt like I was being asked to pledge some kind of loyalty oath, and so I declined to make the changes. Perhaps it was also a case, at the outset, of me being thought of as "one of them," meaning that I ought to be able to agree to a premise that might have seemed reasonable to the editors given their assumptions about who I was supposed to be, according to "given identity profile." This phenomenon gained greater and greater velocity and destructive force in the world at large during the corona period, particularly through censorship, banning access on social media platforms, and repercussions that even extended to employment. Stridency of behavior or position was increasingly codified into emergency regulations regarding the use or even discussion of natural immunity, preventative treatments, the efficacy and or potential dangers of the vaccines, and various other restrictive protocols, to the point of people — originally lauded as "pandemic heroes," and "front-line workers" — being terminated from their jobs. In the face of a relentless onslaught of propaganda, data manipulation, and disinformation campaigns, rational scientific reasoning, questioning and debate, all face unprecedented challenges. Yet, at root, in addition to establishing authoritarian control mechanisms and reaping financial gain, all of the procedures employed were also meant to make it appear as if there was uniformity of thought and opinion, that any dissent at all had to be made to appear as not only abnormal but even dangerous. I was not asked to point things out in greater detail — that, for example, while one of the figures brought to the US to join the diplomatic corps under the auspices of the covert operations I was writing about was largely responsible for the deaths of some four million Soviet prisoners, Pound was being held in an outdoor cage for radio broadcasts that, by any reasonable standard, should have been the protected speech of a US citizen acting under Constitutional principles. And yet, I was being asked to categorize Pound in some way that was already "common knowledge," as a means of supposedly identifying which "side" I was on. It was this implication that most irked me about the editorial exchange and what I was being asked to do.

Be that as it may, as a parting shot, the piece on Pound, as below, appeared in the last round up of our somewhat disruptive and muckraking online journal, *Dispatches from the Poetry Wars*,[1] before we closed up shop and went into archival mode:

---

[1] *Dispatches from the Poetry Wars* originally began through the energies of poets Michal Boughn and Kent Johnson, soon joined by the late Benjamin Hollander, André Spears, myself, and, eventually, others. The run of the journal has been archived and can be accessed here: https://wayback.archive-it.org/12142/20201104192943/https://www.dispatchespoetrywars.com/

This very notable canto by Ezra Pound has been with me for a long time and I've found myself coming back to it again and again during the ongoing pandemic, particularly as politicians roll out various figures in the trillions and bankers and corporations lick their chops at the idea of a virtually endless supply of newly printed money and the ensuing financial chicanery that will transfer even more wealth to even fewer people.

The idea that private banks exert such enormous leverage on society through charging interest for the use of currency is a practice that outraged Pound, and that he felt to be one of the primary roots of the perversion and loss of value in the human community.[2]

Whatever one might think about that, the line "Usura slayeth the child in the womb" is, actually, quite literal, since the ability to use or borrow funds affects the very possibility of life. Think of IMF "restructuring," followed by bread riots in the so-called "developing world," or red-lining to prevent the accumulation of wealth by African-Americans, to mention just a few obvious examples. If one thinks of interest as a means of social engineering — almost like a thermostat that can be set to have the kinds of sweeping effects that a famine or a war might have — suddenly our perspective shifts, as interest rates can actually determine the fates of whole peoples or a whole generation. Like a mortgage foreclosure, horizons also foreclose, fewer children are born, the past is no longer transmissible or else is simply eradicated and

---

[2] In a 1939 reading of this Canto, recorded at Harvard, Pound prefaces the poem with these remarks: "So that you don't continually misunderstand, usury and interest are not the same thing. Usury is a charge made for the use of money regardless of production and often regardless of even the possibilities of production." In my piece, I refer to interest detached from production, as part of the process of the financialization of the economy, regardless of commodity values. "Ezra Pound Reading His Usura Canto, 1939," *Renegade Tribune*, July 3, 2019, http://www.renegadetribune.com/ezra-pound-reading-his-usura-canto-1939/.

whole societies and cultures shrink into themselves, to eventually disappear.

Pound was famously captured in Italy in May of 1945, interrogated by an agent assigned by FBI Director J. Edgar Hoover, then imprisoned in a 6x6 foot outdoor steel cage at a US Army Training Center in Pisa, and eventually charged with treason for radio broadcasts he had made in support of Mussolini. In the cage at Pisa, as Pound wrote in Canto LXXX, "the raft broke and the waters went over me."

What rarely gets told in this complex story is that, while Pound was one of the few American citizens charged with treason following WWII, during the same month, May of 1945, key Nazi officers, intelligence personnel, and scientists were quietly shipped to Washington, D.C., having been recruited by the burgeoning US National Security state to eventually serve in a series of operations with macabre and absurd names like Overcast, Paperclip, Pajamas, Dwindle, Apple Pie, Panhandle, Credulity, and Sunrise. In other words, while Pound — never having actually been put on trial — remained incarcerated at St. Elizabeths Hospital for the Criminally Insane (a building now partially used as the headquarters of Homeland Security), people that, under different political circumstances, would have rightfully been considered war criminals, became key players in US Cold War policy and its clandestine operations that assassinated leaders, destroyed peoples and economies, and insured the hegemony of the American Empire and the US dollar.

In the present context, as politicians of all stripes grandstand and go to great lengths to cover their collectives asses, we would do well to reconsider basic questions of GROUND: on whose ground does authority rest? In what is it vested? Beyond the hysteria and narcissism that characterizes the whole spectrum of our official current political discourse, where do "we the people" even find representation? For myself, as unfashionable as it might be, returning to Pound's *Cantos* has proven a revelatory and unsettling source.

"FOLLOW THE PERSON"

Shortly after the piece appeared in *Dispatches,* Irakli Qolbaia, a young poet from Tbilisi, Georgia that I had started corresponding with, asked if he could translate it into Georgian. The day after it came out, Irakli forwarded me the following message from an older Georgian poet that he is close to, Dato Barbakadze:

> I notice that you published a piece by Ammiel Alcalay — the author I didn't know about. What an aerobatics of the highest order!!! And that you would translate that in Georgian is also aerobatics of the highest order!!! "As the spectrum of permissible speech becomes more and more circumscribed..." that is to say, right NOW, this is exactly the precision that will always protect the nobility of poetry from the enemies of freedom. The force of this tiny piece is so immense that all the powers taken together would not even seem the size of a flea next to it.

Before I knew it, Dato proposed a book centered on my piece, published bilingually in English and Georgian, accompanied by commentaries and translations of the canto by different Georgian poets. Soon enough, copies of this book, with a stunning black and white photo of Pound on the cover, actually arrived from far off Tbilisi, and I was truly speechless. I proceeded to send a copy to old friend Richard Sieburth, translator and scholar extraordinaire, and he sent it on to Mary de Rachewiltz, Pound's daughter, who sent Richard back a pithy and enlightening comment, to the effect that she was happy to see people still able to think with her father. And if that wasn't enough, around the same time I saw mention of Pound in a column by Brazilian journalist Pepe Escobar, one of the last real foreign correspondents left, and someone whom I have turned to and relied on for many years for views of the world completely unavailable in what generally passes for the Anglo-American press. I found a way to send the piece to him, along with the Georgian cover, and he quickly wrote back: "Many thanks. I'm a huge Pound fanatic. One day I will publish a long essay on *il miglior fabbro.*"

Yet again, this very core principle proved to yield more than I could have imagined: Just "follow the person," and before you know it, whole new lines of transmission and communication begin to open before you.

Bibliography

Original Publications

1. Alcalay, Ammiel. "'Follow the person': A Manifesto for *Lost & Found*." *Cambridge Literary Review* 11 (2018): 14–15.
2. Alcalay, Ammiel. "Let me show you something." In *Jayce Salloum: History of the Present (Selected Works, 1985–2009)*, edited by Jen Budney. Exh. cat. Kamloops Art Gallery, 2009.
3. Alcalay, Ammiel. "What I Found Out." *Amerarcana: A Bird & Beckett Review* 1 (2010): 10–16.
4. Alcalay, Ammiel. "Relieving the National Debt: W.D. Ehrhart and the Wages of Memory." In *Last Time I Dreamed About the War: Essays on the Life and Writing of W.D. Ehrhart*, edited by Jean-Jacques Malo. McFarland & Co., 2014.
5. Alcalay, Ammiel. "The Body Is a House." *The Worcester Review* 31, nos. 1–2 (2010): 77–82.
6. Hadbawnik, David. "Interview with Ammiel Alcalay: The Archive and CUNY's Lost and Found Document Series." *Kadar Koli* 9 (2014): 84–97.
7. Alcalay, Ammiel. Afterword to *A Walker in the City: Elegy for Gloucester*, by Peter Anastas. Back Shore Press/Lost & Found Elsewhere, 2013.

8. Alcalay, Ammiel. "Out of the Schools & Into the Archives." *Academy of American Poets* 48 (2015): 45–48.
9. Alcalay, Ammiel. "On Robert Creeley's 'Contexts of Poetry.'" In *The 1963 Vancouver Poetry Conference / Robert Creeley's Contexts of Poetry; with Daphne Marlatt's Journal Entries,* edited by Ammiel Alcalay. Center for the Humanities, 2009.
10. Alcalay, Ammiel. "On *R.D.'s H.D.*" In *R.D.'s H.D.*, by Diane di Prima, edited by Ammiel Alcalay. Center for the Humanities, 2011.
11. Alcalay, Ammiel, and Megan Paslawski. "the whole thing has no meaning if it is not signed." In *Robert Duncan in San Francisco, with an Interview & Letters,* by Michael Rumaker, edited by Ammiel Alcalay and Megan Paslawski. City Lights, 2013.
12. Alcalay, Ammiel. "Robert Duncan's Olson Memorial Lecture." In *Charles Olson Memorial Lecture: Robert Duncan.* Center for the Humanities, 2011.
13. Alcalay, Ammiel. "Letters to & from Joanne Kyger." In *"Communication is Essential": Joanne Kyger: Letters To & From,* edited by Joanne Kyger and Ammiel Alcalay. Center for the Humanities, 2012.
14. Alcalay, Ammiel, with Jacqui Cornetta, Alison Macomber, and Alexander Soria, *"Querido Pablito"/"Julissimo querido," Selected Correspondence, 1958–1971.* Center for the Humanities, 2017.
15. Alcalay, Ammiel. "Of Suckers and Gulls." Afterword to *Captain Poetry's Sucker Punch: A Guide to the Homeric Punkhole, 1980–2012,* by Kenneth Warren. BlazeVOX, 2012.
16. Alcalay, Ammiel, and Kate Tarlow Morgan. "Vincent Ferrini: Before Gloucester." In *Before Gloucester,* by Vincent Ferrini, edited by Ammiel Alcalay and Kate Tarlow Morgan. Center for the Humanities, 2013.
17. Previously unpublished.
18. Alcalay, Ammiel. "You Don't Know Jack: Doing Justice to Jack Kerouac in Todd Tietchen's *The Unknown Kerouac.*" *BOMB Magazine,* February 10, 2017. https://

bombmagazine.org/articles/2017/02/10/you-don-t-know-jack/.
19. Gloucester Writers Center. "Fourth Annual Charles Olson Lecture - Featuring Amiri Baraka." *YouTube,* January 17, 2017. https://www.youtube.com/watch?v=bvCLi8pmak4.
20. Akıman, Özge Özbek. "An Interview with Ammiel Alcalay." *Journal of American Studies of Turkey* 51 (2019): 115–21. https://dergipark.org.tr/en/pub/jast/issue/64844/993427.
21. Alcalay, Ammiel. "For Jimmie Durham, Poet." Liner notes for *Poems: Written, Drawn, Selected and Read by Jimmie Durham* (Rumpsti Pumsti Musik, 2022). LP.
22. Alcalay, Ammiel. "Getting Out of the Western Box: Dennis Tedlock's *The Olson Codex.*" *BOMB Magazine,* February 20, 2018. https://bombmagazine.org/articles/2018/02/20/getting-out-of-the-western-box-dennis-tedlocks-the-olson-codex-projective-verse-and-the-problem-of-mayan-glyphs/.
23. Alcalay, Ammiel. "Digging Our Way through the Data Midden: On Ed Sanders's *Investigative Poetry* and *Broken Glory: The Final Years of Robert F. Kennedy.*" *BOMB Magazine,* September 25, 2018. https://bombmagazine.org/articles/2018/09/25/ed-sanders/.
24. Alcalay, Ammiel. "Q&A." Interview by Marwa Helal. *The Poetry Project Newsletter* 256 (2018). https://www.poetryproject.org/publications/newsletter/256-october-november-2018/q-a-ammiel-alcalay.
25. Alcalay, Ammiel. "'a dance of freedom' / In the Worlds of Etel Adnan." In *To look at the sea is to become what one is: An Etel Adnan Reader,* by Etel Adnan, edited by Thom Donovan and Brandon Shimoda. Nightboat, 2014.
26. Alcalay, Ammiel. "In Friendship, for John Wieners." Preface to *Stars Seen in Person: Selected Journals,* by John Wieners, edited by Michael Seth Stewart. City Lights Books, 2015.

27. Alcalay, Ammiel. "Still Standing: A Memoir for Gil Sorrentino." *The Review of Contemporary Fiction* 31, no. 2 (2011): 89–99.
28. Alcalay, Ammiel. "In & Out of Place: Memories of Nissim Rejwan, Shimon Ballas, and Samir Naqqash." *Banipal* 72 (2021): 21–25.
29. Alcalay, Ammiel. "From the Citadel: 'I must have been an Arab once….'" *Revue française d'études américaines* 170, no. 1 (2022): 51–63.
30. Previously unpublished.

References

Abu Toha, Mosab. *Things You May Find Hidden in My Ear: Poems from Gaza*. City Lights Books, 2022.

Adnan, Etel. "Growing Up to Be a Woman Writer in Lebanon." In *Opening the Gates: A Century of Arab Feminist Writing*, edited by Margot Badran and Miriam Cooke. Indiana University Press, 1990.

———. *Journey to Mount Tamalpais*. Post-Apollo Press, 1985.

———. *Paris, When It's Naked*. Post-Apollo Press, 1993.

———. *To look at the sea is to become what one is: An Etel Adnan Reader*. 2 Volumes. Edited by Thom Donovan and Brandon Shimoda. Nightboat Books, 2014.

Akıman, Özge Özbek. "'Finding Out For Yourself,' Or Poets Re-Writing History." PhD dissertation, Hacettepe University Graduate School of Social Sciences, 2009.

Alcalay, Ammiel. *a little history*. Edited by Fred Dewey. Re:public/UpSet Press, 2013.

———. *After Jews & Arabs: Remaking Levantine Culture*. University of Minnesota Press, 1993.

———. *from the warring factions*. Edited by Fred Dewey. Re:public/UpSet Press, 2012.

———. "Imperial Abhorrences (& Other Abominations)." *Paideuma* 47 (2020): 231–45. https://www.jstor.org/stable/48714059.

———. "Intellectual Life." In *The Jews of the Middle East and North Africa in Modern Times,* edited by Reeva S. Simon, Michael M. Laskier, and Sara Reguer. Columbia University Press, 2003.

———, ed. *Keys to the Garden: New Israeli Writing.* City Lights Books, 1996.

———. *Memories of Our Future.* City Lights Books, 1999.

Anastas, Ayreen, and René Gabri, dirs. *Black Bach Artsakh.* Parks Luksemburg, 2021.

Anastas, Peter. *A Walker in the City: Elegy for Gloucester.* Back Shore Press, 2013.

Anastas, Peter, and David Rich. "Reading Ferrini: A Gallery Talk." CAM Video Lecture Series, vx09. Cape Ann Museum Library & Archives, Gloucester, MA. Transcript archived at: http://gloucesterwriters.org/mp3test/.

Arendt, Hannah. *The Human Condition.* Doubleday, 1959.

Avrich, Paul. *Sacco and Vanzetti: The Anarchist Background.* Princeton University Press, 1991.

Bacha, Julia, dir. *Naila and the Uprising.* Rula Salameh and Rebekah Wingert-Jabi, 2017.

Barrett, Faith, and Cristanne Miller, eds. *"Words for the Hour": A New Anthology of American Civil War Poetry.* University of Massachusetts Press, 2005.

Barry, Jan, and W.D. Ehrhart, eds. *Demilitarized Zones: Veterans after Vietnam.* East River Anthology, 1976.

Basso, Keith H. *Wisdom Sits in Places: Landscape and Language Among the Western Apache.* University of New Mexico Press, 1996.

Bayrakdar, Faraj. *A Dove in Free Flight.* Edited by Ammiel Alcalay and Shareah Taleghani. Translated by Ammiel Alcalay, Sinan Antoon, Rebecca Johnson, Elias Khoury, Tsolin Nalbantian, Jeffrey Sacks, and Shareah Taleghani. UpSet Press, 2021.

Blackburn, Paul, and Julio Cortázar. *"Querido Pablito" / "Julissimo Querido": Selected Correspondence, 1958–1971.* Edited and translated by Ammiel Alcalay, Jacqui Cornetta,

Alison Macomber, and Alexander Soria. Center for the Humanities, 2017.

Boldt, Lindsey, Steve Dickison, and Samantha Giles, eds. *Homage to Etel Adnan*. Post-Apollo Press, 2012.

Brotherston, Gordon. *Book of the Fourth World: Reading the Native Americas Through Their Literature*. Cambridge University Press, 1992.

Césaire, Aimé. *Discourse on Colonialism*. Translated by Joan Pinkham. Monthly Review Press, 2000.

———. *Lyric and Dramatic Poetry, 1946–82*. Translated by Clayton Eshleman and Annette Smith. University of Virginia Press, 1990.

———. *The Collected Poetry*. Edited and translated by Clayton Eshleman and Annette Smith. University of California Press, 1983.

Coe, Michael. *Breaking the Maya Code*. Thames & Hudson, 2012.

Cortázar, Julio. *Around the Day in Eighty Worlds*. Translated by Thomas Christensen. North Point Press, 1986.

———. *La vuelta al día en ochento mundos*. Volume 2. Siglo XXI Editores, 1968.

Creeley, Robert. *The 1963 Vancouver Conference / Robert Creeley's Contexts of Poetry. With Daphne Marlatt's Journal Entries*. Edited by Ammiel Alcalay. Center for the Humanities, 2009.

———. *The Collected Essays of Robert Creeley*. University of California Press, 1989.

Cruz, Juan. "Edith Aron, su propia 'maga.'" *El País*, April 19, 2007. https://elpais.com/diario/2007/04/20/cultura/1177020004_850215.html.

Darwish, Mahmoud. *Memory for Forgetfulness*. Translated by Ibrahim Muhawi. University of California Press, 1995.

Denning, Michael. *The Cultural Front: The Laboring of American Culture in the Twentieth Century*. Verso, 1998.

di Prima, Diane. *"Old Father, Old Artificer": Charles Olsen Memorial Lecture*. Edited by Ammiel Alcalay and Ana Božičević. Center for the Humanities, 2012.

———. *R.D.'s H.D.* Edited by Ammiel Alcalay. Center for the Humanities, 2011.
———. *Revolutionary Letters.* City Lights Books, 2021.
Dorn, Edward. *Charles Olson Memorial Lectures.* Edited by Lindsey M. Freer. Center for the Humanities, 2012.
———. *Collected Poems.* Edited by Jennifer Dunbar Dorn. Carcanet Press, 2012.
———. *Derelict Air: From Collected Out.* Edited by Justin Katko and Kyle Waugh. Enitharmon Press, 2015.
———. *Ed Dorn Live: Lectures, Interviews, and Outtakes.* Edited by Joseph Richey. University of Michigan Press, 2007.
———. *Gunslinger, Book II.* Black Sparrow Press, 1969.
———. *The Poet, the People, the Spirit.* Talonbooks, 1976.
Duncan, Robert. *Bending the Bow.* New Directions, 1968.
———. *Charles Olson Memorial Lecture.* Center for the Humanities, 2011.
———. "Charles Olson Memorial Lecture, Fourth Lecture." *PennSound.* http://media.sas.upenn.edu/pennsound/authors/Duncan/Duncan-Robert_Fourth-Lecture_Charles-Olson-Memorial-Lectures.mp3.
———. *Fictive Certainties: Essays.* New Directions, 1985.
———. "The Homosexual in Society." *Politics* 1, no. 7 (1944): 209–11.
———. *The Opening of the Field.* Grove Press, 1960.
Dunne, Gregory. *Quiet Accomplishment: Remembering Cid Corman.* Ekstasis Editions, 2014.
Edwards, Brent Hayes. *The Practice of Diaspora: Literature, Translation, and the Rise of Black Internationalism.* Harvard University Press, 2003.
Ehrhart, W.D. *Beautiful Wreckage: New & Selected Poems.* Adastra Press, 1999.
———, ed. *Carrying the Darkness: The Poetry of the Vietnam War.* Texas Tech University Press, 1989.
———. *In the Shadow of Vietnam: Essays 1977–1991.* McFarland & Co., 2016.
———. *Thank You For Your Service: Collected Poems.* McFarland & Co., 2019.

———, ed. *Unaccustomed Mercy: Soldier-Poets of the Vietnam War.* Texas Tech University Press, 1989.

———. *Vietnam-Perkasie: A Combat Marine Memoir.* University of Massachusetts Press, 1995.

"Ezra Pound Reading His Usura Canto, 1939." *Renegade Tribune,* July 3, 2019. http://www.renegadetribune.com/ezra-pound-reading-his-usura-canto-1939/.

Fanon, Frantz. *Écrits sur l'aliénation et la liberté.* Éditions la découverte, 2015.

———. *The Wretched of the Earth.* Translated by Constance Farrington. Grove Press, 1963.

Ferrini, Henry, dir. *Poem in Action: A Portrait of Vincent Ferrini.* Ferrini Productions, 1990.

Ferrini, Vincent. *Before Gloucester,* with facsimile edition of *Tidal Wave: Poems of the Great Strikes* (1946). Edited by Ammiel Alcalay. Center for the Humanities, 2013.

———. *Hermit of the Clouds: The Autobiography of Vincent Ferrini.* Ten Pound Island Book Company, 1988.

———. Letters and Papers, Archive Collection. The Cape Ann Museum, Gloucester.

———. *The Whole Song: Selected Poems.* Edited by Kenneth A. Warren and Fred Whitehead. University of Illinois Press, 2004.

Franklin, H. Bruce, ed. *The Vietnam War in American Stories, Songs, and Poems.* Bedford Books of St. Martin's Press, 1996.

Freeman, Ru, ed. *Extraordinary Rendition: (American) Writers on Palestine.* OR Books, 2015.

Giedion, Siegfried. *Mechanization Takes Command: A Contribution to Anonymous History.* W.W. Norton, 1975.

Goldberg, Jacob Max. "The Mizrahi Black Panthers of Israel." *Ha'Am: UCLA's Jewish Newsmagazine.* https://haam.org/the-mizrahi-black-panthers-of-israel/.

Gottlieb, Adolph. *The Pictographs of Adolph Gottlieb.* Hudson Hills Press and the Adolph and Esther Gottlieb Foundation, 1994.

Griffin, David Ray. *The New Pearl Harbor: Disturbing Questions About the Bush Administration and 9/11.* Olive Branch Press, 2020.

Henning, Taylor. "D.H. Melhem: Biographer and Friend of Gwendolyn Brooks." *Rare Book and Manuscript Library.* https://www.library.illinois.edu/rbx/2019/11/11/d-h-melhem-biographer-and-friend-of-gwendolyn-brooks/.

Hussein, Rashid. *The World Of Rashid Hussein: A Palestinian Poet in Exile.* Edited by Kamal Boullata and Mirène Ghossein. Association of Arab-American University Graduates, 1979.

Jeffrey, Ian. *ReVisions: An Alternative History of Photography.* National Museum of Photography, Film & Television, 1999.

Jabès, Edmond, with Marcel Cohen. *From the Desert to the Book.* Station Hill, 1990.

Joans, Ted. *Poet Painter/Former Villager Now/World Traveller.* Edited by Wendy Tronrud and Ammiel Alcalay. Center for the Humanities, 2016.

"Kamal Boullata." *The Khalid Shoman Foundation Darat al Funun.* https://daratalfunun.org/?artist=kamal-boullata.

Kerouac, Jack. *La vie est d'hommage.* Edited by Jean-Christophe Cloutier. Boréal, 2016.

———. *The Haunted Life and Other Writings.* Edited by Todd Tietchen. Da Capo Books, 2014.

———. *The Unknown Kerouac.* Edited by Todd Tietchen, with translations by Jean-Christophe Cloutier. Library of America, 2016.

Kyger, Joanne. *"Communication is Essential": Letters to and From Joanne Kyger.* Edited by Ammiel Alcalay and Joanne Kyger. Center for the Humanities, 2012.

Laâbi, Abdellatif. "The Abdellatif Laâbi Interview." Interview by Christopher Schaefer. *The Quarterly Conversation,* June 11, 2013. https://revue-traversees.com/2014/12/15/the-abdellatif-laabi-interview-by-christopher-schaefer/.

Libedinsky, Juana. "Edith Aron: La maga de Julio Cortázar." *La Nacion,* March 7, 2004. https://www.lanacion.com.ar/lifestyle/edith-aron-la-maga-de-julio-cortazar-nid577957/.

Lowenfels, Walter, ed. *Where Is Vietnam? American Poets Respond.* Anchor Doubleday, 1967.

Lyon, Danny. *The Destruction of Lower Manhattan.* Aperture, 2020.

Majaj, Lisa Suhair, and Amal Amireh, eds. *Etel Adnan: Critical Essays on the Arab-American Writer and Artist.* McFarland & Co., 2001.

Matlin, David. *Prisons: Inside the New America: From Vernooykill Creek to Abu Ghraib.* North Atlantic, 2005.

McClure, Michael. *Scratching the Beat Surface: Essays on New Vision from Blake to Kerouac.* Penguin, 1994.

———. *Star.* Grove Press, 1970.

McGilvery, Laurence, ed. *The Floating Bear: A Newsletter.* L. McGilvery, 1973.

Meding, Jason von. "Fifty Years Later, Agent Orange Still Kills in Vietnam." *The National Interest,* November 28, 2020. https://nationalinterest.org/blog/reboot/fifty-years-later-agent-orange-still-kills-vietnam-173463.

Meltzer, David. Interview by David Hadbawnik, March 2010. Archived at: https://web.archive.org/web/20240723032354/http://www.bigbridge.org/BB14/2010_diprima/DiPrima_Meltzer_Interview.HTM.

Morgan, Kate Tarlow. *Circles & Boundaries.* Factory School, 2011.

Nacer-Khodja, Hamid. *Albert Camus, Jean Sénac, or The Rebel Son.* Translated by Kai Krienke. Michigan State University Press, 2019.

Nelson, Cary. *Repression and Recovery: Modern American Poetry and the Politics of Cultural Memory, 1910–1945.* University of Wisconsin Press, 1989.

———. *Revolutionary Memory: Recovering the Poetry of the American Left.* Routledge, 2003.

Nelson, Truman. *The Truman Nelson Reader.* Edited by William J. Schafer. University of Massachusetts Press, 1989.

Nichols, Miriam. *Radical Affections: Essays on the Poetics of Outside.* University of Alabama Press, 2010.

Olson, Charles. Charles Olson Research Collection. Archives & Special Collections at the Thomas J. Dodd Research Center, University of Connecticut Libraries at Storrs.

———. *Collected Prose*. Edited by Donald Allen and Benjamin Friedlander. University of California Press, 1997.

———. *Selected Letters*. Edited by Ralph Maud. University of California Press, 2000.

———. *The Maximus Poems*. Edited by George F. Butterick. University of California Press, 1983.

Olson, Charles, and Robert Creeley. *Charles Olson & Robert Creeley: The Complete Correspondence*. 10 Volumes. Edited by Richard Blevins and George F. Butterick. Black Sparrow Press, 1980–1996.

Pound, Ezra. *ABC of Reading*. New Directions, 1960.

Prynne, Jeremy. "Lectures on Maximus." Transcribed by Tom McGauley. *Iron* (October 1971). Reprinted in *Minutes of the Charles Olson Society* 28 (April 1999). https://charlesolson.org/Files/Prynnelecture1.htm.

Randall, Margaret, and Sergio Mondragón, eds. *El Corno Emplumado / The Plumed Horn: Selections*. Full run digitized at: http://opendoor.northwestern.edu/archive/collections/show/5.

Rasula, Jed. *The American Poetry Wax Museum: Reality Effects, 1940–1990*. National Council of Teachers of English, 1996.

Rimbaud, Arthur. *Oeuvres de Rimbaud*. Edited by Suzanne Bernard and André Guyaux. Classiques Garnier, 1991.

———. *The Complete Works*. Translated by Paul Schmidt. Harper Perennial, 2008.

Robb, Graham. *Rimbaud*. Norton, 2000.

Rukeyser, Muriel. *"The Difficulties Involved": Selections from* A Season in Hell *by Arthur Rimbaud*. Edited by Chris Clarke. Translated by Muriel Rukeyser. Center for the Humanities, 2019.

———. *The Life of Poetry*. Paris Press, 1996.

Rumaker, Michael. *"Like a great armful of wild & wonderful flowers": Selected Letters of Michael Rumaker*. Edited by Megan Paslawski. Center for the Humanities, 2012.

———. *Robert Duncan in San Francisco*. Edited by Ammiel Alcalay and Megan Paslawski. City Lights, 2013.

Sacco, Nicola, and Bartolomeo Vanzetti. *The Letters of Sacco and Vanzetti*. Penguin, 2007.

Salloum, Jayce. *everything and nothing (from the on-going project, untitled)*. 1999–2005.

———. *"…In the Absence of Heroes…"* Warfare/A Case for Context, 1984.

———. "Occupied Territories: Mapping the Transgressions of Cultural Terrain." Interview-essay with Molly Hankwitz. *Framework* 43, no. 2 (2002): 85–103. https://www.jstor.org/stable/41552335.

———. *Once You've Shot the Gun You Can't Stop the Bullet*. 1988.

———. *So Cal*. 1988.

———. *This is Not Beirut / There was and there was not*. c. 1995.

———. *untitled part 1: everything and nothing*. 2001.

———. *untitled part 2: beauty and the east*. 2002.

———. *untitled part 3a: occupied territories*. 2001.

———. *untitled part 3b: (as if) beauty never ends…*. 2003.

———. *untitled part 4: terra incognita*. 2005.

Salloum, Jayce, and Walid Raad. *Talaeen a Junuub/Up to the South*. 1993.

Sanders, Ed. *Broken Glory: The Final Years of Robert F. Kennedy*. Illustrations by Rick Veitch. Arcade Publishing, 2018.

———. *Investigative Poetry*. Spuyten Duyvil, 2018.

Sauer, Carl O. *Land & Life: A Selection from the Writings of Carl Ortwin Sauer*. Edited by John Leighly. University of California Press, 1963.

Scott, Ramsey. "In the Butcher Shop of Subjectivity: Autobiographical Works from the Black Liberation

Movement, 1970–1987." PhD dissertation, City University of New York, 2009.

Sells, Michael. *Stations of Desire: Love Elegies from Ibn 'Arabi and New Poems.* Ibis Editions, 2000.

Sénac, Jean. *Oeuvres Poétiques.* Actes Sud, 1999.

Solnit, Rebecca. *Storming the Gates of Paradise: Landscapes for Politics.* University of California Press, 2007.

Szwed, John F. *Space is the Place: The Lives and Times of Sun Ra.* DaCapo, 1998.

Tedlock, Dennis. *Popol Vuh: The Definitive Edition of the Mayan Book of the Dawn of Life and the Glories of Gods and Kings.* Simon & Schuster, 1996.

———. *Rabinal Achi: A Mayan Drama of War and Sacrifice.* Oxford University Press, 2003.

———. *The Olson Codex: Projective Verse and the Problem of Mayan Glyphs.* University of New Mexico Press, 2017.

The 9/11 Commission Report: Final Report of the National Commission on Terrorist Attacks Upon the United States. W.W. Norton, 2004.

Vidaver, Aaron. "Vancouver, 1963." *Minutes of the Charles Olson Society* 30 (April 1999). http://vidaver.files.wordpress.com/2009/09/1963-vancouver-poetry-conference-charles-olson-society-minutes-1999-guest-ed-aaron-vidaver.pdf.

———. "Warren Tallman: 'Poets in Vancouver' (1963)." *vidaver.wordpress.com,* August 10, 2009. http://vidaver.wordpress.com/category/poetry-and-poetics/.

Warren, Kenneth. *Captain Poetry's Sucker Punch: A Guide to the Homeric Punkhole, 1980–2012.* BlazeVOX, 2012

Wieners, John. *Stars Seen in Person: Selected Journals of John Wieners.* Edited by Michael Seth Stewart. City Lights Books, 2015.

www.ingramcontent.com/pod-product-compliance
Lightning Source LLC
Chambersburg PA
CBHW070836160426
43192CB00012B/2208